ALCOHOL AND DRUGS, DELINQUENCY AND CRIME

Alcohol and Drugs, Delinquency and Crime

Looking Back to the Future

Lyle W. Shannon
Professor Emeritus of Sociology
and Director
Iowa Urban Community Research Center
The University of Iowa
Iowa City

with the assistance of

Judith L. McKim

Kathleen R. Anderson

William E. Murph

First published in Great Britain 1998 by
MACMILLAN PRESS LTD
Houndmills, Basingstoke, Hampshire RG21 6XS and London
Companies and representatives throughout the world

A catalogue record for this book is available from the British Library.

ISBN 0–333–71912–3

First published in the United States of America 1998 by
ST. MARTIN'S PRESS, INC.,
Scholarly and Reference Division,
175 Fifth Avenue, New York, N.Y. 10010

ISBN 0–312–21437–5

Library of Congress Cataloging-in-Publication Data
Shannon, Lyle W.
Alcohol and drugs, delinquency, and crime : looking back to the
future / Lyle W. Shannon ; with the assistance of Judith L. McKim,
Kathleen R. Anderson, William E. Murph.
    p. cm.
Includes bibliographical references and index.
ISBN 0–312–21437–5 (cloth)
    1. Juvenile delinquency—Wisconsin—Racine—Longitudinal studies.
    2. Youth—Drug use—Wisconsin—Racine—Longitudinal studies.
    3. Youth—Alcohol use—Wisconsin—Racine—Longitudinal studies.
    4. Narcotics and crime—Wisconsin—Racine—Longitudinal studies.
    I. McKim, Judith L.   II. Anderson, Kathleen R.   III. Murph, William
E. IV. Title.
HV9106.R33S53 1998
364.36'09775'96—dc21   98–11064
                                                            CIP

This book is printed on paper suitable for recycling and made from fully managed and
sustained forest sources.

10   9   8   7   6   5   4   3   2   1
07   06   05   04   03   02   01   00   99   98

Printed in Great Britain by
The Ipswich Book Company Ltd
Ipswich, Suffolk

Contents

Acknowledgments

Literally hundreds of graduate and undergraduate students from the University of Wisconsin in Madison, the University of Wisconsin-Parkside, and the University of Iowa have assisted us in our research in Madison and Racine over a period of more than 40 years. They assisted us in interview schedule construction and pretesting, in self-report construction and pretesting, and later in many waves of interviewing for our two major projects. They coded official records, checkcoded, entered data in the computers, helped us construct tables, collapse categories of data, and wrote preliminary assessments of the findings. We sat around the table and discussed what we were learning and what we should be doing that we were not doing. The students said that it was not just a job because they had become part of the project. Many developed research papers based on the data and some did their MA and PhD theses with the data. We welcomed their participation and always told them that if they eventually did a reanalysis of the data which found that something the professors concluded must be modified or completely thrown out, that would indeed be a feather in their hats. Numerous citations in the text and items in the bibliography are to theses and papers by graduate students and now more and more to professors of sociology in other academic institutions, many of whom got their start at interviewing and data collection on the Madison and Racine projects.

Most of the funding for research on juvenile delinquency and adult crime came from the National Institute of Juvenile Justice and Delinquency Prevention and the National Institute of Justice of the Department of Justice. The numerous lengthy reports which we have made to these agencies are cited and listed in the bibliography. Our basic data have been made available by the Department of Justice though the National Institute of Justice's Data Resources Program on a CD-ROM, *Violence Research*, NCJ – 151523, and through the Inter-university Consortium for Political and Social Research at the University of Michigan. More recent data may be obtained from the Consortium and the Sociometrics Corporation in Los Altos, California, Data Set JU 86, *Patterns of Drug Use and Their Relation to Improving Prediction of Patterns of Delinquency and Crime*. The College of Arts and Sciences at the University of Wisconsin was generous in their support during the early years of our research when activities were located in Madison. The Vice-President for Research, Dr Duane C. Spriestersbach and Deans Dewey B. Stuit and Howard Laster of the College of Liberal Arts at the University of Iowa were very generous in their assistance for many years. The facilities of the Weeg Computing Center continue to be a mainstay for the project.

Three people who are listed on the title-page deserve special mention. Judith L. McKim has been involved in the Racine research on the economic absorption and cultural integration of inmigrant workers since 1970 and in the birth cohort research on delinquency and crime since 1972. She worked on the research design, instruments for data collection, and supervised data collection in Racine and data processing in Iowa City. She was involved in analysis and report writing from the beginning. In more recent years and since becoming a social science research assistant emeritus, she has spent most of her time critiquing and editing our reports and publications, most recently this volume.

Kathleen R. Anderson joined the Iowa Urban Community Research Center in 1977 as an undergraduate assistant. She has become more and more involved in data analysis and report writing. Her chapters in several reports to the National Institute of Justice made a major contribution to understanding the complexity of the connection between juvenile and adult crime and the problem of errors in prediction. She is currently writing her PhD dissertation with some of the most challenging data that we have collected.

William E. Murph is no longer in the Iowa Urban Community Research Center but, fortunately for us, is a Programmer Analyst at American College Testing in Iowa City. His computer-generated typologies for delinquency and crime and substance involvement have enabled us to conduct numerous tests that, however they turned out, provided more satisfying answers to continuity questions than we had had before. He continues to assist us from time to time with his computer expertise and knowledge of the Racine data.

Lyle W. Shannon

Preface

Persons who have read our first three volumes describing a variety of social problems in Racine, Wisconsin, including race relations, unequal work opportunities, juvenile delinquency, adult crime, substance involvement, and the failure of the justice system's approach to controlling delinquency and crime, may wonder why we have written yet another. Each of the previous books reported the findings from large segments of our continuing research and referred to the relevant research of others, but with little emphasis on how our findings related to the national and international picture and the extent to which a variety of problem behaviors including illegal drug use and sale are interrelated.

Our now updated and more recent research shows how our work fits into the totality of what we know about delinquency and crime. This book is not repetitious of the earlier volumes. The extended findings describe changes in delinquent and criminal behavior with age, or over time periods, and changes which have presaged the intense national attention now devoted to the problems of delinquency and crime, alcohol and drugs.

This is also a book about the community, the extent to which its members are involved in crime, how their delinquent behavior has sometimes developed into adult criminal careers, and how some adults become involved in crime without having had juvenile careers in crime. To give it a wider context, we refer to data on delinquency and crime for the various states in the United States.

The current national and international debate about what to do about delinquency and crime, alcohol and drugs, dramatized by relatively uninformed executives, members of their administrations, and the media has led us to look back at our own research and experiences and that of others with a different focus than in earlier published articles and books.

Those who have had the opportunity to travel are aware of the broader understanding of problems at home that such travel experiences generate. For example, in 1978 a group of sociologists visited St Petersburg (Leningrad for most of the twentieth century) on a trip arranged by Premier Alexsei N. Kosygin's sociologist son-in-law. We were placed in a hotel for visiting socialist dignitaries and had what amounted to complete freedom to roam about; were even given a map of the city.

On the first evening, a number of us, as sociologists are likely to do, set out for the nearest inner-city area. There the glories of socialism (Soviet state capitalism) lay before us, rows of apartment houses with open windows and blaring American rock music, brightly lit streets, a soldier with fixed bayonet and a policeman standing on almost every corner, and shabbily dressed, unshaven men in baggy pants shuffling along without fear of being assaulted by either Soviet youth or young adults. A virtual paradise free of street crime!

During the daylight hours we visited suburban areas where apartment balconies were a riot of color, where well-dressed women with fancy perambulators strolled their children, and where yet others walked their well-groomed white poodles. Were it not for the lack of warning signs and pooper-scoopers, we might have been in Paris. Surely it was not too long ago that the language of then St Petersburg's elite was French – a life to which some petit-Czarists still dream of returning.

In a way we were viewing what we can see every day in the United States. To be more like Leningrad though, we need better street lighting and more police officers. An expansion of our own already huge state and federal prison system is unnecessary. It is already a growth industry financed by the middle class whose members groan under their heavy tax burden. Our prisons are spread throughout the country, however, rather than far away as was the Soviet Gulag.

After we had toured the area for a few days and had been well-received everywhere (some of us were able to tell them that we had been in the American armed forces at the same time that they had been in the Great Patriotic War) we flew to Helsinki, Finland and, as we left the plane, some of the less sophisticated in the group dropped to their knees with cries of 'Free, free again!' Free from what? That depends on what we wish to be free from and how one looks at it.

Should we now take steps in the United States which will free us from fear in the streets but perhaps infringe upon other freedoms, this before we have even examined the extensive literature on the causes of delinquency and crime or the use of illegal drugs? Maybe we should question why some mind-altering drugs are legal and some illegal. This is not the point to go into how much the Department of Justice (The National Institute of Justice and the National Institute for Juvenile Justice and Delinquency Prevention) has learned about delinquency and crime by supporting research. They have not done as much as they might have by way of summarizing the multitude of research projects that they have financed, but their reports and serial publications are improving. It is not easy to summarize a multitude of conflicting findings from research projects whose definitions and designs are not quite comparable.

Numerous more or less plausible explanations of underlying 'causes' have been presented in the media and in professional forums for every deviant behavior or condition that has been identified as a pressing social problem. Some of these explanations compete with each other and some are compatible, for together they account for more of the delinquency and crime than each alone.

Ameliorative programs which may or may not follow from the various professional explanations of delinquent and criminal behavior and substance involvement have been advanced by both political parties. Some proposals acquire even greater public currency as they are dramatized and superficially dealt with in the media. Persons in positions of political and economic power, many well-meaning to be sure, have seized upon these problems and programs and have showered the relatively naive public with promises of how they will, if given the opportunity and public money, solve the problems, or at least take a bite out of crime. That was what the expensive dog, McGruff, was supposed to do. So why is crime considered to be an even greater threat than ever? Are gated communities becoming more popular not only because they reduce certain types of crime and annoyances within the area, but because they also give those who are fenced in an illusion of security and are a visible sign of higher social status?

Unfortunately, explanations of how social problems have been generated and perpetuated are more often than not based on anecdotal material or personal experiences ('I know because my brother or my cousin . . .') and less frequently on the results of hard, scientific research. The vast body of empirical research on delinquency and crime (government-sponsored and otherwise) has seldom been carefully examined and its totality taken into consideration in planning remedial programs. Some well-intended efforts to do so have been made, but the magnitude of the task escapes even people who have spent a lifetime in that academic and research domain. Looking back one can see that most programs for amelioration have had limited success because they have not been developed from thoroughly tested propositions about the genesis of delinquency, crime, and, now added to that, substance abuse.

Lest we be too harsh with those who at least think about these problems, perhaps with a vision of hope, there are other groups of people who contribute even less – for example, those who, bereft of explanations and the time to even look at what we do know, say that these problems cannot be solved because they are so incomprehensible. Almost worse, there are still people whose ideas went out with bloomers, those who attribute misbehavior to greed and avarice, the inner nature of human beings. There are yet others, well-meaning and democratically oriented, who misguidedly say that we should sit down in town hall fashion and decide what to do about all manner of complex problems that have not yet been clearly defined. For sure, the latter approach appeals to folk who like to talk – and there is never a shortage of them, nor, of course, of those who appeal to divine guidance – for want of a mind that can really absorb the complexity of problems.

Of course, it was not too many years ago that sociology was a talking enterprise. For some it still is. Unfortunately, it takes more than talk, but talk at least sometimes leads to conceptualizing problems in a way that leads to research. Research most often results in the rejection of popular explanations of phenomena. Even the greatest of the great in public life believe that they understand problems about which they haven't a whit of knowledge. Unsophisticated persons tend to react by saying that much research has no value because it doesn't give the answer – it has no bottom line that specifies the solution to problems. It is, however, just as important to know what the answer isn't or that we need more research to determine the definitive answer. Research seldom provides the complete answer but does reject a lot of incorrect ideas about how people come to behave the way that they do.

The conclusions reached by one research project may be quite correct considering the data that have been utilized, how the variables have been derived and coded, which statistical techniques have been utilized, and even which computer programs were used. But it takes more than one specific study to generalize. We may sometimes err in rejecting an idea or supporting a proposition based on the results of one or even a few studies, all of which may be criticized for one reason or another. Cumulatively, however, research reveals which explanations best account for the phenomena.

As a general theory of how behavior comes about is developed from extant research, it provides a basis for the construction of and rigorous testing of more specific hypotheses. If the hypotheses generated by theory are rejected by a number of properly designed and comparable research projects, then the theory must be rejected or at least revised. The same may be said when we turn to programs that claim to be remedial. If a series of well-designed experiments, including control groups, determines that the remedial approaches which are tried do not bring about the hypothesized results, they should be rejected or revised.

The data in this volume, along with numerous other studies to which we have referred, suggest that we should reject some explanations of delinquency and crime and the relationship of delinquency and crime to alcohol and drug use or involvement. This is a disappointment to those who know the answers. Knowledge of delinquency and crime rates, by states, by regions, by different types of neighborhood in urban areas, by sex, and by race/ethnicity, cast enormous suspicion on the usefulness of any general or specific innate propensity explanation of how people develop into delinquents and/or criminals or become involved with substances. Other data cast grave doubt on the success of the juvenile justice and adult criminal systems' approach to dealing with these problems.

Even more, the Racine research makes us wonder if we – that is, various professionals and members of the larger society – have properly conceptualized some social problems, or have at least failed to conceptualize them within a sociological framework. Have many of us taken the wrong road at the outset by examining the characteristics of individuals rather than looking at how these behaviors develop in various patterns in different social milieus? Certainly, the history of our research turns us back toward sociology's social and structural and social process explanations of delinquency, crime, and, now, substance involvement. That is not to say that rigorous tests have been conducted of all of the hypotheses drawn from sociological theories of the behaviors in question and how they develop in various societies. We have, in this volume however, described our research and cited other research which would reject various propensity types of hypotheses and have, even more importantly, presented research which provides data supportive of sociological explanations.

Structural and processual explanations of juvenile and adult misbehavior place emphasis on the organization of society as a determinant of human behavior. This is directly counter to the idea that there are delinquent and criminal types whose behavior is based on inner compulsions or, for that matter, childhood treatment that produces some kind of delinquent or criminally oriented psyche.

The demographic variables of race/ethnicity and sex (so often at least intimated as having a causal nexus with all forms of misbehavior) are not explanatory in themselves. They do enable us to better understand how people are positioned in the larger society and have quite different chains of experiences during the process of socialization, even throughout their lives or, as it is now put, life courses or life histories. It should make those who are in a position to bring about modifications in the organization of society reflect upon the fact that their misinformed concern has sometimes made them unwitting accomplices to what they see as 'terror in the streets.'

This book is the product of 40 years of research on juvenile delinquency and adult crime in Wisconsin, commencing with cross-sectional studies of delinquency in Madison. Wolfgang, Figlio, and Sellin's (1972) *Delinquency in a Birth Cohort*, a longitudinal study of approximately 10 000 of Philadelphia's male juveniles born in 1945, was the model for our longitudinal birth cohort research commencing in 1974 in Racine. The findings are based on official police and court records for three Racine birth cohorts totalling 6127 males and females born in 1942, 1949, and 1955, of whom 4079 were continuous residents in the community. Interviews were conducted with 889 members of the 1942 and 1949 Cohorts.

We had originally selected two birth cohorts, 1942 and 1949. A meeting with local leaders of the community was subsequently arranged by Attorney Edward E. Hales, later President of the University of Wisconsin Board of Regents, and a third cohort, 1955, was added to make the findings as current as possible. It is the 1955 Cohort's data brought up to 1988, heretofore unpublished, that we have emphasized in many of the chapters in this book.

The three cohorts, especially when the 1955 Cohort was updated, enabled us to introduce a dynamic aspect to the analysis and to measure and describe the nature of changes in delinquency and crime over a period of years greater than that encompassed by one birth cohort. This expensive longitudinal design permitted an analysis that foresees the present focus of national and international attention on those who terrorize us in the streets – but at the same time, and some would say unfortunately, pays less attention to the inner workings of the institutions of finance, investment, and corporate plundering. The cohort data have also been buttressed by official police records for the entire city for the period 1969–88.

The reader will soon realize that this is not just a book about delinquency and crime, drug trafficking, or even a book about serious, violent crime in the United States, England, Ireland, or Tasmania. Its focus is on how behavior comes about and what additional behavior may be evoked from the community as a consequence.

Many of the topics which we do not treat in this volume are dealt with in the Bureau of Justice Statistics' *Drugs, Crime and the Justice System* (1992). It is highly readable and replete with charts, diagrams, and maps showing the effect of illegal drugs, their street usage names, geographical variation in use, the dynamics of their production and distribution, and the 'effectiveness' of drug law enforcement.

Beyond the threat to human life and happiness in inner-city neighborhoods, crime and substance involvement have wreaked havoc upon youth and adults in other neighborhoods where it was once not a serious problem. The expense of misdirected attempts to control alcohol and drugs and delinquency and crime have thus been added to a multitude of other burdens on the economy. Many nations are also beset by structural changes in the world of work (for example, the decline of the old smokestack cities and the growth of rust belts), more heterogeneous populations, rising health costs, and the ambivalence of the public about what is a 'right,' all of which become important in a world in such turmoil that the monetary peace dividend has disappeared like dew in the July sun.

No easy solution is presented for the problems of delinquency and crime, alcohol and drugs. There is no easy solution when it is not simply a matter of changing the individual but a matter of changing the structure of society. We encourage the reader to reflect on whether public concern has been properly directed toward the interrelatedness of alcohol and drugs with delinquency and crime. We would probably further erode public confidence if we supported the call for a war on drugs as a war on crime, particularly if we continue to ignore the social and structural basis for the generation of delinquency and crime in the inner city and its growing interstitial or transitional neighborhoods.

To some readers, this will appear to be a very complex book and they will express their disappointment in its failure to provide a detailed explanation of how people become involved in excessive alcohol or illegal drug use and the relationship of these behaviors to delinquency and crime. These readers will be even more disappointed in our failure to provide a simple or, for that matter, any answer to the problem. Understanding the complexity of social relationships must precede the development of effective approaches to amelioration. As long as intervention and institutionalization are followed by career continuation, that approach, however much heralded by the leaders of major political parties, cannot be considered a solution. Any real solution will require the integrative efforts of programs which bring people back into society as useful members rather than policies which remove them from society only to exacerbate the problem in the long run. Unfortunately, for many of our most powerful leaders, the latter is the popular solution, the one with voter appeal.

1 Delinquency and Crime in the United States

A SOCIOLOGICAL PERSPECTIVE

Explanations of delinquency and crime have multiplied and become more complex since the beginning of the twentieth century with the development of sociology and other social and behavioral sciences. Much delinquency is now seen as a form of exciting leisure-time activity, some delinquency and crime are seen as a means of adjustment to one's social environment (gangs), and some are seen as types of career activity that develop in settings where other opportunities are scarce, just as legitimate careers develop in settings where attractive opportunities are present. Other sociological explanations focus on delinquent and criminal behavior as a reaction to perception of the larger society as hostile and impenetrable. Those who view the world about them in this reactive way are provided with little hope of attaining satisfying statuses in the larger society. Crime, on the other hand, may develop as an enhancement of existing, ongoing legitimate activities as opportunities arise (Steffensmeier, 1986).

There is also an extensive literature on delinquency and the family, a revival of earlier emphasis by sociologists on the importance of the family as a primary socializing group, which shows how the characteristics of families are sometimes important in the generation of delinquent and criminal behavior and how youthful behavior in turn influences family life (Wright and Wright, 1994). This concern may serve as a retreat for some people who prefer not to face up to the social and structural position which we shall further elucidate in this introductory chapter.

Those unfamiliar with the sociological framework and its various competing theories, as well as with non-sociological theories, may have some difficulty as they labor through the first few pages of this chapter. A modicum of effort will prepare the reader not only for what follows, but will permit the reader to evaluate presentations in the media and the comments of peers who propose simplistic explanations of behavior and remedies that are without

1

empirical foundation. An overview of several of the major theoretical positions being argued today will set the stage for the approach that we shall take in considering the relationship of alcohol and drugs to delinquency and crime and, even more so, the generation of delinquency and crime as on-going forms of human behavior.

Social control theory posits that the propensity to delinquency or crime is universal and that the relative strength of social controls, rewards, and punishments account for individual and group differences in the incidence (amount) and prevalence (how widespread) of misbehavior. In opposition to those who posit a universal propensity, there are those who contend that there is an inner propensity or predisposition to delinquency and crime that varies from person to person or group to group. Both are points from which some sociologists commence their arguments.

We have commenced with the basic proposition that the organization of society and differences in the opportunity structure for various segments of any society underlie differences in delinquency and crime rates. This position was originally encapsulated within a social disorganization and ecological framework by Shaw, Zorbaugh, McKay, and Cottrell (1929) and even more recently by Bursik (1984, 1986a, 1986b, 1988, and 1989), Bursik and Grassmick (1992 and 1993), Bursik and Webb (1982), and Vila (1994). Time and research will undoubtedly reveal the value of Vila's attempt to organize the patchwork of research on delinquency and crime within an ecological/sociological framework, as well as its use in organizing future research.

Analysis of official police or court and self-report data for the Racine birth cohorts has supported our position, but has revealed, as has other research, that definitive answers are elusive because persons with officially recorded and self-reported, alleged delinquent or criminal acts may or may not rank the same on both measures. Such differences between official and self-report studies have long been cited as evidence of contradictory findings in regards to hypotheses drawn from the same theoretical position. They are two types of data and provide findings based on different perceptions of events, one involving immediate recording and the other memory of events. Both are valuable and what they mean requires an understanding of different data collection techniques.

Although the Philadelphia (Wolfgang, 1972 and 1987), London (Farrington and West, 1977), and Racine (Shannon, 1988 and 1991) longitudinal cohort studies have sufficient similarities in their research designs and operationally defined variables that it has been possible to compare their basic findings (e.g. Petersillia, 1980) there are commonalities and differences in the findings. This is probably because the research was not conducted within exactly the same basic theoretical framework, thus finding agreement at one level but disagreement at another.

Among the other sociological theories of delinquency and crime that are relevant to our approach would be strain theory if the hypothesis of frustrated needs and wants specifies the basis for an unequal distribution of opportunities that creates strain within and between different segments of society and even types of neighborhoods. As Cloward and Ohlin (1960) stated long ago, 'adolescents feel pressure for deviant behavior when they experience marked discrepancies between aspirations and opportunities for achievement.' Elliott and Voss (1974) have contended that persons in the middle class are just as likely to aspire beyond their means as are those in the lower class (lower socioeconomic status, SES). While the life experiences of persons in lower-class neighborhoods differ considerably from those in middle-class neighborhoods, the impact of SES is more complex than many sociologists have considered it to be. Access to their aspirations is usually more available to middle-class youngsters than to lower-class youngsters, but just how to specify the impact of SES has not yet been fully addressed (Tittle and Meier, 1990).

The extent to which persons are integrated into society and later absorbed into the economy varies with how different segments of society are organized for this purpose. Our position is that delinquency and crime are usually the products of various chains of life experiences which differ with SES and neighborhood surroundings, rather than being the products of defective genes, inherited physical characteristics or mental capacity, or mental aberrations. Thus, the effects of SES within an ecological framework become the starting point in the analyses which follow this and the next chapters' presentation of data on delinquency and crime in the United States and, more specifically, in Racine.

A position completely different from ours may be found in Wilson and Herrnstein's *Crime and Human Nature* (1985, p. 70), in which the authors proceed to the position 'that there is some psychological trait, having a biological origin, that predisposes an individual to criminality.' Wilson and Herrnstein have a 'propensity' to overlook the fact that some have a greater probability of becoming criminals because they are born in starkly different life settings – as anyone should know from reading the daily newspaper in any metropolitan community.

Reviews of *Crime and Human Nature* by sociologists Gibbs (1985) and Cohen (1987) point out the major error that Wilson and Herrnstein have made by dwelling upon individual differences (not clearly defined or operationalized) and their rationale for considering them before acknowledging the major contribution made by the organization of society and the difference in chains of social experiences that are created as a consequence.

Unfortunately, the Wilson and Herrnstein volume, issued as 'the most significant social science work of the decade' (see dust jacket), but not carefully read, may well have played a part in a growing pseudo-scientific approach to understanding the genesis of delinquency and crime.

Much of the discussion which follows became even more relevant with the National Institute of Health's violence initiative in 1995 which proposed to identify potentially violent types of inner-city children based on genetic 'markers.' Such a program would focus on inner-city youth in a quite different way than have sociologists. Instead of types of people, we would focus on chains of life experiences within social settings which early on may lead to delinquent and later to criminal behavior.

One need only pick up a daily newspaper (*The New York Times*, September 13, 1992, for example) to read about temporal continuities in delinquency and crime:

> The day Theodore Russell got out of jail after a long stay, a group of neighborhood boys, including his little brother, surrounded him as if he were a rap star passing out concert tickets.
>
> They followed him down the street of the struggling neighborhood on the South side of Chicago, admiring his crudely drawn cellblock tattoos and marveling at the new muscles he had developed from hours of lifting weights in the yard. Then they sat on the steps of his mother's porch, looking up at the man they call Dirty Red, and fired questions at him about life in the world behind bars, the same questions that he asked when he was their age.

The totality of life experiences also includes the community's efforts to control delinquency and crime as well as the reactions of those who have been dealt with by the justice system. The *Times* story to which we have just referred continued:

Just this month, a study by the National Center for Institutes and Alternatives said that on any given day in Baltimore, 56 percent of the city's black men between 18 and 35 were either under the control of the criminal justice system or being sought on warrants. In 1981, just as the term 'war on drugs' was coming into vogue, a total of 15 white juveniles were arrested for sale of drugs in Baltimore, compared with 86 black juveniles. In 1991, 13 white juveniles were arrested in Baltimore for selling drugs – as were 1,304 black juveniles.

It is unnecessary to be a sociologist to suspect (theorize and then hypothesize) how the changing ratio of black to white arrests has developed. As a resident of the Robert Taylor public housing development in Chicago put it, '"A lot of people lose hope," he said. "Every day is a struggle. It seems like going to prison is destiny for a lot of young brothers. But we know what time it is. White folks be committing crimes, too. But they get probation. We go to jail. They get in drug rehab, we go to the cemetery."'

The *Times* continued: 'The so-called "war on drugs" has exposed the racism that has always driven the criminal justice system in this country,' said Jerome C. Miller, president of the center. 'This is the situation in virtually every urban center. We've so overused incarceration, that we've succeeded in socializing a whole generation to going to jail.'

Put differently in Snyder's article in the Department of Justice's Office of Juvenile Justice and Delinquency Prevention, January 1992, *Update on Statistics,* 'In 1980 the rate of drug abuse arrests for white and black youth were nearly equal.' The drug abuse arrest rate for white youth declined by 38 percent by 1987. 'Between 1984 and 1989 the rate of drug abuse arrests for black youth increased by 200 percent.' Whether these statistics are evidence of racism (the behaviors of persons in the criminal justice system) or the absence of attractive opportunities in the larger society is a matter of interpretation, for the arresting officers have become more and more likely to be blacks.

To understand delinquency and crime, the various chains of life experiences must be identified and examined through research in the community rather than through psychologically or physiologically oriented clinical research. As Elliott, Huizinga, and Ageton (1985) concluded, prior delinquency and involvement with delinquent peer groups are the main factors influencing the development of careers in delinquency and drug use. And as has been shown by sociologists since the 1930s, this is more likely to be a continuing pattern of behavior in some kinds of neighborhoods than in others.

Neither we nor most other researchers have been completely satisfied with the models which have been developed of the process by which some juveniles become involved in delinquency and continue from delinquency to adult crime. Surely we cannot accept, as did Nagin and Farrington (1992), the position that the continuity which does exist between past and future behavior is based on individual differences within people – perhaps some sort of underlying criminal potential. At the same time, it is difficult to dispute some of the points in Farrington's 'deliberately provocative' critique of the research of Shaw and McKay and his later research on neighborhood influences (Farrington, Sampson, and Wikstrom, 1993). Farrington states that his 'focus is particularly on influences on offending by individuals rather than influences on offender rates, offense rates or victimization rates of larger units such as neighborhoods.' He would better commence with the characteristics of neighborhoods (place of residence as well as place of work and leisure) and then turn to families and individual characteristics in the fine-tuning process. Beyond what is taking place in the neighborhood of socialization he might then determine which individual characteristics play a part in the chains of events or life experiences which produce delinquent and criminal behavior. While this may sound repetitive, it is important to clarify the difference in approaches which the psychologically vs. sociologically oriented bring to the field of criminology.

Neither we nor others have markedly increased predictive efficiency for members of a birth cohort from juvenile to adult careers with official, self-report, or interview data, at least not very much over chance or that which is possible based on marginal distributions (to be explained later) in tables of juvenile vs. adult categories. Looking back, what aspects of social settings have we missed and what chains of experiences have we failed to encapsulate in past efforts to predict the future from the past? How have we, as sociologists, failed to conceptualize the nature of the human experience so as to better predict future behavior from past and present experience?

Furthermore, we must not fail to mention the importance of chance, not only in the statistical sense, but in terms of important occurrences that may alter the life course and may interface with the chain of events that would otherwise take place. Howard Becker (1994) has explicated this in his article, 'FOI POR ACASO: Conceptualizing Coincidence' (a Brazilian expression – it happened by chance). While social science theory attempts to determine causal relationships, think, for example, of the events that occur by chance on the Copacabana and other magnificent beaches of Rio de Janeiro. Most correlations between predictor variables (hopefully explanatory variables) and the behavior to be predicted are probably reduced by the elements of chance and perhaps increased by coincidence.

If we commence without some idea of the connection between a set of independent, antecedent, explanatory variables and the dependent or set of related dependent variables, or with too narrow an explanatory framework or theoretical perspective, we will: 1) overlook the range of variables which are explanatory, 2) base our predictive effort on the use of variables which are correlated with what we wish to predict but are not antecedent, or 3) base our prediction effort on antecedent variables that are not the crucial ones.

At a different level, well-meaning persons, politicians, agency bureaucrats, and some researchers wish to commence with 'control' without adequate knowledge about the nature, extent, and causal settings of the phenomenon to be controlled. The simplest correlations between the deviant behavior to be controlled and some other behavior are sometimes accepted as evidence of predictability and maybe even 'causation.' To show that two variables have a statistically significant relationship, that is, greater than chance, is still insufficient from our perspective. Rejection of the null hypothesis that there is no relationship (therefore there is a relationship, even if it is so small that very little of the variance is accounted for) is sometimes taken as evidence that hypotheses and a theoretical position have been supported by scientific research. This is not good science and it is not the strategy that we should employ.

All of this may seem sophomoric to some, but the state of the art as represented by much of the literature, beyond that which we have already mentioned, suggests that those who have made many attempts to determine the relationship of delinquency to crime or to predict career continuity have not thought about or sufficiently considered the complexity of the problems which they face. And, as McCord stated in her 1989 presidential address to the American Society of Criminology, 'Whatever evidence confirms one theory in fact confirms a multitude of competing ones.' Most recently, the difficulty in settling on a single explanation of either delinquency or crime has been dramatized by three articles in a single 1994 issue of the *Journal of Quantitative Criminology* (Ward and Tittle, 1994; Burton, Cullen, Evans and Dunaway, 1994; and Triplett and Jarjoura, 1994). One must conclude that it is almost necessary to ask whose delinquency, crime, or continuity in either behavior or between behaviors is best explained by which model for which sub-groups or segments of the population. We shall soon come to this with the Racine data, where predictive efficiency varies between segments of the cohorts.

Our look back after many years of birth cohort research on the relationship of juvenile delinquency to adult crime brings us to a concern that we have not previously addressed. Does the relationship between drugs and/or alcohol and delinquency and/or crime enable us to better understand the development and continuation of these behaviors and to predict continuity in delinquency and crime?

MEASURING DELINQUENCY AND CRIME

Official Records of Delinquency and Crime

The task of determining which sociological explanation or combinations of explanations account for most of the variation in the incidence and prevalence of delinquency and crime is in itself an enormous task. Unfortunately, it does not seem to have warranted more than a piecemeal and poorly funded attack upon problems which have, in a manner of speaking, left tens of millions of urban and even rural dwellers imprisoned in their homes, at least believing so, as dusk falls upon their neighborhoods. At times the largely unsophisticated Congresses have postured by passing legislation which appropriated hundreds of millions for ameliorative programs which had little chance of success because they addressed the problem from emotion rather than accumulated research findings.

Going beyond the structural and organizational bases for rural/urban and within urban area differences, the social nature of the process of constructing delinquency and crime from delinquency statutes and criminal codes becomes clear. For this one need only note state-by-state variation in measures or indices of offenses based on police, court, probation, or institutional records and their variation over either short or long periods of time. These variations are so large (even considering the shortcomings of official measures) that non-sociological explanations of delinquent and criminal behavior may, for the most part, be discarded without further delay.

To wit, if non-sociological explanations have any probability of being supported by sophisticated research, then there should be some extant evidence that biological, psychological, or any other non-sociological explanations are based on the existence of non-sociological antecedent variables which have a distribution very highly correlated with the various measures of crime. Without some idea of the spatial distribution of theoretically appropriate, non-sociological antecedent variables, it is difficult to conceive of the possibility of a relationship that could even be remotely considered as causal.

The research problem becomes even more complex when, realizing that many measures of crime are not highly correlated, we must still select a yardstick by which the success or failure of a program may be determined. An examination of various measures that are often cited as evidence of the success of ameliorative programs suggests that political variables are of major importance in the interpretation of the findings. Politicians do not often say, 'If such and such delinquency or crime rates do such and such over a specified period of years we can consider the program a success.' More often politicians wait until a statistic can be found which is favorable to their programmatic position.

Offenses Known to the Police
The Department of Justice's *Uniform Crime Reports* have provided the data for several indices of crime. The Total Crime Index is based on offenses known to the police: murder and non-negligent manslaughter, forcible rape, robbery, aggravated assault, burglary, larceny, theft, motor vehicle theft, and arson. The Violent Crime Index includes the first four offenses, while the Property Crime Index commences with burglary and includes the remaining offenses. In 1960 the Total Crime Index was less than 2000 per 100 000 population, up to 5500 per 100 000 population in 1987 and up again to 5741 by 1989. We could use any recent year from the *Uniform Crime Reports* data, but our own data for Racine extend only into 1988 and there is no point in using later index or statistical data for the 1990s. These indices have had enormous state-by-state variation that may be encapsulated into regional differences in the incidence

of crime (particularly for specific offenses) as related to cultural differences (Lottier, 1938; Shannon, 1954).

Although official measures of violent crime have increased, most of the rapid rise, which by now has tripled the 1960 rate, may be accounted for by an increase in property crime. The Total Crime Index rates which follow are for 1987. Florida had the highest index offenses rate (8503), Texas second (7722), Arizona third (7189), and Washington fourth (7017). At the other extreme were West Virginia (2191), South Dakota (2678), North Dakota (2833), and Pennsylvania (3163).[1] While the ranking of states by Total Crime Index rates varies from year to year, the states with the highest offense rates have rates almost four times as high as those with the lowest rates.

Arrest Rates

Arrest rates, another official measure of criminal behavior, ranged from 101.2 and 98.2 per 1000 population (Alaska and Nevada – have you thought of either as being centers of crime in the United States?) to 23.8 and 31.6 (Vermont and Iowa) (*Sourcebook – 1988*, pp. 485–8). Politicians of both parties in Iowa have been posturing about crime for the last several years, as though Iowa was a borough of New York City. While these and other variations in rates have been presented in numerous articles, our focus is on how variation reflects on support for genetic or any other explanation vs. sociological explanations of crime.

Of the 2.2 million arrests in the United States in 1990, 16 percent were under 18 (25.7 percent of the population was under 18). Youth of this age accounted for 33 percent of the burglary arrests and 43 percent of the motor vehicle theft arrests. While the number of drug arrests of youth has increased during the past ten years, they have not increased as much (except in specific urban areas) as have more serious index offenses such as murder and aggravated assault. That youth accounted for only 7 percent of the drug abuse arrests may be attributed in part to the fact that the single most serious offense in multiple charge offenses is reported, thus not calling for a drug offense report along with many serious offenses.

Offense Rates vs. Arrest Rates vs. Justice System Expenditures

Florida had the highest Total Crime Index rate and the 14th highest arrest rate and, with the exception of Nevada which had next to the highest arrest rate and was highest in its proportion of govern-

ment funds spent on its justice system, spent the largest proportion of its government funds on its justice system in 1986 (*Sourcebook
– 1988*, pp. 14–18). What did either of them get for their expenditures? Maybe a small bite out of crime? Why are their crime rates
so high? Certainly not because they fail to address the problem by
spending. West Virginia had the lowest Index rate (and the third
lowest arrest rate) and spent the lowest proportion of its funds on
its justice system. Does it spend a low proportion of its funds on
the justice system because it has little crime or do lower expenditures on the justice system produce less crime on paper? Texas'
Total Crime Index rate was almost as high as that of Florida and
its arrest rate was the 17th highest, but it tied for 26th with a number of other states in terms of the proportion of state expenditures
for its justice system. Virginia had a low crime rate (3960), the
18th highest arrest rate, but spent one of the largest proportions
of its funds (ninth highest) on its justice system.

Which comes first, crime or justice system expenditures? Are
increases in one almost surely to be followed by increases or decreases in the other? If propensity is evenly distributed, arrest rates
and justice system expenditures provide little support for the effectiveness of arrests and justice system expenditures as devices for
social control. All of the above makes it even clearer that offense
rates are social constructs. The larger the list of proscribed behaviors, the higher the crime rates. Going even further, do these figures
also suggest that public reaction to offense measures may produce
institutional behavior which influences not only official rates but
the behavior itself? To put it very simply, why is there so little
relationship between offense rates and variables that many people
believe to be closely related to crime rates, that is, institutional
activities that are supposed to have a depressing rate on crime? If
genetic variables underlie crime, do they have state-by-state variation that generates indirect effects if not direct effects?

Let us go back again and this time examine per capita justice
system expenditures (*Sourcebook – 1988*, pp. 14–18, 21). Alaska
had the highest per capita expenditures and the highest arrest rate
(excluding the District of Columbia). West Virginia, which we have
just mentioned, had the lowest Total Crime Index rate and the lowest
per capita expenditures, followed closely by Arkansas, which ranked
35th on Index rates and 40th on arrest rates. Texas, with the second highest Index rate, was 23rd on per capita expenditures. How
do we account for such differences and inconsistencies in ranking?

Are per capita expenditures the product of social interaction between professionals, politicians, and their voting constituents? Are offense rates variable and without a definitive relationship to propensity, evenly or unevenly distributed, and to expenditures on the justice system? Watch what goes on, particularly when an election is close at hand. We have seen it in 1996 in the United Kingdom and the United States, in the parliament and the legislature, and in the media in both countries. Does all of this confuse you? It should.

Crimes of Violence vs. Property Offenses

Perhaps we should go further into Index offenses as a background for the Racine research. For example, in the US there were 610 violent crimes known to the police per 100 000 population in 1987 vs. 4940 property crimes. Wisconsin had a violent crime rate of 250 and a property crime rate of 3919 (*Sourcebook – 1988*, p. 437). Metropolitan Statistical Areas had 720 violent crimes per 100 000 vs. 351 in other cities and 178 in rural areas. Property offenses also differed, but not as sharply as between metropolitan and other cities (*Sourcebook – 1988*, p. 428). Is Wisconsin's population genetically different from that of other states? Do metropolitan dwellers have a greater predisposition or propensity to engage in delinquent and criminal behavior than do others or differ genetically from the residents in smaller urban areas and rural areas? Or is it a matter of the urban subculture and opportunities?

What Do the Figures Mean?

One must only look at the inconsistencies in state rankings from Index rates, arrest rates, and proportion of expenditures and dollars per capita of state expenditures on the justice system to recognize that the demographic characteristics of the population, the structure or organization of society, cultural differences, and the nature of human interaction in one area vs. another account for huge differences in any measure of delinquent or criminal activity. We are not trying to say that one state is better than another by selecting the measure that supports our position, as the politicians and media entertainers do. You can trust them on facts about as far as you can fling an Aberdeen Angus bull by the tail. Thus far we have presented only a few examples to spark your concern and make you think about what may lie behind these figures. Thinking is a dangerous thing. You may lose your faith in someone for whom you have voted.

The Complex Interrelationship of Official Measures

Look at the figures for all states, dividing the distribution for each variable as close to the midpoint as possible. When this is done for Total Crime Index offenses per 100 000 vs. arrests per 1000, for example, about three-fifths of the states had either high offense rates and high arrest rates or low offense rates and low arrest rates, but two-fifths were in inconsistent categories. Michigan and Oregon are examples of states that had high Index rates but low arrest rates, and Mississippi and Virginia had low Index rates but high arrest rates. While Index rates had a low correlation with arrest rates (0.165), an arrest rate based on only persons 18 years of age or older produced a higher relationship (0.332). Remember that we are referring to positive correlations, for example, states with low Index rates have low arrest rates and states with high Index rates have high arrest rates. A correlation of 0.165 from a range of 0.000 to 1.000 does not indicate that the variables have much relationship to each other.

What produces a high arrest rate is obviously not the same as what produces a high Index rate, and vice versa. We shall refer to correlations from time to time in order to show that variables which might be assumed to be closely related to each other are not. When the number of sentenced prisoners per 100 000 was substituted for arrests, the relationship between the crime index and sentenced prisoners was 0.224. Three-fifths of the states were in the High High or Low Low segments of the tables, but some states shifted their position on the scattergram because state arrest rates and sentencing rates were no more highly related than were other distributions (*Sourcebook – 1988*, pp. 6–13). Although Nevada in the far west had the highest sentenced prisoner rate, states in other regions such as Louisiana, South Carolina, and Oklahoma were also high. North Dakota was the lowest, followed by Minnesota, West Virginia, and New Hampshire. Washington and Colorado were highest on the crime index but low on sentenced prisoners, while Mississippi and Alabama were low on the crime index but high on sentenced prisoners.

If any of the statements that you have read in the past few pages upset you, buy a copy of *Crime State Rankings: 1994* (eds. Morgan, Morgan, and Quitno) and do your own analysis for the latest years available. Select your own measures from this volume if you do not like the ones that we picked from the Department of Justice's *Sourcebook*.

Regional Differences

Although we have spoken of regional differences in rates, none of the distributions which we have mentioned produced consistent regional differences. The data set to which we referred and which did produce regional differences did so by examining each of the index offenses separately (Shannon, 1954).

From 1946 to 1952, there were 11 states with murder rates lower than 2 per 100 000 population, North Dakota the lowest and Connecticut the highest of the 11, all in the New England or North Central States. A dozen states had murder rates above 10 per 100 000, ranging to 21, and all were in the South Atlantic, East South Central, or West South Central states, the last the highest. The pattern for aggravated assault was similar.

In 1987, rates for murder ranged from 1.5 per 100 000 population in North Dakota and 1.8 in South Dakota, 2.0 in Wyoming, and 2.1 in Iowa to 11.3 in New York, 11.4 in Florida, 11.7 in Texas, 11.8 in Georgia and 12.2 in Michigan (*Sourcebook – 1988*, pp. 429–37). Does the propensity for violence in a population gradually increase from North and South Dakota's low density to higher population density states and those with other crime generating characteristics? Or does the effectiveness of social controls decrease?

What happens if one looks at Hong Kong and other Asian high density cities with very little of the crime, at least to the present, about which we are so concerned? References to animal studies (rats) as examples of high density life are relevant only if their society is similar to ours. Reference to urban life as a 'rat race' are not sufficient.

How many of those who hypothesize a difference in propensity as an explanation of differences in delinquency and crime rates have been in a railhead cattle-loading community (a low population density community) at the end of a long cattle drive and seen the boisterous activity that almost equals Hollywood's version of Western violence? Pity the back bar and the chairs and tables. What kinds of other situations provide an arena for violence in North Dakota, a state that otherwise has very low rates for crimes of violence?

Regional patterns for burglary, for example, have also varied over time. Rates for burglary in 1987 ranged from 455 and 534 per 100 000 population in North Dakota and South Dakota and 603 in West Virginia to 1787 in New Mexico, 1783 in Oregon, 1904 in Washington, 2118 in Texas and 2256 in Florida. By contrast, between 1946 and 1952, there were 14 states with burglary rates below 300 per 100 000 population and all were in the New England, Middle Atlantic, and North Central States (with the exceptions of Maryland and Louisiana). Seven states with rates over 600 were in the Pacific and Mountain States (with the exception of Florida). Variation in offense patterns by states and regions has changed from the 1920s and 1940s and 1950s to the late 1980s. That in itself should put to rest explanations based upon the idea that some people are inclined toward delinquency and crime, that is, the idea of individual propensity. What could be proposed as the basis for change in individual propensity in some states and not in others? Or can rate differences be accounted for by differences in the effectiveness of programs for social control?

What Do Regional Differences Mean?
As stated over 40 years ago (Shannon, 1954),

> This research lends additional emphasis to the contention that crime, as reported and recorded in the United States, is largely a function of social and cultural factors rather than biological or psychological factors. In the absence of significant biological variations or significant differences in basic mental processes on a regional or sectional basis, all other things being equal, one would expect a rather even crime rate from state to state. Since vast differences in crime rates on a sectional basis are found to persist over a period of time, one may hypothesize that subcultural variations of a regional or sectional nature are responsible for these regional or sectional patterns of crime.

Self-reported Delinquency and Crime and Victimization

Self-reports of Delinquency and Crime
There are two approaches to measuring delinquency and crime other than official records of offenses known to the police, police contacts and referrals, arrest data, court data, and institutional commitments. The first approach consists of self-reported delinquency and crime and the second approach consists of victimization data. The most extensive study of the incidence and prevalence of delinquency and crime over the past 50 years with national samples has been conducted by Elliott *et al.* (1983). They have laid to rest the earlier position that there is little variation in delinquency/crime

rates by SES. We shall also see that there are inequities in how the justice system works which enhance the effects of socioeconomic differences.

To put it even more strongly, the inclination of earlier researchers to believe that official rates which varied by SES were essentially an artifact of the operation of the justice system led to a willing acceptance of the idea that ordinary delinquency and crime were more evenly distributed than had been thought. Elliott's more balanced self-report device found out differently. Even then, the questions asked in Elliott's National Youth Survey Report are in large part less serious examples (for example, joyriding) of the Index offenses which they represent and are scarcely comparable to offenses known to the police or police contact behaviors that place one in the various index categories. There are sufficient comparable offenses, however, to see that aside from disorderly conduct, public intoxication, and the use of marijuana, only a small proportion of the juveniles have engaged in felony-level or serious misdemeanor-level misbehavior.

Marijuana use among Elliott's national youth samples was reported by 17 percent in 1976, rose to 44 percent by 1980, and was irregular but below that rate until 1986 when it declined to 37 percent. Public intoxication rose from 14 percent to 44 percent. For some offenses the proportion of the sample involved (prevalence) rose slightly between 1976 and 1980 and for others it remained the same or declined (*Sourcebook – 1988*, pp. 382–3). As far as the incidences of offenses are concerned, minor assaults such as hitting a student, disorderly conduct, and illegal substance use were highest. Marijuana use exceeded the other illegal substances and alcohol use had an incidence higher than marijuana. Does this mean that the genetic composition of samples of youth has been changing and/or that some inner propensity for substance use and/or abuse has been increasing over the years? Or was propensity the same but controls variable? Have you seen a study which has a measure of societal controls and a negative correlation with illegal substance use?

Victimization Reports

Victimization data differ in that they present a picture of what victims perceive happened to them, really more than that, what a sample of persons and households report for a given year. This provides an opportunity to compare official trend data with victim trend data. Each measures a different dimension of the problem.

The National Crime Survey is conducted for the Bureau of Justice Statistics of the US Bureau of Census. In terms of personal victimization, the rate was 32.6 per 1000 persons age 12 and older in 1973, a rate which slightly increased to 35.3 by 1981 and then declined to 28.6. Household burglary had a rate of 91.7 per 1000 households in 1973, a rate which was somewhat erratic but on the decline since 1981 to a low of 61.3 in 1987 (*Sourcebook – 1988*, p. 283).

The National Crime Survey reveals that from 1975 to 1987 those juveniles who reported receiving a traffic ticket or moving vehicle violation in the previous six months increased from 26.8 percent to 31.2 percent (*Sourcebook – 1988*, pp. 348–9). This question was followed by one which inquired about whether the respondent had been drinking alcoholic beverages, smoking marijuana or hashish, or using other illegal drugs. While there were some fluctuations, the 17.6 percent involvement with alcohol had declined to 13.8 percent by 1988, that with marijuana had declined from 10.4 percent to 3.9 percent, and other illegal drugs declined from 2.3 percent to 1.5 percent (*Sourcebook – 1988*, pp. 351–3). Explaining these changes is difficult and, again, if you examine the patchwork of research which attempts to explain them, you will realize why it is so difficult.

Perceptions of Harmfulness of Substance Use

How do people look at drugs? Although the manufacture, transportation, sale, and possession of drugs has been illegal since passage of the Harrison Act in 1919, it has only been in recent years that the larger public has had the concern evidenced in the 1980s and 1990s, a phenomenon related to the spread of drug use from inner-city, lower SES use to higher SES groups. Thus, the 'dope fiend' image was replaced by that of unfortunate youth with a chemical dependency. Similarly, the inner-city drunkard has been transformed into the diseased, sickbed alcoholic (Peele, 1989; Mulford, 1984).

Tobacco use was once indicative to many of a character defect (Henry Ford and Thomas Edison), but is now looked at as an unfortunate and dangerous addiction. In the middle 1980s there were about 60 million cigarette smokers in the US compared with 113 million drinkers (NIDA, 1989) but only 6 million who non-medically used (in the past month) stimulants, sedatives, tranquilizers, or analgesics.

Not everyone agrees on whether drug use and/or involvement in drugs as an enterprise is a serious crime. When a 1986 sample of the US population was asked how they perceive drug use as a problem, 20 percent answered that it was a very serious problem and another 42 percent said that it was somewhat serious. Although there were demographic variations, they were relatively small. High-income persons were less likely to see drugs as a serious problem than were low-income persons. Similarly, when asked about crime as a serious problem in their neighborhood, although only 10 percent acknowledged it, low-income persons (15 percent) were twice as likely to do so as high-income persons (7 percent) (*Sourcebook –1988*, p. 261). Both were probably making an assessment consistent with their neighborhoods.

What should be done about illegal drug use or any other social problem is a controversial matter. In 1991, 46.7 percent of the Federal defendants sentenced to prison were there for drug offenses (Bureau of Justice Statistics, July 1992). Some would see this as evidence that the problem was being effectively addressed, but others wonder why the space is taken up with drug offenders rather than with violent offenders. While 61 percent of the US population in 1986 believed that stopping the importation of drugs from other countries was the most effective approach to the control of drugs and 68 percent in 1985 agreed that the US government should spend as much money as necessary to stop the flow of drugs into this country, 83 percent believed that drug abuse will never be stopped because a large number of Americans will continue to want drugs and be willing to pay lots of money for them (*Sourcebook – 1988*, p. 264).

The law differs by states in what is considered criminal behavior and what is not. California has now legalized the sale and use of marijuana for medical purposes – loosely defined. Its Cannabis Buyer's Club of San Francisco, the nation's largest distributor of marijuana for medical use, is open after winning a court challenge to the law. Arizona sells official cannabis duty stamps to licensed marijuana dealers, for which a certificate from the State of Arizona costs $100. Neither 1996 US presidential candidate wished to be associated with the Arizona decision by a state legislature controlled by Republicans (*The Sunday Telegraph*, London: October 13, 1996, p. 30). The Arizona law, passed in 1983, was introduced to serve as a method of confiscating drug dealers' profits but did not work out that way. The outcome of this has not yet been determined.

In another poll at the same time, stiffer penalties, more educational programs about drug abuse, and drug testing in the workplace were approaches that were thought to be effective, that is, they would reduce illegal drug use a great deal (*Sourcebook - 1988*, p. 265). In a 1988 poll, educating young people was considered to be the approach that would do the most to halt the drug epidemic (47 percent). It takes more than 'Just Say No.' Making it harder for drugs to enter the country was in second place (35 percent) (*Sourcebook - 1988*, p. 266).

Most people have also been ambivalent about the best strategy for controlling excessive use of alcohol, tobacco, and other drugs. We shall not go into the argument for or against the wisdom of developing an anti-drug program that emphasizes either destruction of drugs at the source or interdiction at the borders of the country, nor the inconsistency in taking the position that tobacco use must be curtailed by directing programs at individuals when it would be so easy to destroy (prohibit its growth) at the source. What if we did say 'no' to the production of tobacco and bourbon whiskey in Kentucky and Tennessee? What would happen to the poor families of tobacco growers and workers and the families of those employed in distilleries?

High school seniors have changed their perception of drugs. In 1977 only 13.4 percent believed that smoking marijuana occasionally would put them at great risk of harming themselves (physically or in other ways) but this increased to 31.7 percent by 1988. Smoking it regularly was believed to be a great risk by 36.4 percent in 1977 and 77.0 percent in 1988. LSD, cocaine, amphetamines, and barbiturates were thought to constitute a 'great risk' in 1977 and their regular use was considered to be such a risk by even larger percentages in 1988, up to 89.2 percent for regular use of cocaine and 88.8 for heroin. By contrast, the risk of regular use of amphetamines and barbiturates was considered high in 1977 (66.6 percent and 68.6 percent) but increased by only 1 to 3 percent over the years.

Juveniles did not exhibit such dramatic changes in their evaluation of the risk of harming oneself for the various categories of alcohol use, For example, the risk of harm by taking four or five drinks nearly every day increased from 62.9 percent to 68.5 percent. The risk of smoking one or more packs of cigarettes per day increased from 58.4 percent in 1977 to 68.9 percent in 1988 (*Sourcebook - 1988*, p. 253). Young adults had similar responses to the smoking questions from 1980 to 1987, but were more concerned about the risk of heavy drinking (*Sourcebook – 1988*, p. 254). Persons who believed their health problems to be related to substance use blamed alcohol (32 percent) and tobacco (33 percent) in the National Institute for Drug Abuse's 1985 National Household Survey (NIDA, 1989).

There is little doubt that samples of high school seniors have in one way or another been convinced that there is considerable risk in substance abuse. By 1988 they disapproved of drug use, alcohol use, and cigarette smoking, disapproval having risen by as much as 30 percentage points for some categories of use since 1977 (*Sourcebook – 1988*, p. 256). The percent believing that marijuana should be entirely legal had dropped from 33.6 percent to 15.4 percent between 1977 and 1987 and the percent who thought that it should be a crime had increased from 21.7 percent to 45.3 percent (*Sourcebook – 1988*, p. 257).

What do these changes in perception of the danger of substance use and abuse suggest about the very nature of delinquency and crime, tobacco, alcohol, and drug use? Doesn't it emphasize the ·social and definitional nature of misbehavior in contrast to the idea that those who engage in misbehavior should be dealt with as clinical entities with psychological or physiological proclivity to become involved in deviant behavior?

SUMMARY

State-by-state and regional comparisons of official crime statistics reveal that the offense rate for serious crime (Total Crime Index) is four times as high per 1000 population in the four states with the most serious problem as in the states with the lowest offense rates. Differences in arrest rates between the highest and lowest states had a similar range as did the rate of sentenced prisoners, but none of these rates were highly correlated. The pattern of relationships between measures of offenses and efforts to control became even more complex when we examined efforts to deal with crime in terms of the proportion of state budgets and per capita expenditures designated for the justice system and/or its component parts.

When state and regional differences were considered for specific offenses, burglary, for example, there were not only greater differences than had been found for overall rates but regional differences consistent with the research going back to the 1930s, 1940s, and 1950s. In each case we know of no data that would suggest that there was a basis for genetic, psychological, or any innate propensity explanations of difference in offense rates. Instead, the findings, as they have in the past, suggest that social, structural, and cultural factors lie behind state and regional differences in crime rates.

Self-report and victimization data presented a mixed picture of delinquency and crime increases and declines as well as downward changes in alcohol use and drug involvement. Still, alcohol and drugs are considered to be serious problems by persons of all ages and SES groups, with variation by demographic and social characteristics of respondents. Nor was there agreement on how to deal with the problems of delinquency and crime, alcohol and drugs.

How does Racine fit into the national scene and what is Racine's representativeness as a research site for those who wish to better understand the social genesis of delinquency and crime? Here we will have more detailed data on people and their neighborhoods and measures of delinquency and crime for individuals and for neighborhoods which will enable us to go beyond what we have learned from a picture painted with a broad brush.

NOTE

1. The various index figures, offense rates, arrest rates, sentencing rates, and other justice system statistics as well as a number of national survey findings were taken from or based on tables in Maguire and Flanagan (eds.), *Sourcebook of Criminal Justice Statistics – 1987 and 1988*, Washington: US Department of Justice, 1988 and 1989, in the present case from pp. 429–37, *Sourcebook – 1988*. Additional references in this chapter to material from the *Sourcebook – 1988* were made by citing appropriate pages.

2 Delinquency and Crime in Racine

FOCUSING ON THE URBAN SCENE IN RACINE

Having established the social nature of delinquency and crime in the United States and their changing types and patterns we shall now examine the nature of delinquency and crime in Racine. Racine's urban scene is a miniature of Chicago. As the sociologist sees it, human behavior is a product of how people have been socialized to deal with life problems in the sub-sector of society of which they are a part. These problems are encapsulated to a considerable degree within neighborhoods and clusters of neighborhoods. It is how the elements of behavior which are acquired in a given stratum of society or types of neighborhoods are put together to carry out and justify delinquent and/or criminal acts that is the major concern of sociologists. And it is here that sociologists differ from psychologists and psychiatrists.

Gang Murder

For example, to bring the issue home to Racine, *The Journal Times*, February 13, 1992, contained a front-page story about how ten gang members looking for a thrill killed a South Side teenager.

> Ten gang members – one a 15-year-old boy – stalked the South Side last September, randomly hunting for someone to kill in the hours before a Milwaukee man was slain on a street corner, Racine police said.
>
> ... They weren't really particular about who they were going to shoot, according to Detective Jon Soderberg.
>
> ... Gang members reportedly drove around for hours before the shooting, trying to get up the nerve to kill. The adults in the group also tried to convince the juveniles into committing the murder, police said.
>
> The decision to seek out a victim was made after the Vice Lords reportedly became agitated during a minor scuffle at a football game between Park and Horlick High Schools. Police

aren't sure who else was involved in the argument, but [the victim] wasn't even at the game.

After the fight, the North Side gang members piled into three cars and reportedly drove around the South Side – the turf of the rival gang federation known as 'Folks' – looking for a chance to shoot any person they thought might be associated with the group.

... Our investigation has confirmed that (Vice Lords) in at least three vehicles were on a mission to seek out some members of the South Side 'Folks' gang, said detective Lt. Steven C. Molnar.

At one point, the Vice Lords got out of their cars near 17th and Center streets and reportedly pointed guns at, and chased, some people who were gathered nearby. No shots were fired and no one was reported injured in the incident.

Then, at about 11:30 p.m., the Vice Lords found several people standing near 21st and Mead Streets.

After flashing gang signs and cruising the street in a caravan of cars reportedly meant as a show of force, several Vice Lords exited the cars, police said.

Moments later, the gunfire that ended [the victim's] life erupted as the Vice Lords indiscriminately sprayed the neighborhood with about a half-dozen bullets, police said. One of the bullets struck [the victim] in the head. He died several hours later at St. Luke's hospital.

Even a Newspaper Story Tells Us

Does this sound as though the participants were suffering from a mental disorder or an illness? Is this the behavior of persons who were unaware of the nature and consequences of their acts? Similar stories may be found in the media for almost any metropolitan area. An Associated Press story about some of the 4000 people who have been killed or wounded in New York in 1992 (*The Daily Iowan*, September 4, 1992) ran, '12 Injured in Spray Shooting in South Bronx Neighborhood.' It was described as 'a shooting spree of such ferocity and randomness that even the case-hardened cops of the 41st Precinct were amazed.'

This is not the point at which to embark on a description of how a multitude of factors add up to the acquisition of delinquent/criminal attitudes, rationalizations, and knowledge of techniques for delinquent and criminal acts. We must first present a general picture of the extent and nature of delinquency and crime and how they have varied over the years and, even more specifically, from month to month. In short, we shall further establish the social nature of delinquency and crime by examining some data for the entire city and for the groups that were selected for more intensive analysis. This should be sufficient to further dispel any notion that the inner nature of man, his/her biological or psychological functions, are basic to an understanding of how delinquent and criminal behaviors develop.

SEASONAL FLUCTUATIONS IN RATES

Another phenomenon which must be considered from the viewpoint which argues that delinquency and crime are explained by the nature of human life is the degree to which offense rates fluctuate seasonally and the fact that variation on a seasonal basis may be as great or greater within almost any set of spatial units of measurement (Police Grid Areas, Census Tracts, Aldermanic Areas, or Neighborhoods) than that which occur year by year over a period of years.

Plots 1 through 4 for 1969–79 (Shannon, 1981) show that seasonal variation in rates is clearly greater than the change in rates over a period of ten years. For example, the January to July difference in number of offenses committed in Racine in many years was as great or greater than the differences in number of offenses committed in January of 1969 and January of 1979 (Plot 1).

In Police Grid Area 12 (Plot 2) the extreme inner city area, that is, central business district and adjacent deteriorating area, seasonal fluctuation in offenses known to the police (based on place of offense) became greater and greater, particularly during peak years in the 1970s. Fluctuations for Police Grid 12, or any other grid, were the product of offenses in the area not only by people who resided there but by the multitude of others attracted to the central business district as well. The rate was a product of changing patterns of social interaction in a community with four rather distinct seasons which provide climates for varying types of indoor and outdoor activities among the city's population. This is not meant to be an acceptance of turn of the century geographical explanations or, for that matter, even more recent claims that climate influences violence, but to point to the varying nature of human use of time as the seasons change.

In an area with a smaller number of offenses, a high SES residential area (Police Grid 4, for example), the seasonal fluctuation is just as apparent as in an inner city area such as Grid 12 (Plot 3). Although there is a pattern of seasonal fluctuation for theft for the city and for Police Grids 12 and 4 (Plot 4), there are also idiosyncrasies which point to specific offenses as a product of interaction with one's immediate social environment, one's place of residence, place of work, and place of leisure-time activities which may change in some respects from year to year. In short, the seasonal changes in how life is organized in urban areas have a significant effect on total offense rates, specific kinds of offense rates, and the location of offenses, as do a variety of other social variables.

Seasonal fluctuations are not central to the focus of this volume but they do reveal an important aspect of the social nature of crime. Just as recreational and other activities have a seasonal nature, weather influences the likelihood that people will engage in various types of offenses. Do young men chase young women on the beach in January? There are, of course, temporal variations within any 24-hour period by offense types (differences in the frequency with which some offenses are committed by the time of day, early evening, late evening, and so forth) (*Sourcebook – 1988*, pp. 313–14). Although this is not really pertinent to the major issues addressed in this volume, it indicates that those who commit certain kinds of time-spaced offenses are neither engaging in them precipitously nor without some knowledge of the nature of their acts.

THE LONGITUDINAL BIRTH COHORT DATA

Now that we have examined some of the variations in delinquency/ crime rates and public concern in the United States, have touched on the growing apprehension about alcohol and drugs and their relationship to delinquency and crime, and have briefly described annual and seasonal fluctuations in official offense rates for the city of Racine, it is time to look at the Racine birth cohort data. Although the tables in this chapter and their description may not be the most fascinating part of the book, we have found that every new set of readers must have the basic data before them. It is important that we present these data, even in abbreviated form,

Plot 1.
Offenses for City of Racine from January 1969 to December 1979

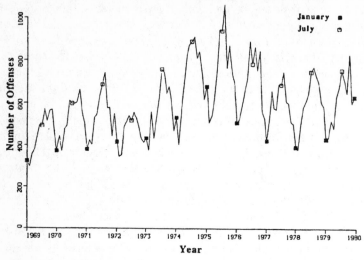

Plot 2.
Offenses in Grid 12 from January 1969 to December 1979

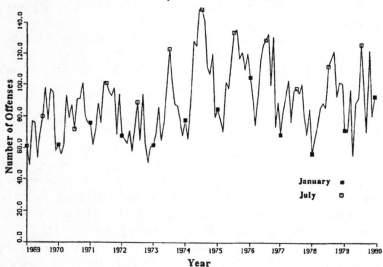

Plot 3.
Offenses in Grids 12 and 4 from January 1969 to December 1979

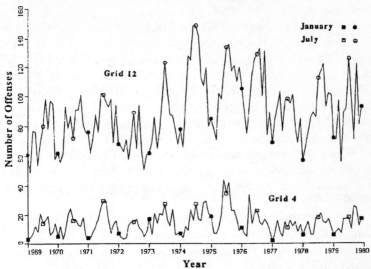

Plot 4.
Theft/Larceny in Grids 12 and 4 from January 1969 to December 1979

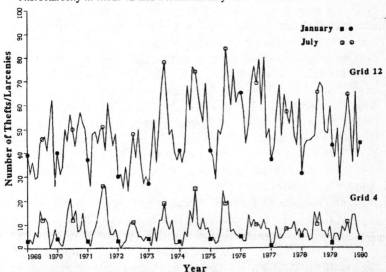

because they are the foundation upon which our argument for a sociological explanation of delinquency and crime and continuity in it rests.

Offense and disposition data for the three birth cohorts (1942, 1949, and 1955) were obtained from Racine's police and court records and originally covered the age periods 6–33, 6–27, and 6–22. Collection of the police record data on the three cohorts began in 1974 and first finished in 1976. More recently, we collected data on the 1955 Cohort to age 33. Although some of the analyses will deal with the 1955 Cohort to age 22, our most definitive analyses will be based on data to age 33. The results that we shall report in the next few pages include the updated 1955 Cohort's data. If anything sounds repetitious of our earlier descriptions of the findings, it is because the updated data only confirmed what had been previously reported.

The first panel of Table 1 presents the race/ethnic|sex composition of the birth cohort samples. They were fairly evenly balanced by sex, but each cohort was predominantly white, although decreasingly so from cohort to cohort.

The second panel of the table includes only those who had continuous residence in Racine. Note that the male-female proportion was less balanced and that, cohort by cohort, there were proportionately even fewer whites (lower percent in the table). The proportion of whites among those with continuous residence declined even further between 1976 and 1988 for the 1955 Cohort. The proportion of blacks and Chicanos increased cohort by cohort.

In the third panel of Table 1 we see that as of 1976, 80.3 percent of the 1955 Cohort had continuous residence, in comparison with 61.8 percent for the 1949 Cohort and 46.8 percent of the 1942 Cohort. The last column of the total figures in the third panel shows that during the 12 years between 1976 and 1988, additional members of the 1955 Cohort were lost so that only 63.1 percent of the cohort members with continuous residence as of 1976 now had continuous residence.

Many members of the 1955 Cohort are now in other states from New York to California, elsewhere in Wisconsin, in foreign countries, have unknown whereabouts, or, if still in Racine, have been out of the city long enough to not be considered continuous residents, that is, absent for more than three years during the older adult period, age 21 or over. Hundreds and hundreds of telephone calls to members of the 1955 Cohort, their parents, siblings, other relatives,

Table 1.
Basic Characteristics of the 1942, 1949, and 1955 Cohorts and Percent of Persons with Continuous Residence in Racine 1976* and 1988**

	Males				Females				Total			
			1955				1955				1955	
	1942	1949	1976	1988	1942	1949	1976	1988	1942	1949	1976	1988
Cohort												
Number	679	1081	1114	1369	673	1018	1035	1307	1352	2099	2149	2676
% by Sex	50.2	51.5	51.8	51.2	49.8	48.3	48.2	48.8				
% White	94.1	90.1	86.3	86.4	94.8	91.5	88.6	88.4	94.4	90.7	87.4	87.4
% Black	4.6	6.8	9.5	9.1	3.0	5.8	8.3	8.4	3.8	6.3	8.9	8.8
% Chicano	1.3	3.2	4.2	4.5	2.3	2.7	3.1	3.1	1.8	2.9	3.7	3.8
Total	100.0	100.1	100.0	100.0	100.1	100.0	100.0	99.9	100.0	99.9	100.0	100.0
Continuous Residence												
Number	356	740	1114	717	277	557	1035	640	633	1297	2149	1357
% by Sex	56.2	57.1	51.8	52.8	43.8	42.9	48.2	47.2	95.6	91.4	87.4	85.6
% White	94.9	91.5	86.3	84.7	96.4	91.2	88.6	86.6				
% Black	4.2	5.9	9.5	10.9	1.8	7.0	8.3	9.8	3.2	6.4	8.9	10.4
% Chicano	.8	2.6	4.2	4.5	1.8	1.9	3.1	3.6	1.3	2.2	3.7	4.1
Total	99.9	100.0	100.0	100.1	100.0	100.0	100.0	100.0	100.1	100.0	100.0	100.1
Percent of Category with Continuous Residence												
% Total	52.4	68.5	81.4	64.4	41.2	54.7	76.7	61.8	46.8	61.8	80.3	63.1
% White	52.9	69.5	81.2	63.2	42.0	54.6	79.3	60.4	47.4	62.2	80.3	61.8
% Black	48.4	59.6	84.8	73.6	25.0	66.1	78.2	73.3	39.2	62.4	81.7	73.4
% Chicano	33.3	59.5	77.0	68.1	33.3	35.7	78.0	71.9	33.3	47.5	77.5	69.6

* Absent from Racine no more than three years during the age period 6 through the original cut-off date for that cohort.
** Continuous Resident of Racine in 1976 and absent from Racine no more than three years between 1976 and 1988.

Table 2.
Distribution of Police Contacts by Type for 1955 Cohort Members with Continuous Residence in Racine in 1976 and 1988 and with Non-Continuous Residence in 1988

| | Ages 6–17 | | Ages 18–20 | |
	CONT	NONC	CONT	NONC
Traffic	9.4	10.3	31.6	28.3
Disorderly Conduct	14.5	15.6	27.5	26.5
Suspicion, Investigation	15.1	15.0	12.5	11.5
Liquor	2.5	2.4	2.1	2.9
Theft	12.7	13.8	5.6	7.7
Incorrigible, Runaway, Truant	27.9	23.9	.3	.6
Vagrancy	1.6	1.5	.6	.4
Auto Theft	2.2	2.9	1.3	1.4
Sex Offenses	.8	1.1	1.5	1.4
Assault	2.5	2.1	2.6	2.3
Burglary	6.5	5.7	4.0	4.2
Weapons	.7	.7	1.6	1.2
Violent Property Destruction	.7	.9	1.2	1.2
Forgery, Fraud	.8	1.3	1.3	2.9
Robbery	1.0	.8	1.9	2.1
Gambling	.1	–	.1	.1
Narcotics, Drugs	1.2	1.7	4.0	5.3
Homicide	–	.1	.1	.1
TOTAL	100.2	99.8	99.8	100.1
Percent Part I	24.9	25.4	15.5	17.8
Part I Mean Contacts per Person	.580	.319	.161	.100
Mean Contacts Per Person	2.3	1.3	1.0	.6
Number of Police Contacts	3170	1635	1412	732

and friends in 1989 revealed that the bulk of those who are not in Racine left after high school or college because they believed that employment opportunities were better elsewhere or because their spouse was pursuing employment opportunities elsewhere – Racine had been transformed into an old smokestack city.

Although we had earlier found that those who were continuous residents were not significantly different from those who were not continuous residents a new comparison of them was made. Table 2 is based on the types of offense that resulted in police contacts for 1357, 1955 Cohort members with continuous residence in 1988 and the 803, 1955 Cohort members who were no longer continuous residents but had been continuous residents in 1976. Those who left had on the average fewer police contacts and fewer serious reasons for police contacts (shown as mean contacts per person) during the age periods 6–17 and 18–20 than had those cohort members who remained in the community, although a slightly higher proportion of their offenses were Part I for those who left than for those who stayed. Remember that the Racine cohort data are for police contacts, referrals, and court dispositions. When we speak about offenses by members of a cohort we are referring to the type of offense for which a police contact was made. Telephone conversations with hundreds of those who were no longer in the community gave the impression that a large proportion has made successful adjustments in their new communities; whether they have had more than the occasional traffic ticket we do not know.

THE CHANGING NUMBER AND DISTRIBUTION OF OFFENSES IN THE RACINE COHORTS

In Table 3, an updated version of data appearing in earlier publications, it is possible to compare cohort offense differences within age periods, differences between age periods within each cohort, and differences between those in the 1955 Cohort with continuous residence to 1976 vs. 1988, as well as to examine total cohort distributions by offense type. The 1955 Cohort distributions are blocked off to facilitate comparison of the 1976 continuous residents and those who were still in Racine and the 1988 continuous residents. The general pattern of offenses for those who remained as of 1988 when compared with the larger group remaining in 1976 does, however, indicate a distribution of the remaining 1988 Cohort members which was a bit more skewed toward the serious end of the continuum and whose career continuity from the juvenile to the adult period will be somewhat greater.

With controls for sex, the number of police contacts during the juvenile period were not significantly different at the 0.05 level for those with continuous residence to 1988 from those who had continuous residence only to 1976. Nor, with race/ethnicity controlled,

Table 3.
Distribution of Police Contacts by Type in Cohorts and Age Periods with 1955 Cohort as of 1988 Added

	Ages 6–17		1955		Ages 18–20		1955		Ages 21+		1955		Total		1955	
	1942	1949	1976	1988	1942	1949	1976	1988	1942	1949	1976	1988	1942	1949	1976	1988
Traffic	25.4	17.2	10.1	9.4	52.2	39.0	31.3	31.6	49.4	36.7	28.9	42.0	42.5	28.4	17.8	23.4
Disorderly Conduct	25.3	22.3	15.0	14.5	15.7	21.7	27.4	27.5	20.9	28.1	35.5	21.3	21.2	23.8	20.3	19.3
Suspicion, Investigation	16.6	19.9	15.1	15.1	16.9	25.1	12.2	12.5	21.0	22.4	15.1	7.3	18.9	21.9	14.2	12.4
Liquor	6.1	5.1	2.3	2.5	4.0	1.9	2.1	2.1	2.0	1.6	1.0	1.6	3.6	3.3	2.2	2.2
Theft	7.8	9.6	12.9	12.7	3.0	3.0	5.4	5.6	1.1	1.9	3.1	5.0	3.6	5.7	9.9	9.0
Incorrigible, Runaway, Truant	9.6	14.0	26.5	27.9	1.0	.2	.3	.3	.1	.2	–	–	3.2	6.5	16.9	14.0
Vagrancy	2.6	2.7	1.7	1.6	1.6	2.1	.7	.6	.5	.7	1.3	.4	1.4	2.0	1.4	1.0
Auto Theft	2.9	1.9	2.4	2.2	1.2	.7	1.5	1.3	.2	.1	.2	.2	1.2	1.1	2.0	1.4
Sex Offenses	.6	1.2	.9	.8	2.0	1.5	1.3	1.5	.9	1.2	1.0	1.1	1.0	1.3	1.0	1.0
Assault	.5	1.0	2.3	2.5	.2	1.0	2.4	2.6	1.2	1.8	2.1	5.3	.8	1.2	2.3	3.3
Burglary	1.6	2.8	6.2	6.5	.6	.6	3.8	4.0	.2	.4	.8	1.0	.7	1.6	5.1	4.4
Weapons	.5	.4	.7	.7	.2	.4	1.4	1.6	.5	.4	1.2	2.3	.4	.4	.9	1.4
Violent Property Destruction	.6	.2	.7	.7	1.0	.7	1.3	1.2	.1	.4	1.0	2.6	.4	.4	.9	1.3
Forgery, Fraud	–	1.0	.8	.8	.2	1.2	1.9	1.3	.7	1.4	1.8	3.0	.4	1.1	1.2	1.4
Robbery	–	.4	.8	1.0	.2	.3	2.0	1.9	.5	.3	.7	.6	.3	.4	1.1	1.1
Gambling	.1	.2	.1	.1	–	.1	.2	.1	.3	.1	–	.3	.2	.1	.1	.1
Narcotics, Drugs	–	–	1.5	1.2	–	.6	4.7	4.0	.3	2.2	5.9	5.3	.1	.8	2.8	3.0
Homicide	–	–	–.1	–	–	.1	.1	.1	–	–	.3	.2	–	–.1	.1	.1
TOTAL	100.2	99.9	100.1	100.2	100.0	100.2	100.0	99.8	99.9	99.9	99.9	99.5	99.9	100.1	100.2	99.8
Percent Part I	12.7	15.9	24.6	24.9	5.2	5.6	15.3	15.5	3.2	4.5	7.2	12.3	6.5	10.0	20.5	19.3
Part I Mean Contacts per Person	.168	.307	.510	.580	.041	.060	.143	.161	.070	.055	.021	.159	.278	.422	.673	.900
Mean Contacts Per Person	1.3	1.9	2.1	2.3	.8	1.1	.9	1.0	2.2	1.2	.3	1.3	4.3	4.2	3.3	4.7
Number of Police Contacts	836	2511	4444	3170	498	1383	2008	1412	1370	1587	608	1765	2704	5481	7060	6347

were the two groups significantly different. If both sex and race/ethnicity are controlled, the only significant differences during the juvenile period were for black males, with those who remained in Racine to 1988 having significantly more police contacts than the larger group that had remained only until 1976.

When comparisons for offense seriousness as reported by the police are made for the juvenile period with controls for sex, both males and females who remained in Racine to 1988 had more serious offense records than did those remaining until 1976. With controls for race/ethnicity, the only significant difference was for blacks, those remaining in Racine to 1988 having significantly more serious reasons for police contacts than the group remaining to 1976. When both controls were applied, white and black females who remained to 1988 had more serious records than did the group who had remained until 1976.

Turning to the 18 through 20 age period, males, whites, and white and black females, who remained in Racine to 1988 averaged significantly more police contacts than did the larger group who had been there in 1976. Offense seriousness comparisons for this age period followed a similar pattern to others, males with continuous residence to 1988 having significantly more serious offenses, whites and blacks with continuous residence having significantly more serious offenses, and white males and females who remained to 1988 having significantly more serious offenses. Black males and females who remained had more serious offenses but the differences were not significant.

The dissimilarities shown for age 21+ are based on changes in the distribution of offense patterns which come with age, an increase in traffic offenses and a decrease in disorderly conduct, for example. This table also reveals that the percent of police contacts which were Part I remains the same for the two comparable age periods, 6–17 and 18–20, 24.6 vs. 24.7 and 15.3 vs. 15.5, and that the number of Part I contacts per person remains about the same: 0.510 vs. 0.580 and 0.143 vs. 0.161.

The data for a longer period of time at risk for the 1955 Cohort now enables us to see that this cohort had a higher mean number of Part I contacts per person (theft, auto theft, assault, burglary, robbery, murder) and higher mean number of contacts in general than did the 1942 and 1949 Cohorts. This is probably a matter of proportionately more police contacts cohort by cohort as well as increased police concern and reporting about delinquency and crime.

THE CHANGING INCIDENCE OF SERIOUS OFFENSES IN THE RACINE COHORTS

Cohort and Age Period Increases in Seriousness

More specific comparisons of the 1955 Cohort's 1976 and 1988 continuous residence persons with the two earlier cohorts were made to show how the incidence of police contacts for various offenses (number of contacts per person) has increased or remained stable across cohorts during each age period and how they had changed from age period to age period for persons in each of the three cohorts. The age period cohort rates were of particular interest because they enabled us to see that the incidence of some more serious offenses had remained stable while some had changed during the life-cycle for members of each cohort, thus increasing or decreasing the mean for the cohort during that age period. Similar comparisons of rates for only persons with contacts allowed us to determine where the increases for specific offenses had been greatest among those in the cohort who did get into trouble.

In later analyses we shall focus on how the 1955 Cohort members had developed a higher incidence of specific kinds of seriousness than had the 1942 and 1949 Cohorts, involving alcohol and/or drugs as well as auto theft, assault, burglary, weapons, violent property destruction, and robbery during the juvenile vs. adult periods. This led into more serious types of delinquent and criminal careers, that is, combinations of specific offenses and levels of seriousness, than those found in the 1942 and 1949 Cohorts.

Increasing Weapons Offenses

It should come as no surprise that weapons offense rates for younger cohort members markedly increased in Racine at the time that increases in weapons offenses provided almost daily headlines on the first page of newspapers throughout the country. Typical was that of *The New York Times* for February 16, 1992, 'Teen-Age Gunslinging Is On Rise, In Search of Protection and Profit.' The *Times* story opens with,

> On a shadowy corner in Brooklyn, a gangly teen-ager slowly opened his jacket to give a peek at the 9-millimeter semiautomatic pistol jammed in the waistband of his jeans.

'When you've got it,' he said, glancing at the weapon, 'you've got the power. It doesn't matter whether you're big or small. You've got the power.'

In a pizza parlor not far away, two young men said they felt naked without their guns. 'It is like an article of clothing,' one explained. 'I put on my shoes, my pants, my shirt, my hat and my gun.'

Throughout New York City these days, there are teen-agers toting guns, armed from the arsenal of tens of thousands of pistols and revolvers, sawed-off shotguns and submachine guns that have been flooding in on the surging currents of riches and violence in the nation's biggest drug market.

But New York is not alone. Experts say that all around the country teen-agers are taking up guns. 'The number of young people arming themselves and dying is reaching epidemic proportions,' said Vanessa Scherzer, a spokeswoman for the Center to Prevent Handgun Violence in Washington. 'It's happening in both cities and small towns.'

In this respect Racine is also a microcosm of urban, industrial society.

How the 1955 Cohort Signaled the Future

Remember that (Table 2) those who left Racine by 1988 had, on the average, fewer police contacts, fewer Part I contacts, but a slightly greater proportion of their offenses were serious offenses (Part I) than had those who stayed. The important point is that offense rates increased cohort by cohort for continuous residents, the 1955 Cohort signaling the higher offense rates in the 1980s. Moreover, the mean rates for felonies and major misdemeanors for white vs. black males aged 6–17 in the 1942 Cohort were 0.305 vs. 0.467, but this rose to 0.619 for white males and 3.858 for black males in the 1955 Cohort. There were similar increases in seriousness rates for only those in the cohorts who had police contacts. It is undoubtedly the increasing incidence of serious offenses (and in a racially and ethnically mixed society with high urban segregation, and a more rapidly accelerating increase for black and Chicano males aged 6–17) which is responsible for such public concern, let alone political posturing by vote seekers of both parties.

In addition to the Total Mean Rates and Part I Mean Rates for cohorts and age periods, total and Part I annualized offense rates increased cohort by cohort for the age periods 6–17 and 18–20. During the age period 21+ the picture was more complex. The cohort to cohort increase was present in comparisons made with the unextended 1955 Cohort but the extended 1955 Cohort with its 13 years of exposure after age 21 had entered Racine's period of declining criminal activity and thus produced a lower annualized rate. A large proportion of the cohort discontinued their, at least observable, criminal activities in five or six years rather than 13.

The annualized rates show that while in most cases mean offense rates were highest during the age period 18–20 and always lowest at age 21+, mean Part I offense rates were always highest during the 6–17 age period and declined thereafter. To this we must add that Part I offenses, such as theft and burglary, make it easy to produce a high juvenile offense rate for public consumption in an effort to highlight the problem of delinquency. Few juveniles can become involved in more sophisticated, less easily detected non-Part I misbehaviors. While the 1955 Cohort rates signaled an increase in serious crime as traditionally measured, this same period was producing a new set of sophisticated white collar crimes that have only recently been confronted by the justice system. Most of these have, in a manner of speaking, been reserved for males.

THE CHANGING DISTRIBUTION OF SERIOUS OFFENSES BY AGE PERIOD, SEX, AND COHORT

Table 4, describing age period and sex differences, is again an update of an earlier table and shows that in every age period in every cohort with one exception (the 1955 Cohort for the 21+ period), males have a higher percentage of their police contacts in the three most serious offense categories and that these differences remain at every age period in the extended (members with continuous residence to 1988) 1955 Cohort. The proportion of female police contacts in serious offense categories has increased cohort by cohort and male–female differences in offense seriousness have decreased from cohort to cohort, a finding consistent with that of other studies in recent years.

When all members of each cohort (males and females) were arrayed according to their most serious offense, members of the extended 1955 Cohort were more skewed toward the serious end of the continuum than were members of the original cohorts whose

Table 4.
Percent of Contacts in Seriousness of Contact Category by Cohort, Sex, and Age Period

Ages 6–17

	Males			Females		
	1942	1949	1955	1942	1949	1955
Felony Against Person	.5	.8	2.7	–	.9	3.2
Felony Against Property	5.3	6.2	11.8	1.0	.3	2.9
Major Misdemeanor	9.1	11.6	16.5	5.2	9.0	13.7
Minor Misdemeanor	47.6	41.1	27.3	33.3	28.8	28.7
Juvenile Condition	9.2	13.0	26.3	12.5	20.7	36.8
Suspicion, Investigation	28.4	27.4	15.4	47.9	40.2	14.7
TOTAL	100.0	100.1	100.0	99.9	100.0	100.0
Mean Seriousness	2.6	2.6	2.9	2.0	2.1	2.6
Number of Contacts	740	2188	2499	96	323	627

Ages 18–20

	Males			Females		
	1942	1949	1955	1942	1949	1955
Felony Against Person	.9	1.1	8.5	3.5	–	5.3
Felony Against Property	2.0	2.8	8.9	–	1.1	2.8
Major Misdemeanor	5.0	6.0	11.2		1.5	6.9
Minor Misdemeanor	46.0	40.3	57.5	35.1	42.6	74.9
Juvenile Condition	1.1	.3	.1	–	.4	.6
Suspicion, Investigation	44.9	49.5	13.8	61.4	54.4	9.4
TOTAL	99.9	100.0	100.0	100.0	100.0	99.9
Mean Seriousness	2.2	2.2	3.2	1.9	1.9	3.1
Number of Contacts	441	1113	1067	57	270	319

Ages 21+

	Males			Females		
	1942	1949	1955	1942	1949	1955
Felony Against Person	1.1	2.1	6.3	1.1	2.5	8.7
Felony Against Property	1.1	2.0	2.3	–	.7	1.5
Major Misdemeanor	3.3	5.5	17.3	1.7	3.9	18.0
Minor Misdemeanor	45.4	47.8	66.5	41.8	50.9	65.3
Juvenile Condition	–	.1	–	.6	.7	–
Suspicion, Investigation	49.1	42.5	7.6	54.8	41.4	6.5
TOTAL	100.0	100.0	100.0	100.0	100.1	100.0
Mean Seriousness	2.4	2.3	3.3	1.9	2.3	3.3
Number of Contacts	1193	1302	1333	177	285	401

Total

	Males			Females		
	1942	1949	1955	1942	1949	1955
Felony Against Person	.9	1.2	4.9	1.2	1.1	5.3
Felony Against Property	2.6	4.2	8.6	.3	.7	2.4
Major Misdemeanor	5.4	8.5	15.6	2.4	5.0	13.4
Minor Misdemeanor	46.2	42.8	44.4	38.2	40.2	50.6
Juvenile Condition	3.1	6.3	13.5	3.9	8.0	17.3
Suspicion, Investigation	41.9	37.0	13.0	53.9	45.0	11.0
TOTAL	100.0	100.0	100.0	99.9	100.0	100.0
Mean Seriousness	2.3	2.4	3.1	1.9	2.1	3.0
Number of Contacts	2374	4603	4899	330	878	1347

* 1955 Cohort reported for persons with continuous residence in 1988.

records had been followed to only 1976, the 1942 and 1949 Cohorts. It was also apparent that sex differences for traditional types of law breaking had declined even more as the 1955 Cohort's period of exposure was increased.

SUMMARY

Several time series were shown to indicate the rather erratic fluctuation in number of offenses from month to month (seasonal) and year to year in Racine and then total offenses vs. specific offenses in two police grid areas. These and the other data clearly indicate that crime rates are in part a product of seasonal variation in patterns of social interaction.

Every comparison of the cohorts has indicated that those members of the 1955 Cohort who left Racine, whether to outlying suburban neighborhoods, to other cities in Wisconsin, to other states, particularly the East and West Coasts, or to foreign countries, were somewhat more middle or upper SES than those who remained in Racine. Every comparison has also shown that during the age periods 6–17 and 18–20, those who stayed (even though they had slightly higher police contact rates and slightly more serious offenses) were sufficiently representative to enable us to describe cohort-to-cohort changes in types and patterns of delinquency and crime.

The 1955 Cohort members had been more involved with the justice system than had those from earlier cohorts and those of that cohort who remained had been somewhat more involved with the police than had those who left. Still, the extended sample produced 1357 cohort members distributed among groups of neighborhoods in a sufficiently balanced way to permit examination of the relationship between alcohol/drugs and delinquency/crime with controls for sex and neighborhood of socialization.

The next question is an old one and, although worried and chewed upon like a dog with a poor rabbit, has not yet been answered. Is it sufficient to speak about delinquency and crime or must we address the varying types of crime and perhaps types of delinquents and criminals? This brings in the complications that almost entirely escape persons who are so willing to proclaim that they have the answer to delinquency and crime prevention.

3 The Ecological Approach to Explaining Delinquency

DANGEROUS AREAS

For those who have spent most of their lives in small-town America, it is no longer surprising if a visit to the city brings words of caution from friends about where not to go for an evening stroll. Whether fear of becoming a victim is completely justified by the facts, or is an artifact of the imagination, or a creation of the media, we are warned to avoid neighborhoods in which ordinary street crime is commonplace and which is frequented by persons on the way to prison or just released from prison.

By the same token, the media's characterization of the type of neighborhood in which one resides may play a part in determining one's perception of the extent and nature of delinquency and crime. Then, again, the simple fact that your neighbor may believe it necessary to carry a baseball bat to and from the grocery store may incline one to be more concerned about the safety of the neighborhood.

Delinquency and crime are part of the way of life of more of the residents in inner-city neighborhoods than in other kinds of neighborhoods. The delinquent neighborhood, the dangerous area, may be so because it not only has a disproportionate number of residents who are law-breakers, but because it has targets which attract other law-breakers, or because it is an arena for night-time recreational activities which may evolve into delinquency and crime. There are, of course, neighborhoods in which few law-breakers reside and to which few are attracted as well as combinations of each type.

Unfortunately, there are many inner-city neighborhoods in which most young males have had contact with the police before the age of 18 and a large proportion are early-on socialized into delinquency as a way of life. Bursik and Grasmick (1993) have dealt with this at length in Chapter 4 of their volume, *Neighborhoods and Crime: The Dimensions of Effective Community Control*.

One sometimes wonders if the urban population has not only unknowingly turned the Chicago model of the city into a guide to safe real estate investments (redlining) but has also used it to create walls within the city. For example, between 1973 and 1987, National Opinion Research Center polls revealed that 38 to 47 percent of the population was afraid to walk alone in some places within a mile of their residence. Almost three times as many females as males expressed this fear. One need not wonder why. Blacks were generally even more fearsome of their own neighborhoods as were others residing in or near the inner city or interstitial areas (*Sourcebook - 1987*, p. 141).

In a 1988 Gallup Poll, a sample of the US population was asked if drug-related crime was a serious problem, somewhat of a problem, or not a problem at all in their neighborhood. Ten percent replied that it was a serious problem and 34 percent said that it was somewhat of a problem. Nineteen percent of the blacks saw this as a serious problem in their neighborhood, but only 10 percent of the whites did so. Drugs were seen as a serious problem by 18 percent of those with less than high school graduation but by only 4 percent of the college graduates. Considering the spatial distribution of the urban population by SES, response differences by educational achievement should not be surprising.

THE ECOLOGY OF RACINE

Delineating and Describing Spatial Units

There are many data collection problems for the researcher who wishes to describe and delineate the various types of neighborhoods, characterizing them by the physical and social aspects of daily life therein on one hand and on the other by objectively measuring events to determine if the neighborhood is an area in which delinquency and crime abound. Events are easier to represent than are the social characteristics of areas. Maume's recent paper (1996), linking objective measures of disorder and fear of crime and both to neighborhood context, is a model of procedure.

Police contacts or arrests may be reported by place of residence of the arrestee and place arrested, but offenses known to the police may only be reported by place of offense. The Racine birth cohort data record place of residence and place of offense so that it is possible, as we have done in numerous lengthy research reports, to present patterns of offenses by place of occurrence and by residence of the offender.

The basic data from the first few years of our research in Racine have been presented in great detail in *Criminal Career Continuity: Its Social Context* (Shannon, 1988) and in *Changing Patterns of Delinquency and Crime* (Shannon, 1991). The neighborhood as an arena for socialization and/or a place in which ordinary activities develop into delinquent behaviors and the special problems of the inner city underlie the complexity of the birth cohort analyses which we have been conducting over a 40-year period in Racine.

The complexity of some of the analyses has been increased even more by the changing ecology of the city and changes in the spatial units of analysis used for reporting arrests and offenses known to the police. The number of the various Part I offenses known to the police were reported by police grids for 14 years; this was followed for five years by aldermanic district reports; in 1989 reporting was changed to police patrol areas. Fortunately, these problems had no effect on either the official or self-report birth cohort data which were analyzed by the neighborhoods and natural areas which we had created.

Map 1 shows the police grids (one mile square) overlaid on the 1970 natural areas created early in our research and based on *U.S. Census of Housing: 1970*, BLOCK STATISTICS and land use data (Shannon, 1981). The Census block data on housing characteristics were: average value of owner-occupied housing, average contract rent, percent of residences lacking all plumbing, percent of units renter-occupied, and percent of units overcrowded. Each block was given a score for 1950, 1960, and 1970 based on factor analyses of the census data (raw scores rescaled with a range from zero to 100) and a Geometric Score (a derivative of Guttman Scaling ranging from zero to 31) based on the same block data. These scores were utilized in the delineation of several types of statistical areas and in numerous mapping procedures.

Although housing variables are good indicators of the social characteristics of areas, housing quality scores were supplemented with other indicators developed from land use data. Factor and Geometric scores indicated that the inner-city spatial units were distinctly different from others and that they were more homogeneous than the areas in transition. The inner-city spatial units differed markedly from all others, but there was also sufficient difference between the areas in transition and all others to make this division for analytic purposes as well. Moreover, the mean Geometric Scores of the inner-city and transitional spatial units showed a steady decline in quality throughout the period from 1950 to 1970.

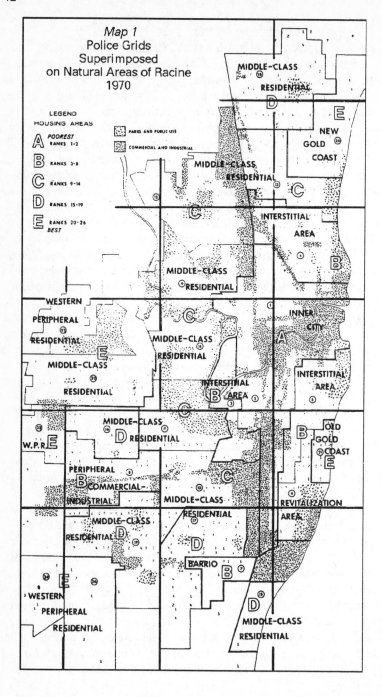

Map 1
Police Grids
Superimposed
on Natural Areas of Racine
1970

LEGEND
HOUSING AREAS

PARKS AND PUBLIC USE
COMMERCIAL AND INDUSTRIAL

A POOREST
   RANKS 1-2

B RANKS 3-8

C RANKS 9-14

D RANKS 15-19

E RANKS 20-26
   BEST

MIDDLE-CLASS RESIDENTIAL

NEW GOLD COAST

MIDDLE-CLASS RESIDENTIAL

INTERSTITIAL AREA

MIDDLE-CLASS RESIDENTIAL

WESTERN PERIPHERAL RESIDENTIAL

INNER CITY

MIDDLE-CLASS RESIDENTIAL

INTERSTITIAL AREA

MIDDLE-CLASS

RESIDENTIAL

INTERSTITIAL AREA

W.P.R.

MIDDLE-CLASS RESIDENTIAL

OLD GOLD COAST

PERIPHERAL

COMMERCIAL-INDUSTRIAL

MIDDLE-CLASS RESIDENTIAL

REVITALIZATION AREA

MIDDLE-CLASS RESIDENTIAL

BARRIO

WESTERN PERIPHERAL RESIDENTIAL

MIDDLE-CLASS RESIDENTIAL

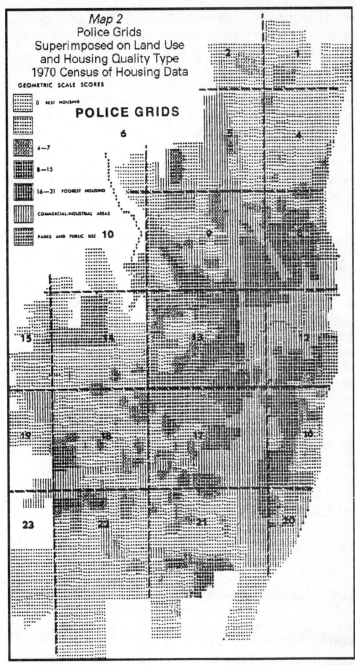

Map 2
Police Grids
Superimposed on Land Use
and Housing Quality Type
1970 Census of Housing Data

GEOMETRIC SCALE SCORES

- 0 BEST HOUSING
- 4—7
- 8—15
- 16—31 POOREST HOUSING
- COMMERCIAL-INDUSTRIAL AREAS
- PARKS AND PUBLIC USE

POLICE GRIDS

Map 2 with police grids overlaid on a 1970 housing quality and land use map clearly indicates the heterogeneity that is present within the units delineated by this type of spatial system. Some police grids had almost 8000 persons in them and some peripheral grids fewer than 1000. Whatever the shortcomings of police grids, data sets based on them gave us an idea of the relationship of demographic change and changing patterns of land use to changing patterns of offenses known to the police. They indicated that traditional notions about the concentration and dispersion of delinquency and crime following the ecological structure of the city should, with recognition of some irregularities in structural development, guide our continuing analyses of the Racine data. These data provide a backdrop for the cohort analyses.

A CITY IN TRANSITION

Changes as Seen in Police Grids

Racine has been in a state of·flux, as have other urban areas (Denton and Massey, 1991). To take a simple example of the changes which have taken place, inner city, interstitial, and transitional Police Grids 8, 12, 13, and 16 contained 49.3 percent of Racine's population in 1950 but only 28.3 percent in 1980, yet their proportion of the Part I offenses known to the police declined very little, 49.4 percent in 1968 to 43.1 percent in 1981. Peripheral Police Grids 1, 2, 5, 6, 10, 15, 19, 22, and 23 contained only 5.8 percent of the population in 1950 but 27.7 percent in 1980; their proportion of the Part I offenses known to the police showed only a relatively small increase from 18.5 percent to 19.9 percent, considering population growth. Doesn't this indicate that the underlying 'causes' of most Part I offenses are social and structural in nature?

The Role of the Tavern

The location of major tavern areas, commercial-industrial areas, and public use areas, indicated to some extent in which police grids high police contact rates were to be expected. As Mott (1990) has found in England and others (Roncek and Meier, 1991) in the United States, drinking is part of a way of life, leading to disorder and fights in and around drinking establishments. Drinking leads to disorder, then to police intervention, and to more disorder. One's conception of disorderly conduct's seriousness as an offense probably varies by SES.

Roncek and Meier found that in the course of their normal activities people are exposed to risks in their own areas and in traveling to other areas, particularly non-residential areas. Taverns had statistically significant effects on ten types of crime, in blocks considered safe and in blocks that already had higher crime rates. Not all bars were linked to crime, of course, in part because control varies across bars (some bar owners haven't the slightest idea of how to effectively control disruptive behavior) and some of the worst crime areas had neither taverns nor lounges. So much for blaming it all on taverns or pubs. As Felson and Cohen (1980) contend, findings are more productively viewed within a routine activities framework than as though alcohol was the 'cause' of higher crime rates.

TEMPORAL TRENDS IN OFFENSE RATES BY SPATIAL AREAS

Part I Offenses in Police Grids

When Part I offense rates by police grids were first considered, we found that offenses against the person and property were correlated 0.905. Assault and rape were correlated 0.921 and burglary and theft were correlated 0.880, the latter being the two Part I offenses with the greatest frequency of occurrence, followed by assault. We concluded that the basic trends for crime within areas were best represented by cumulative Part I offenses regardless of type.

The characteristics of each police grid in Racine (target density, percent of area commercial-industrial, percent residential vacancy, and housing scores) and offense rates and changes in offense rates within the grids showed fairly consistent differences between the inner city and other grids (Shannon, 1988). Delinquency and crime were also generated in some grid milieus, not only among the residents but among those who entered the area because they perceived it as a place of leisure and leisure activity which turned into delinquency and/or crime. Others perceived the areas' establishments as targets. For example, Grids 12, 16, and 13 had higher burglary rates than did other grids. There were, however, some striking anomalies as characteristics of spatial units in the city were related to offense rates and then temporal changes in them in some of the more peripheral areas.

Offense Concentration in Natural Areas

When multi-celled tables based on the 26 natural areas (Map 1) were constructed showing the distribution of offenses for each cohort by place of residence and place of the offense, it was found that 38 percent of the contacts for the 1942 Cohort took place in two adjacent inner-city natural areas, declining to 30 percent for the 1955 Cohort. However, only 31 percent of the offenses by place of residence for the 1942 Cohort were in either of these two natural areas, declining to 18 percent for the 1955 Cohort. There were numerous peripheral natural areas in which less than 1 percent of the offenses took place and/or less than 1 percent of each cohort's offenders resided.

Still another set of tables for each natural area for each cohort revealed that the police contacts in some natural areas were made by persons residing in the area or·contiguous areas while the police contacts in other areas were the product of offenses by cohort members from more distant areas. These patterns also changed by cohort as the city grew and the residential population of many cohorts increased or decreased.

Even more detailed tables revealed that these patterns also differed by the race/ethnic composition of natural areas. Blacks and Chicanos became involved with the law in their own neighborhoods to a far greater extent than did whites. Perhaps that is why it has so often been said that whites from peripheral areas who frequent inner-city bars must just be looking for trouble.

Police Grids, Census Tracts, and Offense Trends

Numerous analyses revealed that no single dimension of area characteristics acts as a consistent and powerful predictor of delinquency and crime rates over time. Housing quality and land use did emerge as important corollaries of crime rates during the 1970s and coupled with classical theory (the Chicago School as represented by Park, Burgess, McKenzie, Shaw, and McKay and others) led us to hypothesize a set of rates for police grids consistent with their demographic and social characteristics. The predicted (expected) rates and trends were closely related, only however at extremes of a constructed ecological (inner-city, transitional, or other areas) or structural continuum (land use, target density, and housing vacancies). Other analyses of event rates and offenses known to the police by census tracts showed that target density, land use, and housing quality accounted for from two-thirds to three-quarters or more of the variance in tract rates. This has been only the briefest account of rates and trends for various sets of spatial units but serves as a preface to and provides the foundation for our closer structurally oriented examination of offender types and trends.

The Hardening of the Inner City

After detailing the relationship of delinquency and crime to the changing ecological structure of the city over a period of 40 years (Shannon, 1982), we were then ready to conduct further research on criminal career continuity and to develop the concept of the 'hardening of the inner city.' The inner-city and interstitial areas in Racine were developing delinquency and crime as traditional patterns of behavior as had Chicago and other major metropolitan areas earlier in the century. Our research had reaffirmed the value of what has been termed the ecological approach at the very time that others in sociology were once again turning to it.

Although we have placed considerable emphasis on the hardening of the inner city, we have also shown (Shannon 1981 and 1984) that Racine had, as have other urban, industrial communities, developed a less than perfect set of concentric circles (as Hoyt showed for numerous US cities in 1939 and was further explicated in reference to delinquency and crime by Bursik in 1988). Peripheral areas that once consisted of only single family dwelling units sometimes grew to contain huge apartment houses, condominiums, town houses, or other forms of multiple dwelling units, some of which attracted highly mobile elements of the population. As desirable or, for that matter, undesirable housing became less available in transitional areas, the decline in population there became the increase in some peripheral areas. Deviations in patterns of land use and population composition have been followed by variations in delinquency and crime patterns.

LIFE IN THE DELINQUENT NEIGHBORHOOD

Neighborhoods and Other Spatial Units

Time went on, and the police grids, census tracts, and natural areas were replaced with 65 smaller and more homogeneous neighborhoods (Map 3). These neighborhoods (Shannon, 1984) were delineated by making use of natural boundaries such as streams, harbors, railroad tracks (which were highly used at that time), commercial-industrial barriers, parks, playgrounds, cemeteries, and other public use facilities that sharply divided residential areas, as well as housing type and quality scores based on block data from the 1960 and 1970 US Censuses.

Neighborhoods and Felony Offenses

Map 4 is a composite based on six computer maps which showed the concentration of felony-level police contacts by cohorts by place of contact and place of residence. The major high crime neighborhoods (high felony rates) were those which we had listed as inner city, portions of several adjacent transitional neighborhoods, and several peripheral neighborhoods adjacent to a large commercial-industrial area on the southwestern edge of Racine. These are illustrative of the deviations from the classical model for the development of metropolitan patterns of delinquency and crime. The Chicago publications on the development of metropolitan patterns of delinquency and crime left room for later developments of this nature if one had not become too attached to the idea of concentric circles.

Neighborhoods and Their Characteristics

Neighborhoods gave us further opportunity to determine not just how delinquency and crime varied within homogeneous spatial units but to see how rates would differ depending on race/ethnicity, sex, and type of neighborhood. For example, Peeples and Loeber (1994) have recently stated, 'several decades of research have not produced a consensus on the relationship among ethnicity, neighborhood, and juvenile delinquency.' They find from their own Pittsburgh data (self-report) that the behavior of black youths in non-underclass neighborhoods was similar to that of whites. With controls for a

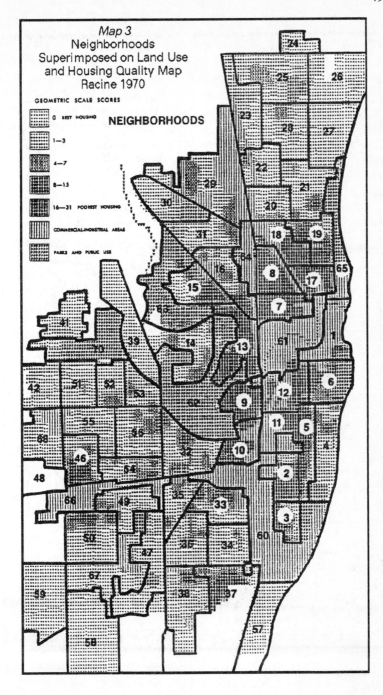

Map 3
Neighborhoods
Superimposed on Land Use
and Housing Quality Map
Racine 1970

GEOMETRIC SCALE SCORES

0 BEST HOUSING

1—3

4—7

8—15

16—31 POOREST HOUSING

COMMERCIAL/INDUSTRIAL AREAS

PARKS AND PUBLIC USE

NEIGHBORHOODS

50

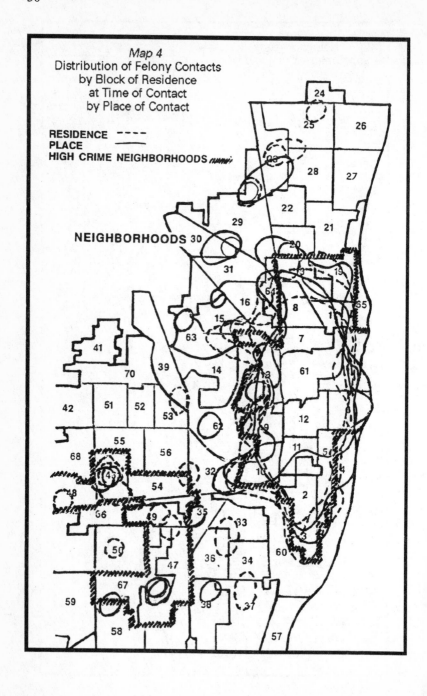

Map 4
Distribution of Felony Contacts
by Block of Residence
at Time of Contact
by Place of Contact

RESIDENCE - - - -
PLACE
HIGH CRIME NEIGHBORHOODS

multitude of individual factors they also showed that residence in underclass neighborhoods was significantly related to delinquent behavior and race was not.

Perhaps one of the most important findings from the Racine data was produced when measures of serious delinquency and serious adult criminal behavior were regressed on interview variables with the 1942 and 1949 Cohorts divided into categories according to the offense rates of the areas (low, medium, and high) and the social and structural delinquency and crime producing character-istics (DCP) of the area (low, medium, and high and combinations thereof). The pattern of variable effects differed for each of the 12 categories of areas, whether measures were for the juvenile or adult period and whether the delinquency/crime measure was official or self-report. In other words, interview variables were related to measures of delinquency and crime in different ways, depending on the characteristics of the area in which the cohort members resided (Shannon, Chapter 4, 1991).

Most frequently appearing as a significant variable for the juve-nile period, in high offense rate and DCP areas, was head of house-hold's employment status. High school graduation, delinquent/criminal self-concept, juvenile friends in trouble with the police, attitude toward the police, and auto use were significantly related to seri-ous juvenile delinquency in a variety of types of areas. But a statis-tically significant relationship to measures of delinquency does not create or support a causal model unless the variables precede or occur with delinquent behaviors in a theoretically defensible way. It may well be that the 'causal' variables are simply reinforcing a pattern of delinquent behavior that has already been developing. Some of these and other variables had significant effects carrying into the adult period and here we have a more solid basis for in-ferring some causative effects. More recently, Sampson and Laub (1990) concluded from their reanalysis of Gluecks' 1950 *Unraveling Juvenile Delinquency* and Eleanor Glueck's (1960) and Sheldon Glueck's (1960) follow-up studies that the largest single influence on overall adult crime is job stability.

During the adult period, for example, level of first job was now significantly correlated with seriousness of adult offense record, in the highest DCP and high crime rate neighborhoods and combina-tions thereof, as were age at which a driver's license had been re-ceived, age of marriage, head of household's employment status, military service, and having adult friends in trouble with the police.

It must be noted, however, that only about half of the variance (0.494 percent for official seriousness and 0.540 percent for self-report seriousness) was accounted for in even that group of neighborhoods (medium DCPs and with medium residential offense rates) where the interview data variables had their highest impact on seriousness of either official or self-report scores for the juvenile period. For the adult period, 0.441 percent of the self-report seriousness variance was accounted for by interview variables in neighborhoods with medium residential offense rates and 0.556 percent for those who were medium in both the DCP and residential offense rates.

When controls were introduced for race, sex, and inner-city residence, each group again had dissimilar patterns of significant interview and other variable effects on career seriousness scores, juvenile or adult. While failure to graduate from high school seemed to have consistently significant effects on the careers of whites and non-inner-city residents, failure to graduate from high school may not in itself be the explanatory variable. For white and non-inner-city youth it does raise the question of what variables explain failure to graduate from high school for this group.

Most of the interview question variables, high school graduation, for example, are probably proxies for integration into the larger society or integration into a peer group society that has goals and values differing from those of the larger society. A given question may or may not be indicative of integration for minority or lower SES youth. Some variables which have been thought of as integrating may not be indicative of integration into those segments of the society which are influenced by agencies of social control; instead, they are indicative of integration into groups for which there are deleterious consequences rather than ameliorative effects.

CONCLUSION

The aforementioned findings are convincing evidence that juvenile delinquency and adult crime are products of life experiences in different types of neighborhoods; these experiences have different effects on people whose lives are framed by their race and sex. This has been stated in the sociological literature (e.g. Taylor and Covington, 1988) in more specific terms but we apply it here as we look back at our earlier research on delinquency and crime.

The fact that Racine's inner-city non-white males had the highest juvenile and adult seriousness scores, that they had the lowest level first jobs, the lowest high school graduation rate, the most negative attitude toward the police, and so forth, may be known to researchers and police, but its meaning, how statuses and responses have been developed, and how these variables are interrelated comes only from examining the data more closely. What we have found is that the answer is not very simple.

The enormity of the problem in America, based on data for Chicago from 1960 to 1980, has been detailed by Chilton (1987). Kasarda (1993) has most recently shown that from 1970 to 1990 there has been an increasing concentration of poverty (20 percent of residents below poverty level) and neighborhood distress (disproportionately high levels of poverty, joblessness, female-headed families, and welfare recipients) in the 100 largest central cities of the United States. Between 1980 and 1990 the greatest deterioration took place in Midwestern cities; poor blacks became even more concentrated, particularly in the poorest and then the more deteriorated tracts and neighborhoods than did the Hispanics and whites. This research, perhaps more than any other that we have cited, provides evidence for what we have termed the hardening of the inner city and the framework within which we have re-examined the Racine data as we look back to the future.

4 The Justice System

THE INCREASING PRISON POPULATION

Whether the justice system is effective or not has been debated longer than it has been carefully researched. Many of us have grown up on accounts of specific events that support one view or another of the effectiveness of quick, stern, harsh, or whatever justice. Persons more recently aware of the issues have been informed, or more likely misinformed, about the merits of this or that policy at various stages of the justice process (Shannon, 1961).

As a surprise to most people, even in the field of sociologically oriented criminology, in April of 1997, a report by Lawrence W. Sherman and Denise Gottfredson, two Universisty of Maryland criminologists, *Preventing Crime: What Works, What Doesn't, and What's Promising*, was made public. This Congressionally mandated report was commissioned by the National Institute of Justice. It was described in *The New York Times* of April 16 as 'The most comprehensive study ever of crime prevention . . . questions the effectiveness of the nation's huge prison construction program in the past two decades.' Their review (the University of Maryland team) of the relevant scientific literature covered over 500 program impact evaluations. It is interesting, though not surprising, that although Congress required that the research be 'independent in nature' and 'employ rigorous and scientifically recognized standards and methodology,' some Congressional reaction was political in nature and represented the most uninformed point of view.

Whether effective or not, the fact remains that the United States spends at least $25 billion per year on prisons and jails. The Bureau of Census reports that by 1988–9, criminal justice spending had increased to $130 per capita compared to $106 for education. With 823 414 prisoners in the Federal and State institutions in 1991, The US expanded its lead over South Africa in rate of imprisonment, 455 persons per 100 000 compared to the latter's 311. Perhaps more astonishing is the United States' imprisonment rate for black males, 3370 per 100 000 compared to only 681 in South Africa (*The New York Times*, February 11, 1992).

How has this almost unbelievable increase in prison commitment rates come about? It has been shown in one study (Cappell and Sykes, 1991) that US World War II and post-World War II and 1960–85 prison commitment rates were related to unemployment, the age composition of the population, and active duty rates in the military before more recent trends to incapacitation as a policy solution to the crime problem. Would updating the Cappell and Sykes study to 1995 with inclusion of variables such as the hardening of the inner city and increasing media attention to street crime have shown that these variables, along with other structural changes in society, played a part in more recent increases in commitment rates? In other words, has it been a matter of both policy change, incarceration of people for offenses that did not seem to require incarceration until recent years, as well as underlying changes in the social structure which have generated crime increases to which society has reacted with imprisonment and calls for even more imprisonment?

THE EFFECTIVENESS OF THE JUSTICE SYSTEM

What Happens Next as the Criterion of Success

The effectiveness of the justice system is best determined by what people do next after an encounter with it. If an officer stops a juvenile or group of juveniles engaged in behavior which constitutes either a status offense or what would be a felony or misdemeanor if engaged in by an adult, several courses of action are permissible depending on police policy in the community. If counseled and released, that may be considered the most effective approach to the problem. If referred, that may be considered to be the most effective approach depending upon the behavior in question. In either case, all things considered, there may still be disagreement as to which disposition was most appropriate. What happens next in each case, however, determines whether policy for police decision-making is effective (Smith and Gartin, 1989).

In 1988, 1 156 000 delinquency cases were heard in courts with juvenile jurisdiction. About half were informally processed and dismissed for lack of evidence or counseled and their cases terminated. Fifty-seven percent of the adjudicated were given probation and 30 percent were placed in a residential facility other than their homes. Less than 2 percent were transferred to the adult courts for trial. Only 6 percent of the delinquency cases involved a violent offense charge such as murder, forcible rape, robbery, or aggravated assault but 7 percent a drug charge.

Some notion of society's growing concern about drugs may be noted from the fact that, of those detained between referral and disposition, the largest proportion was that 33 percent with a drug charge. Of even more concern was the fact that only 21 percent of the whites were detained at this point compared to 57 percent of the non-whites (Sickmund, 1992). This reveals how in one way or another delinquency and crime statistics are a product of interaction between offenders and those members of the justice system who operate as representatives of society.

Even the category of property offenses has shown considerable variation from state to state in the proportion of juvenile offenders who were petitioned to the juvenile court. Some states have petitioned 10 percent of their shoplifters and others 50 percent. Some have petitioned 50 percent of the youthful burglars and others 90 percent (Nimick, 1990).

As juveniles and adults proceed through the justice system step-by-step, what happens next determines whether or not the system is effective. Recidivism (committing another offense) at any stage indicates that the action taken was not effective. The longer a juvenile or adult does not recidivate, the better. Perhaps we must be satisfied if the time to recidivism has been reduced whether it is the time after a street-level disposition or release from an institution. Those who understand how delinquency/crime is generated in various segments of society expect high rates of recidivism for some offenses and low rates for others. Expectations based on knowledge of variation by offense are only one of many considerations in determining whether institutionalization is the appropriate remedy.

The Determinants of What Happens Next

At the national level, 69 percent of the young adults paroled in the United States in 1978 were rearrested within six years, 53 percent were reconvicted, and 49 percent were reincarcerated. Property offenders had higher recidivism rates (73 percent rearrested and 56 percent reincarcerated within six years) than did violent offenders (64 percent rearrested and 39 percent reincarcerated) (*Sourcebook – 1988*, p. 657). The Bureau of Justice Statistics reported that for 11 states in a 1983 study, 68.1 percent of the property offenders had been rearrested within only three years and 47.7 percent had been reincarcerated. Again, violent offenders had lower recidivism rates, 59.6 percent rearrested and 36.5 percent reincarcerated (*Sourcebook – 1988*, p. 658). Burglars (most serious offense in record at time of release) in the 11-state sample were more likely to be rearrested within three years for burglary (31.9 percent) and larceny/theft offenders for larceny/theft (33.5 percent) than for other offenses. Property offenders were more likely to be rearrested for property offenses (49.8 percent). Beyond this there was evidence of considerable offense switching, particularly among violent offenders (*Sourcebook – 1988*, p. 659).

Those who had one prior arrest were least likely to be rearrested within three years (38.1 percent), but those who had 16 or more arrests were most likely to be rearrested (82.2 percent). There were sex and race/ethnic differences in rearrest rates but the greatest differences were based on age at first arrest and number of prior arrests. In other words, early and frequent involvement with the justice system heralded continuity, as we have found in our longitudinal research in Racine (*Sourcebook – 1988*, p. 660).

The debate on the effectiveness of the justice system has often centered on specific vs. general deterrence, particularly as applied to the effects of prison sentences vs. capital punishment. While capital punishment is effective for specific deterrence, that is, those who are executed have ended their criminal behavior, its general deterrent effect has been rejected by research covering many societies and lengthy periods of time. But vengeance is important to some people and that drives them to call for the death penalty.

The Function of Imprisonment

The Impact of Incapacitation
Here we become involved in the debate on how to measure the impact of incapacitation (imprisonment). Incapacitation was a buzzword in the 1970s and 1980s in Washington – it made bureaucrats feel like they knew something! Practitioners and researchers have been willing to accept failure upon release, with or without parole, as a measure of justice system failure. In other words, the recidivism rate, often quoted as 80 percent, is taken as evidence of failure of the system, for example, institutionalization is not an effective remedy.

One could even say that prison has made some of its inmates more adept, has taught them how to cover their tracks (be more discreet), or perhaps has even taught them skills that permit them to engage in fraudulent behavior which is less recognizable as illegal. After all, crime is only what the public's representatives have defined as crime. Stealing sheep, cattle, or horses has long been understood by the general populace as an impermissible form of theft, but stealing electronic representations of goods is not as well recognized by the public or by those who are charged with enforcing the law.

With the recidivism rate represented by that proportion of the offenders who, after institutionalization and release, have engaged in behavior which has returned them to the system, that is, reinstitutionalization, the question is still not answered as to whether this is entirely because the justice system has failed. Has the system made bad actors worse because they have some inner criminal propensity that could not be eliminated or overcome but was only intensified by institutional programs, or has it made incarcerated offenders worse even though they are not 'criminals' by nature, or is it because the offender had been returned to the same social situations that produced his/her delinquent and/or criminal behavior? This has been the focus of much debate. A review of the literature gives little solace to those who claim that prison has specific deterrent effects, that is, the imprisoned offender becomes penitent as a direct result of time in the penitentiary. Society has even been known to laud those who cannot be 'broken.' Politicians seem oblivious to all of this but not to public outcries which are translated into votes.

Changing the offender into a law-abiding person is not usually considered by the public to be the only goal of the justice system. Coterminous goals may be to protect society, to punish, or to hopefully produce specific and/or general deterrence. Do we know how much general deterrence (fear of imprisonment reduces crime) occurs because some criminals are institutionalized? How much specific deterrence occurs because offenders who are institutionalized cannot commit crimes outside of prison? The specific deterrence answer depends on which offender types have been institutionalized, are still institutionalized, and their ages. There is also the question of cost for lengthy institutionalization.

Unfortunately, self-report studies do not provide, any more than do official statistics, a basis for saying that a substantial proportion of serious crime in the United States has been eliminated through institutionalization, nor do they provide evidence that a substantial proportion of crime would be eliminated if more persons of a specific type were institutionalized, for example, drug offenders. They do not even provide evidence that institutionalization and treatment has been an effective way of dealing with drug offenders, although there are many opportunistic professionals and politicians who will argue the effectiveness of in-house therapy of this or that type.

Between 1975 and 1987 National Opinion Research Center polls indicated that from 79 percent to 89 percent (*Sourcebook - 1987*, pp. 142–3) of the population believed that courts are not harsh enough. It is not surprising that blacks were less inclined to believe that the courts were not harsh enough, considering the extensive literature on the subject of differences in rates of institutionalization, than were whites.

The Cost of Incapacitation

One would be hard-pressed to produce evidence that the cost of the justice system's operation against any specific type of serious offense is a bargain or even reasonable considering the quantity of crime eliminated for the cost. Still, in 1976, 66 percent of those interviewed in a national survey by the National Opinion Research Center thought that we were spending too little on halting the rising crime rate. This varied by 1 to 3 percent from then until 1987. Most categories of the population continued to believe that too little was being spent to halt the rising crime rate, and females thought too little by as much as 5 percent more than males in some years (*Sourcebook - 1987*, pp. 124–5). How would the population respond if they had a tax increase that was related to increases in spending on crime?

For those who wish to see the offender punished, to receive his/her just deserts, the picture becomes even more complex. Historically, institutions have been of different types and sizes, just as they are today. At the turn of the century if the comforts of life (however unsavory) were not available in some institutions they could be brought in it at the expense of the prisoner or family. In some other institutions inmates were forced to spend their time in silence at hard labor, in idleness in their cells, or in some combination of these. No one could doubt that life in most penitentiaries was punishing even if it did not produce repentance.

The house of correction was notorious for its failure to correct. Even then there was a conflict between the goals of different segments of the population, which continues today as some institutions are charged with being country clubs where the criminal may enjoy a life of comfort watching television, playing billiards, tennis, the entire range of sports, reading books, acquiring computer skills, and so on. In some tent city types of institutions, however, incarceration in itself is punishment. The increasing number of inmates in some states and the cost of building traditional institutions is likely to produce even more prisons that some citizens will describe as country clubs.

Again, evidence to support the effectiveness of institutionalization for general deterrence is even more scarce than for specific deterrence. Residents of the inner city and interstitial neighborhoods are more likely to be institutionalized than are persons from other neighborhoods. Supporters of general and specific deterrence effects would expect a drop in inner city neighborhoods' offense rates as a consequence. Such a drop is seldom found. More frequently, severe sanctioning is followed by what we have called the 'hardening of the inner city' and higher offense rates.

While there has been considerable interest in deinstitutionalization (Fabricant, 1980), including half-way houses which would theoretically reduce recidivism, neither programmatic nor bottom-line research has yet provided sufficient evidence of their success. It is easier to obtain funds for institution-building than to finance evaluation research. Never before has Congress been so concerned about evaluation research. We shall await the outcome.

PUBLIC PERCEPTIONS OF CRIME

Perception of 17 Selected Offenses

Although perceptions of the seriousness of selected offenses have varied greatly over the years and by the demographic and social characteristics of populations, there has been a measure of agreement in national surveys in the United States in recent years. For example, the National Survey of Crime Severity in 1977 ranked forcible rape of a victim, a consequence of which she died, as the most serious of selected offenses, followed by robbery in which the victim struggled and was shot to death. The same ranking was obtained in the National Punishment Survey in 1987.[1] While there were some differences on the entire continuum of serious offenses, there was a degree of consensus on the seriousness of Index Offenses.

The fact that two surveys produced similar average conceptions of seriousness does not eliminate the fact that there is vast disagreement about the seriousness of offenses within the larger population which means that no matter how even-handed the police and courts are in dispensing justice, there are differences in what demographic and spatially distributed segments of the population consider even-handed. Thus, any finding that is made about courtroom consistency or inconsistency will produce different responses from different segments of the population. These response differences apply even more as one observes responses to questions about the kind of punishment preferred for different offenses. These are the kinds of thing that you must keep in mind if you sit down with the idea of proposing responses to crime.

Punishment Preferred

Beyond the perceived seriousness of offenses, the severity of sanctions preferred for offenses is another thorny issue. In the case of the offender who has committed rape which resulted in the death of the female, 41.7 percent of the sample preferred the death penalty. Thirty-seven percent also preferred the death penalty for the robber who killed his victim. Although drunk driving that caused a fatal accident was considered twice as serious as selling cocaine to others for resale, 90 percent of the respondents preferred prison or jail for both. Note that in practice juvenile court cases involving drugs are dealt with more severely than those involving alcohol (Sickmund, 1991). In the case of robbery with a gun which resulted in wounding the victim, 92 percent preferred prison or jail, a disposition more serious than the drug sales but less serious than drunk driving which had caused a death (*Sourcebook – 1988*, p. 219).

All of this was made more complex when specific cases with mitigating factors were brought into the equation and both judges and laymen saw the desirability of taking these factors into consideration. This goes on at the same time that others are calling for sentencing guidelines for judges in order to reduce disparities in sentencing. At the moment, a large segment of the population calls for mandatory sentencing, three strikes and you're out included, but when it becomes law they back away, particularly if it is someone whom they know to be only a 'bad boy.'

Purpose of Punishment

Behind the public's ideas about the type of sanction preferred for various types of offenses is their conception of the purpose of sanctions. We have already addressed this issue but now examine it in the framework of the survey reported in *Sourcebook – 1988*. Not surprising is the fact that what people prefer as a sanction may be totally ineffective as a means of accomplishing what they perceive to be the goals of the justice system. For example, 71.5 percent of the respondents thought that the sentence they had selected for a crime should be to treat the offender, to change whatever in him/her made him/her do the crime, that is, rehabilitation. At the same time, 69.8 percent also selected the sentence to give the offender what he/she deserves, that is, just deserts. The reason most often selected (79.2 percent), however, was 'to scare the offender so he/she will not do it again,' that is, specific deterrence (*Sourcebook – 1988*, p. 221). How naive can they be to think that perpetrators of the most heinous crimes scare so easily?

When respondents were asked about the purpose of punishment for selected offenses from robbery-generated murder to misdemeanor theft, reasons for 'punishment' varied with specific deterrence most frequently mentioned for serious property offenses as well as offenses injurious to persons. The same respondents could select more than one reason and, as a consequence, high percentages of the samples also mentioned boundary setting (this behavior will not be tolerated), rehabilitation, general and specific deterrence, incapacitation, and just deserts. While relatively few mentioned retribution, the highest mentions for it were for offenses leading to the death of a victim. That people have very mixed notions about the function of the justice system (*Sourcebook – 1988*, p. 222) is not surprising, considering the varied explanations of delinquency and crime that are accepted by different segments of the population.

Attitudes toward the death penalty varied by offense committed and demographic and socioeconomic characteristics (*Sourcebook – 1988*, p. 223). Between 1936 and 1988 support for the death penalty was lowest in 1965–6 and highest by 1988. While 67 percent of the males believed that the death penalty was a deterrent in 1986, only 58 percent of the females, 62 percent of the whites and 49 percent of the blacks did so (*Sourcebook – 1988*, p. 229). Considering that a sizable proportion of the population believes that the death penalty is a deterrent, it is notable that in 1986 only 32 percent of the population believed that it is carried out fairly, again with considerable variation based on social and demographic characteristics of the respondents (*Sourcebook - 1988*, p. 231).

The Question of Self-Defense

Although a sizable proportion of the population (28 percent) believes that they should take the steps which they consider necessary to defend themselves, that is, based on their response that having a gun in the home made it safer, 36 percent of the 1986 US sample believed that it was more dangerous. There were sizable demographic differences, for example, only 30 percent of the Protestants thought that a gun made the home more dangerous but 44 percent of the Catholics and 66 percent of the Jewish respondents did so (*Sourcebook - 1988*, p. 233). Following this, however, 69 percent of the Protestants, 63 percent of the Catholics, and 62 percent of the Jewish respondents thought that people should have the right to shoot someone who breaks into their home, even if they don't know whether the person is armed (*Sourcebook - 1988*, p. 233). One could go even further with questions about Federal laws controlling the sale and registration of all guns; close to 80 percent supported such legislation (*Sourcebook - 1988*, p. 234). The question about banning all handguns except for the police did not receive such favorable responses, 37 percent in 1988, with, as in the case of every other question, more females (45 percent) in favor of control than males (28 percent) (*Sourcebook - 1988*, p. 234). Although the British Parliament had decided not to ban all handguns after weeks of controversy, adopting a less stringent policy, the new Labour Government plans to extend the ban. And some people in the US still seem to believe that they need an AK47 type of assault weapon to defend themselves - or shoot rabbits.

THE EFFECTS OF SANCTIONS IN RACINE

Juvenile Offenses and Sanctions vs. Adult Offenses

During early stages of the analysis numerous rather simple tables were constructed which revealed that institutionalization of Racine's cohort members did not break their continuity in delinquent and criminal careers. These tables also showed that persons with the same level of seriousness of behavior prior to 18 who had not been sanctioned so severely had apparently modified their behavior in such a way that relatively few were involved with the justice system after age 18.

It is peculiar, if the justice system has any claim to effectiveness, that fewer of those in each offense seriousness group who received no sanctions ages 6–17 had failed to behave in such a fashion as to be incarcerated after 18 while such a large proportion of the same group who had been institutionalized or otherwise sanctioned during the juvenile period were incarcerated or otherwise sanctioned as adults. Furthermore, step by step, the process of social interaction worked to place a disproportionate number of inner city blacks in institutions before the age of 18 and continued to place them in institutions following that age.

A series of tables were also constructed in which members of the Racine cohorts were arranged by number and seriousness of police contacts and severity of sanctions through age 18 vs. number and seriousness of police contacts at and after age 19 (Shannon, 1980b). That the number and seriousness of police contacts and severity of sanctions as juveniles were positively related to number of adult police contacts was clear. The results were similar when juvenile career seriousness and adult career seriousness were substituted for the number of police contacts. The relationship was not as clear for females but their careers involved fewer contacts, less serious offenses, and less severe sanctions.

Even with controls for offense frequency and seriousness, the more severely juveniles were sanctioned, the more numerous and serious were their offenses as adults. When the number of contacts and seriousness scores through ages 15, 17, and 21 were controlled and measures of association calculated between severity of sanctions through these ages and number of police contacts and seriousness scores after these ages for males and for females, there was not a single coefficient that would indicate that, on balance, those who received more severe sanctions during the earlier period had fewer police contacts or lower seriousness scores later than did those who received less severe sanctions. Most of the correlations were low and out of 45 correlations there were only four that exceeded 0.300, indicating a positive relationship between early severity of sanctions and a lower number of police contacts or seriousness scores after that age.

It might be argued that we have yet to show that what we see is not simply an extension of patterns of misbehavior that were so well learned by some juveniles during the process of socialization that the best efforts of the justice system were of no avail. We could also say that in the case of those who showed a decline in their misbehavior following sanctions, that it was a part of the general attrition in misbehavior that takes place after the late teens among those who have not been sanctioned as well as those who have.

A Multivariate Approach to the Effectiveness of Intervention

Analysis of covariance and path analysis (Shannon, 1980a and more recently in *Criminal Career Continuity*, Shannon, 1988), showed that among males, although the more severe the juvenile sanctions and the more serious the adult career, seriousness of juvenile career was still the most powerful determinant of adult seriousness. In other words, juvenile justice system effects (effects of referrals and sanctions) contributed to seriousness of adult careers but were not as powerful as were juvenile careers in themselves. In essence, severe sanctions seemed only to push offenders to further offenses.

Essentially the same findings were made for females but justice system effects on adult career seriousness were not as strong, although they had increased for the 1955 Cohort's females. Of course, the females were only a small part of the problem. How many of us worry that either a young or old female will hold us up, steal our auto, break into our house during the middle of the night, or, for any reason at all, kill us – unless we beat them too often?

A series of path analyses bolstered the findings from the analyses of covariance and furthered our conclusions that intervention by agencies of social control had little to do with later careers, except to the extent that they may have crystallized patterns of misbehavior acquired in youth. Path analyses did, however, indicate that in the case of the 1955 Cohort, juvenile seriousness was reflected in severity of juvenile sanctions to a greater extent than in the other cohorts. While there were some differences between males and females in the various analyses, these and dozens of other earlier analyses of juvenile vs. adult measures or age by age analyses revealed that the experiences of females were becoming similar to those of the males.

In conclusion, we can say that, 'all other things held equal,' judicial intervention as carried out in Racine was ineffective even though intervention had become increasingly severe – the opposite of what many people thought.

A More Precise Evaluation of the Effects of Sanctions

What Happened at Each Police Contact?
As the various phases of the larger project progressed, the focus again and again turned to the effectiveness of the justice system, more specifically to the effects of increasing severity of sanctions on future offense seriousness. A laborious recoding and multiple regression analysis included demographic and independent experience variables such as behavior and justice system responses to behavior (seriousness of each police contact, type of juvenile neighborhood, sex, race, age at each police contact, severity of prior sanctions, total prior sanctions, number of prior sanctions, and severity of present sanction). This type of analysis introduced a dynamic element in that the regression coefficients (standardized estimates) for the antecedent variables were calculated at each contact – thus we could observe the changing weight of the different antecedent variables on future offense seriousness from contact to contact.

When Could Effects of Sanctions be Predicted?
Future juvenile offense seriousness for the combined cohorts could best be predicted at the fifth or sixth contact but only about 38 percent of the variance was accounted for. The first adult contact, which would be relatively early chronologically in the adult period, provided the best prediction of future adult behavior but accounted for only 28 percent of the variance (Shannon, 1985a). Police contacts three through eight revealed, perhaps more clearly and more surely with Lisrel analysis, that the effects of independent processual (experiences and behaviors) and demographic variables differed and were in general different for the juvenile and adult careers. When juvenile and adult careers were combined, the best prediction of future contacts with the police could be made after the eighth or ninth contact, accounting for 40 percent of the variance.

What Effects were the Greatest?
Age at contact and race contributed the most to explaining the variance in future total offense seriousness following the first through the tenth contacts. Race (non-white) was associated with future

offense seriousness and age (contacts early in life were predictive of future contacts) with future offense seriousness. When the effects of age at contact (which represents more years at risk for future trouble as well as early identification) and race (which represents status and life experiences rather than predisposition to delinquency and crime) were removed from the multiple regression analysis, *total prior seriousness* and *number of prior sanctions* became the most important variables accounting for *future total offense seriousness*.

Furthermore, number of prior sanctions had either the most important or the second most important effect when age and race were eliminated from the set of independent variables. This finding, along with later analysis (Shannon, 1985a) indicating that increasing severity of sanctions does not result in desistance or lower future offense seriousness, suggests that frequent intervention of a less severe nature may be more effective than sporadic or infrequent severe sanctions.

The association between a large number of prior sanctions and a low future offense seriousness may also be a function of the relationship of age at the contact of instant to each of the other two variables. An older age at that contact may have had as its antecedent a large number of prior sanctions and be followed by a low future total offense seriousness because the cohort member had a shorter time to acquire future contacts and future seriousness. Thus what we perceive as a relationship between numerous prior sanctions and low future offense seriousness may, in part, be a reflection of the age at contact, particularly the interrelationship of variables at age of first contact.

Other analyses were made on an age-by-age basis. Regardless of the basis of the analysis (age or contact sequence) there was no evidence that severity of sanctions reduced future offense seriousness. Number of prior court interventions seemed to be the only aspect of the justice process that reduced delinquent/criminal career continuity and this was not found consistently (Shannon, 1986 and 1991). The most important finding in this lengthy series of analyses was the lack of a significant relationship between the severity of prior sanctions and total future offense seriousness, that is, severity of sanctions did not reduce future offense seriousness.

Continuation vs. Discontinuation

Multiple discriminate analysis was used to investigate whether or not a career would continue or discontinue after a given contact. The various experiential and demographic variables at the first through ninth contacts had little effect; age of contact was clearly the best discriminating factor, such discriminators as total prior seriousness and number and severity of prior sanctions becoming important only after the fourth, fifth, or sixth contact, but without sufficient consistency beyond the fifth or sixth contact to have predictive value for persons in decision-making positions.

Excluding Traffic Contacts

We also conducted a number of analyses in which traffic contacts were excluded unless they included alcohol as part of the offense. Every cohort member was placed in one of ten different seriousness and severity of sanctions categories for each two-year period commencing at ages 15–16, and proceeding in two-year intervals to 21–22. These categories ranged from persons with no police contacts during that period to those with felonies which culminated in institutionalization. The more severely juveniles were sanctioned or the more severely young adults were sanctioned, the more serious was their misbehavior in the following two years. This suggested that institutionalization in the earliest years had more deleterious effects and was slower to wear off than did institutionalization during later years.

CONCLUSION

It should almost go without saying that there are varieties of demographic and demographic-related structural factors that make the problem of delinquency and crime more difficult to deal with in some states than others. Thus it is not surprising that the data indicate that there is little relationship between per capita expenditures on the justice system or a measure of effort in terms of total state expenditures and measures of crime or responses to it, for example, arrests and incarcerations.

We have already argued that cultural differences have produced different offense patterns historically, and they still do. If the population of a state is stable, not in much contact with national and international criminal elements (organized crime), crime control is less difficult than in states such as California, Florida, and New York with highly mobile populations containing representatives of organized crime. Besides this, there are socioeconomic differences between states, compounded by rapid influxes of people who have not been absorbed into the larger society and are thus less oriented toward all forms of law-abiding behavior than are long-term residents who may even be poorer. It is difficult to conclude, at least in the context of the statistics that we have presented, that the justice system of one state is more effective than that of another, all things being equal, when all things are not equal.

From time to time as our research results have found their way to the desks of practitioners and into the media, the findings have been roundly criticized, rejected, because 'everyone knows' that judges and professionals are dealing with miscreants in a way that is effective. Few judges will say that they may be doing more harm than good (one of our juvenile court judges in Racine was an exception). Few psychiatrists and other professionals will say that their efforts have been fruitless.

Moreover, some other researchers have said that we must be wrong because our findings differ from theirs. Quite aside from the fact that our design is longitudinal and based on birth cohorts, there are many other analytic steps that produce diversity in findings, coding, collapsing categories, measurement techniques for determining the amount of relationship between variables, and so forth. Cross-sectional studies based on samples of delinquents and criminals have produced different results in different types of urban areas. Studies of only those who have appeared in court may produce some differences in findings from those based on institutionalized populations. But what we have reported is what we have found in three birth cohorts with the justice system as it existed at that time in Racine.

As far as Racine is concerned, our conclusion that the justice system is ineffective is based on statistical analyses which show that intervention has not had much impact on delinquent and criminal careers. Maybe the behavior patterns that constitute delinquency and crime have been so internalized during the process of socialization that we should reframe our conclusion by saying that the larger society has been ineffective in socializing its youth rather than that the justice system has failed. Perhaps society has presented members of the justice system with an impossible task, particularly in neighborhoods whose residents have so little stake in conforming to the norms of the larger society. Some people may believe that the only alternatives available to them are illegal and indeed may prosper by behavior which places them in conflict with the larger society.

NOTE

1. The various index figures, offense rates, arrest rates, sentencing rates, and other justice system statistics as well as a number of national survey findings were taken from or were based on tables from the *Sourcebook of Criminal Justice Statistics – 1987* or the *Sourcebook of Criminal Justice Statistics – 1988,* Washington: U.S. Department of Justice, 1989, in the present case from the 1988 volume, p. 218. Additional references in this chapter to material from the *Sourcebook* were made by citing appropriate years and pages.

5 The Prediction Problem

INTRODUCTION

Substance involvement has long been used as a predictor in devices that are meant to guide probation and parole decisions. Whether substances are the cause of delinquency and crime or not, the Racine data suggest that alcohol and drugs may have a catalytic influence on some patterns of continuity in delinquency and crime. Substance use may influence behavior to the extent that employment becomes unstable or impossible with property crimes becoming the best alternative to work.

Graham (1987) has further suggested that drugs may be a catalyst for violent crime, but Chaiken and Chaiken (1991) have found that several factors commonly perceived as indicative of high rate dangerousness are not, among them alcoholism and number of prior arrests for drug distribution or possession. Haapanen, Houstin-Hencken, and Duncan (1991), based on their analysis of arrest data in California, developed four violent offender types including an assaulter type linked to drinking and, while this pattern was the most stable in the group, the overall probability of repeating a pattern of behavior was so low that they concluded these types to be of little use in predicting future behavior from past behavior. Whether or not knowledge of alcohol and drug involvement may improve our ability to predict career continuity remains to be seen.

Before continuing with an investigation of the extent to which predictive efficiency from the juvenile to the adult period may be enhanced through alcohol use and drug involvement as a predictor we shall review our prior prediction research. As the chapter develops, you will better be able to see why the book has been subtitled *Looking Back to the Future*.

EARLY ATTEMPTS TO PREDICT CRIME FROM DELINQUENCY IN THE COHORTS

Predicting from Number and Seriousness of Contacts

Predicting from Number of Contacts
Table 1 in this chapter (Shannon 1985b) reveals that the proportion (percentage) of those persons who had continuity (five or more police contacts) after any given age was greatest for those who had frequent and early police contacts. The effect of number of contacts on police contact continuity is clearly shown at age 17 for each cohort. For example, 62 percent of the 1949 Cohort members who had five or more police contacts through age 17 had five or more police contacts after that age. Early police contacts and exposure to the juvenile justice system and to some extent the opposite, that is, no early police contacts and no exposure to the justice system, produced an indication of what would be likely to happen to cohort members in the extreme ends of each distribution. In other words, records of contacts with the police enabled us to predict from the past to the future for people who were presumably very well behaved or people who were quite troublesome to the police but not for those who were in between the extremes.

Measuring the Advantage of Using a Predictor Variable: Age 18 as the Predictor Age
It is always possible to engage in cutting point roulette, that is, to select a cutting point on the juvenile period predictor continuum which produces the best prediction of what will happen to people with specified characteristics after that age. Rather than that we have taken the legal age of 18 for an example. There are two kinds of errors, *false positives*, those who were predicted to be serious adult offenders but were not, and *false negatives*, those who were predicted to not be serious adult offenders but who were indeed serious adult offenders. In Table 2 (Shannon, 1985b) we see that knowing whether a 1942 Cohort member was involved with the police four or more times as a juvenile enabled one to predict who would be involved five or more times as an adult with a 14.0 percent error and a 23.2 percent proportional reduction in error over the modal category of the marginals.

Before we go further, the language of prediction and the mechanics of this approach should be detailed a bit. Reference is frequently made to the modal category of the marginals. This is the largest or most frequently appearing category of one or more categories to be predicted. In our case we wish to predict what cohort members will be like as adults, that is, have serious or non-serious criminal records. Five or more police contacts as an adult is a widely accepted definition of a serious criminal record. We shall often refer to this as a serious vs. non-serious criminal career.

If about half of the cohort had a serious criminal record and the other half did not, use of the modal category of the marginals would result in an error of about 50 percent. If most of those who as juveniles had a serious juvenile record also had a serious adult record, and if those who as juveniles did not have a serious juvenile record did not have a serious adult record, then the best prediction would be that everyone will have a record as an adult similar to that as a juvenile. There would be only a few errors in prediction, a few *false negatives* and a few *false positives*, a huge improvement over using the modal category of the marginal which had generated 50 percent errors. The proportional reduction in errors would be close to 100 percent. It seldom works out quite that well and if it seems to one had better check the numbers. We have found that some knowledge of what youth are like and the experiences that they have had as juveniles does decrease errors of prediction that would be made by using the modal category into which they fall as adults.

To go back to Table 2, if we predicted that no one would have more than four police contacts after 18, 116 errors would have been made. Utilizing the predictor, three or fewer vs. four or more police contacts to the age of 18, 89 errors would be made, 35 *false positives* and 54 *false negatives*. This produced the 23.2 percent proportional reduction in error that was mentioned on the previous page. The 1942 Cohort's proportion of *false positives* (35 divided by 97 = 0.36 percent) was quite high compared with the proportion of *false negatives* (54 divided by 536 = 0.10 percent).

Which type of error can society tolerate the best – *false positives* or *false negatives*? Most of the false positives would probably be given no more than counseling. The false negatives have, in most cases, probably had few police contacts which would be classified as felonies were they adults, but if they did commit serious offenses, they would then be dealt with. If the table was constructed based on felony-level offenses, then a false negative classification would be more serious and, in actual practice, a false positive classification

Table 1.
Police Contact Continuity in Birth Cohorts
Percentage of Cohort with Five or More Contacts After Age (Years) by Number of Contacts Prior to and at Age (Years): 1942, 1949, and 1955 Cohort Members with Continuous Residence

1942 COHORT

Number of contacts through age	Percentage of 1942 cohort with five or more contacts after age											
	8	9	10	11	12	13	14	15	16	17	18	19
0	27	26	26	25	24	23	19	14	10	7	5	4
1	88	90	86	88	70	69	58	52	30	19	15	11
2	–	67	80	100	100	86	74	67	58	38	19	11
3	–	–	–	50	86	80	75	67	67	53	35	24
4	–	–	–	–	–	100	100	89	67	56	58	35
5 or +	–	–	–	–	–	50	71	83	76	75	65	59
Median number of contacts by age at first contact	11.0	14.5	17.5	16.0	6.0	10.5	8.0	8.3	3.7	2.4	3.3	2.0

PERCENT INCREASES

Number of contacts through age	Percentage of 1942 cohort with five or more contacts after age										
	20	21	22	23	24	25	26	27	28	29	30
0	2	1	1	0.4	0.4	0.4	0.4	0.0	0.0	0.0	0.0
1	11	8	6	3	2	2	2	1	0.0	0.0	0.0
2	6	2	7	3	3	0.0	0.0	0.0	0.0	0.0	0.0
3	8	11	3	3	3	2	0.0	0.0	0.0	0.0	0.0
4	43	35	13	0.0	4	4	0.0	0.0	0.0	0.0	0.0
5 or +	51	45	44	39	31	27	24	13	9	5	2
Median number of contacts by age at first contact	3.6	1.9	2.0	2.1	1.3	1.4	1.5	1.2	1.5	1.1	1.1

PERCENT DECREASES

1949 COHORT

Percentage of 1949 cohort with five or more contacts after age

Number of contacts through age	8	9	10	11	12	13	14	15	16	17	18	19	20	21	22	23
0	24	23	22	20	18	16	14	10	6	3	2	1	0.6	0.2	0.2	0.0
1	67	61	56	54	45	38	35	30	22	12	5	2	2	1	0.8	0.0
2	100	90	80	75	71	59	47	42	33	20	12	8	4	0.6	0.6	0.0
3	100	100	100	100	93	77	83	69	48	25	18	10	5	2	–	0.0
4	–	–	100	100	88	93	63	72	67	49	28	19	10	7	4	0.0
5 or +	100	100	100	100	100	100	100	83	80	62	51	42	33	23	12	5
Median number of contacts by age at first contact	9.0	12.0	10.5	6.8	6.2	4.3	5.3	5.0	3.5	2.4	2.0	1.5	1.4	1.5	1.2	1.2

1955 COHORT

Percentage of 1955 Cohort with five or more contacts after age

Number of contacts through age	8	9	10	11	12	13	14	15	16	17	18	19	20
0	17	15	14	12	11	9	7	5	3	1	0.5	0.0	0.0
1	58	47	43	36	32	30	20	15	8	4	2	0.5	0.0
2	85	76	76	67	50	45	38	28	18	8	4	2	0.0
3	100	100	82	71	76	68	57	40	29	17	7	3	0.0
4	100	100	100	91	72	71	68	58	40	24	16	3	1
5 or +	100	100	92	96	94	86	79	75	62	46	34	21	7
Median number of contacts by age at first contact	6.1	5.1	5.3	4.2	3.4	5.0	3.0	2.4	2.2	2.1	1.2	1.1	1.5

Table 2.
Predicting Police Involvement After Age 18

		1942 Cohort		
		Involvement with police after age 18		FALSE NEGATIVES 54
Involvement through age 18		0–4	5 or +	Total
0		333	(17)[a]	350
1–3	FALSE	149	(37)	186
4 or +	POSITIVES →	(35)	62	97
Total	35	517	116	633

14.0% error with prediction device
18.3% error from modal category of marginals
23.2% proportional reduction in error using prediction device

a. False positives and false negatives appear in parentheses.

would for sure result in counseling which may or may not have a detrimental effect on them. That there is often a higher proportion of errors based on a prediction device then is produced by using the modal category of the adult marginals does, however, question what use should be made of number of police contacts as a juvenile as a predictor in any decision-making process.

In recent years a measure, RIOC (Relative Improvement Over Chance), has been frequently used as an indication of the relative value of one prediction device over another. Although RIOC ranged from 51 percent for the 1942 Cohort to 33 percent for the 1955 Cohort, and some people would equate this with inventing the wheel, we take the stance that a measure of proportional reduction in error is a more meaningful measure. Even if there is considerable improvement over chance, the modal category of the marginals may still be the best predictor. The measure of proportional reduction in error and the type of error remaining tells us if and how the prediction device should be used.

What concerns the public and, even more so, those who must make decisions is whether or not it is possible to predict who will commit serious offenses as young adults. Schmidt and Witte (1988) expressed similar concern about false positive rates which are so high that decision-makers would deal with a sizable proportion of non-recidivists or non-continuers as though they would be in the recidivist or continuer category.

Adding Self-Report as a Predictor

The stochastic nature of official careers, a finding with which we and others have dealt (Shannon, 1988; Haapanen, 1988), has been one of the prime reasons we believe that combining official and self-report measures would generate a better estimate of total careers than would either alone. Haapanen's research suggests that 'models in which rates of offending are assumed to be stable will overestimate the amount of crime that could be prevented by locking up individuals who, at any particular time, were identified as high-rate offenders.' In other words, the stochastic nature and general decline in offending rates (particularly as represented by official offense records) produce positive errors of prediction.

The 1949 Cohort members who were interviewed were divided into four groups on a basis of their official records and responses to a question about being stopped by the police and a question about what they had done for which they could have been stopped. Less official record continuity at the police contact level or the felony or misdemeanor level was found for those who stated that they had not been stopped and who stated that they had not done things than was found for those who had admitted that they had been stopped and had done things. False positives (24.2 percent and 42.4 percent) were lowest for both groups that had been stopped and had done things while false negatives were lower in all of the other groups. Again, while improvement over chance (RIOC) was considerable, ranging up to 65 percent, if the marginal distributions do not permit much improvement over chance, a high RIOC does not mean much in reference to the basic prediction problem. The highest measures of proportional reduction of error indicated an improvement over the modal category of the adult marginals of only 24 percent, and this is the bottom line, so to speak.

The prediction problem became increasingly difficult as the level of seriousness to be predicted was raised. Only 310 (56.3 percent) of the persons interviewed in the 1949 Cohort with police contacts had felony or misdemeanor contacts at that age or later. However, if having had a felony or misdemeanor contact and having admitted that they had been stopped by the police before 18 and done things for which they were not caught is used as the predictor of those who will have a felony or misdemeanor as an adult, 93 errors are made (70 false positives and 23 false negatives), 25 fewer than the prediction that no one would have a felony or misdemeanor contact (a 21 percent improvement over the modal category).

You have heard people say that we must conduct research to predict who will kill or commit the most heinous crimes at a higher level of seriousness than other felonies. Knowing how difficult it is to predict the future from the past, would you expect that this could be done? As an event that has a very small probability of occurring it will be unpredictable but not inexplicable if one can look back at all of the facts – too late to take action, of course.

In addition to the exercises in prediction that we have just described, we also examined the relationship of past referrals to number of future contacts and seriousness of future contacts at ages 15 and 21, with and without controls for juvenile place of residence (inner-city and interstitial areas), number and seriousness of past contacts to number of future court dispositions, number of past dispositions to number and seriousness of future dispositions, and many other combinations. There was little increase in predictive efficiency over the modal category of the marginals, seldom over 20 percent, that increase occurring most often when utilizing past referrals as a predictor of future police contacts. Persons who have had police referrals in the past are better known to the police than others and are more likely to have their future misbehavior noted and recorded. Although number of dispositions during the teens and early twenties and contacts or dispositions in the future were related (a high number of juvenile dispositions meaning frequent contacts or dispositions as adults), there was little increase in predictability over the modal category of the adult marginals.

The issue of predictability over chance or even the modal category of the marginals has been raised so frequently because some measures of association, that is, various coefficients of correlation, give the impression that there must indeed be such a substantial relationship between delinquent and criminal careers that it may be a basis for decision-making. Giving the false impression that we had developed a predictive instrument that could be a basis for decision-making process would be an error, particularly if it were to serve as a basis for proceeding down the path to selective incapacitation.

Suggesting that certain categories of juveniles are unlikely to have criminal career continuity might be a more appropriate strategy considering the distribution of the data and the overall relationship of delinquent to criminal careers. Any strategy involving judicial or quasi-judicial action must be pursued with caution until it has been shown that multiple cohorts in diverse settings produce similar results beyond the well-known fact that a small percentage of each cohort is responsible for a major proportion of the cohort's serious delinquency and crime. A good statistic is not always the foundation for immediate action.

Even when we reached the point of relating severity of past sanctions to number and seriousness of future contacts, we reduced errors of prediction very little except in the case of severity of past sanctions and severity of future sanctions. Here we found, particularly in the inner-city and interstitial areas, that errors of prediction were reduced (but no more than 30 percent). It is not surprising, of course, that those with severe past sanctions are more likely to acquire severe sanctions in the future.

A DIFFERENT WAY OF LOOKING AT THE PREDICTION PROBLEM

The Expanded Cohort and Its Police Contacts

The nature of the relationship between juvenile and adult careers becomes more obvious when careers are dichotomized as shown in Diagrams 1A, 1B, 1C, 1D, and 1E, based on the 1955 Cohort as expanded to include persons with continuous residence from age 13 to 22. Cohort members were partitioned into four categories depending upon the total number of police contacts that each had as juveniles and adults. The contacts which they had as juveniles and adults include traffic offenses, contacts for suspicion, investigation, or information, and status offenses.

Note the career progression of the 260 cohort members in Diagram 1A who had five or more contacts as juveniles. Only 97 of them (37.3 percent of 260) were there as adults. These 97 were only 3.6 percent of the cohort but accounted for 37.4 percent of the police contacts by the 1955 Cohort and 58.9 percent of the 5024 career police contacts by those who had five of more contacts as juveniles (Diagram 1B). These 97 constituted 61.0 percent of the 159 frequent adult offenders and were responsible for 2960 (84.1 percent) of the career police contacts of the frequent adult offenders.

The 163 cohort members who were *false positives* (predicted to be frequent adult offenders but who were not) constituted 6.1 percent of the cohort and 6.5 percent of those who were non-frequent adult offenders. They had 2064 police contacts. That is 47 percent

Diagrams 1A, B, C, D, and E
Offender Types, Number of Offenders Produced by Them, and Mean
Number of Offenses per Offender, Dichotomized

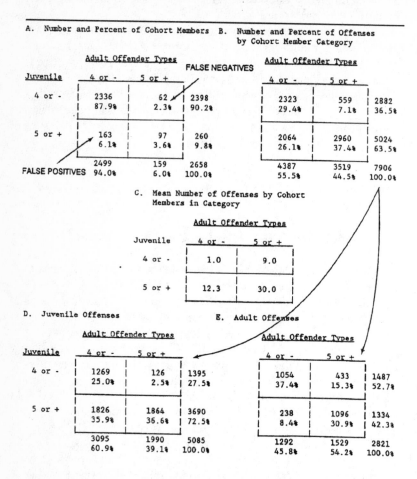

A. Number and Percent of Cohort Members

Adult Offender Types

FALSE NEGATIVES

Juvenile	4 or -	5 or +	
4 or -	2336 87.9%	62 2.3%	2398 90.2%
5 or +	163 6.1%	97 3.6%	260 9.8%
FALSE POSITIVES	2499 94.0%	159 6.0%	2658 100.0%

B. Number and Percent of Offenses by Cohort Member Category

Adult Offender Types

	4 or -	5 or +	
	2323 29.4%	559 7.1%	2882 36.5%
	2064 26.1%	2960 37.4%	5024 63.5%
	4387 55.5%	3519 44.5%	7906 100.0%

C. Mean Number of Offenses by Cohort Members in Category

Adult Offender Types

Juvenile	4 or -	5 or +
4 or -	1.0	9.0
5 or +	12.3	30.0

D. Juvenile Offenses

Adult Offender Types

Juvenile	4 or -	5 or +	
4 or -	1269 25.0%	126 2.5%	1395 27.5%
5 or +	1826 35.9%	1864 36.6%	3690 72.5%
	3095 60.9%	1990 39.1%	5085 100.0%

E. Adult Offenses

Adult Offender Types

	4 or -	5 or +	
	1054 37.4%	433 15.3%	1487 52.7%
	238 8.4%	1096 30.9%	1334 42.3%
	1292 45.8%	1529 54.2%	2821 100.0%

of the career police contacts by non-frequent adult offenders and
26.1 percent of all of the police contacts for the cohort. This is a
large error in the view of those who remain critical of the enterprise. The 62 cohort members who were *false negatives* (predicted
to be non-frequent adult offenders but were frequent adult offenders) constituted 2.3 percent of the cohort, 39.0 percent of the frequent adult offenders, but had accrued only 559 (15.9 percent) of
the career police contacts by frequent adult offenders and 7.1 per-

cent of the cohort's total police contacts (Diagram 1B). The *false positives* and *false negatives* were responsible for a disproportionately greater share of the career police contacts than would be expected for their numbers in the cohort.

The *false negatives* were on the average (Diagram 1C) far more frequent offenders than the true negatives and far less frequent than the true positives. The *false positives* were less frequent offenders than the true positives and more frequent than the false negatives.

In sum, Diagram 1A indicates that there was no increase in predictive efficiency over the modal category of the marginals in terms of reducing incorrect predictions of what people would be like as adults. If juvenile contact frequency is utilized as a predictor of adult frequency, 225 errors (8.4 percent errors) are made (163 false positives + 62 false negatives) while the modal category would suggest that we predict that no one would have extensive careers (5 or more police contacts) which would net us 159 errors (6.0 percent).

When the cohort was partitioned, omitting traffic offenses, contacts for suspicion, investigation, or information, and status offenses, there were only half as many persons in the three cells which involved five or more police contacts and proportionately fewer false positives. Still, using juvenile category as a predictor of adult status produced more errors of prediction than did the modal category. The more serious the event to be predicted, the more difficult it is to better a prediction based on the modal category of the marginals, as we have said more than once before.

Another Look at Predictive Efficiency

There is yet another way of looking at prediction and for this we shall turn to Diagrams 1D and 1E. In 1B, the juvenile contacts are arrayed according to the career seriousness category that each cohort member was in as a juvenile and as an adult. Diagrams 1D and 1E array the contacts in the same manner but, of the 7906 contacts, 5085 were as juveniles and 2821 were as adults. Thus, it is possible to see which of the contacts shown in each cell in Diagram 1B took place before 18 (Diagram 1D) and which took place after 18 (Diagram 1E). The latter distribution is forced by the table design and the continuity/discontinuity process. These additional diagrams reveal, as they should, that *false positive* cohort members' total careers consisted to a greater extent of contacts which occurred when they were juveniles (1826) while *false negative* career contacts, those which incorrectly suggested serious career continuity, consisted to a greater extent of contacts (433) accrued during the adult period.

Diagram 1D contains only those police contacts which took place during the juvenile period for the cohort members as distributed in Diagram 1A and only those which were police contacts as juveniles in Diagram 1B. As we have so often said, however, the bottom line is what juvenile period behavior enables us to predict about adult period behavior. For this we turn to Diagram 1E which presents the distribution of police contacts during the adult period for the cohort distribution in Diagram 1A and the adult contacts from the distribution of total contacts in Diagram 1B. Note that 68.3 percent of the adult contacts (37.4 percent + 30.9 percent) are in the cells in which juvenile offender types were consistent with adult offender types. There were only 671 police contacts as adults (433 + 238) in the opposing cells while chance based on the marginals would have placed 1324 contacts in these cells.

Had the modal category of the marginals been used as the predictor, that is, had we predicted that no one would be a serious adult offender, 1529 offenses as adults would have been committed by 159 persons who actually did turn out to be serious adult offenders (Diagrams 1A and 1E). The 225 error type persons (*false positives* and *false negatives*) in Diagram 1A had, however, only 671 police contacts as adults (Diagram 1E). The 62 *false negative* cohort members produced 15.3 percent of the adult police contacts and most of the errors. On the other hand, the *false positives* produced only 8.4 percent of the police contacts as adults. Thus, those who were missed by use of the juvenile police contact status as a predictor accounted for more error than did those who would be wrongly identified as likely adult serious offenders. Use of the predictor, juvenile status, reduces the errors of prediction in terms of number of police contacts but misses more police contacts by those whom it predicts will not become serious offenders but do, than police contacts it wrongly predicts will be made by serious juvenile offenders who will not continue as serious adult offenders.

It is difficult to determine the social cost of a procedure that mislabels 6.1 percent of the cohort who did not become serious offenders but committed 8.4 percent of the adult police contacts and misses positive identification of 2.3 percent of the cohort who have committed 15.3 percent of that cohort's adult police contacts. How much better is this than whimsical judgments that sometimes take place in the justice system?

PREDICTING FROM NUMEROUS BACKGROUND VARIABLES

One last mention should be made of our earliest attempts at predicting seriousness of adult criminal careers as measured by either official record data or self-report data. When a variety of juvenile records, background, and attitudinal variables were utilized as the independent variables, as high as 52 percent of the variance in adult seriousness was accounted for, differing by sex and cohort. Although type of neighborhood of socialization and juvenile seriousness usually had the greatest direct effects, attitudes toward school and performance in school, type of juvenile associates, automobile use, race, and head of household's sex also had significant effects in the various analyses.

What all of this means is that those juveniles who lacked integration into the larger society were most likely to become involved in delinquency and continue into adult crime, that the kinds of areas in which they were socialized played a part in the process, and that involvement with the justice system produced interaction that increased and generated continuity and/or more serious involvement. Understanding this and constructing measures which better represent the crucial predictor variables would enable us to move on to more effective prediction focusing attention on the organization of society as well as on the individual whose behavior we wished to predict.

CONCLUSION

This presentation of the prediction problem suggests that while we and others have been critical of the prediction enterprise, there are possibilities that are worth pursuing. Diagrams 1A through 1E reveal the complexity of the problem but also indicate that juvenile offender careers are a useful starting point in predicting who will or will not make significant contributions to the totality of adult offenses, particularly as predictions are bolstered by breaking down the distribution of police contacts for each offender type into those which occurred as juveniles and those which occurred as adults. This is the most positive contribution that our research has made to the prediction enterprise.

We have looked back to the future in two ways: 1) through a look back at the changing patterns and types of delinquency and crime over a period of more than 40 years and 2) through a variety of statistical analyses which reveal the difficulty of predicting what individuals will do in the future based not only on their past official records of police contacts, police dispositions, and court adjudications, but on background, associations, attitudes, and integration into the larger society.

6 Career Continuity in Delinquency and Crime and the Prediction Problem

THE TYPOLOGICAL APPROACH TO REPRESENTING CRIMINAL CAREERS

Thus far, whether describing the extent and nature of changes in delinquency and crime or presenting our early attempts to predict adult careers from juvenile careers, we have dealt with the incidence and seriousness of offenses and severity of sanctions (events) as converted into descriptive statistics which represent the careers of individuals or groups of individuals. When events, individuals, and groups of individuals are confused the discussion sometimes becomes confused because everyone is not referring to the same phenomena represented by the statistic before them. The Racine cohort data in this chapter have been arrayed in categories of offenders and typologies which reveal the extent to which data on juvenile careers differ from those for adult careers.

Related to all of this have been the controversies over which are the best measures of offense seriousness, of severity of sanctions, and, even more, the seriousness of a person's career. To address these questions, several ways are now presented of arraying cohort members according to the type of career that they have had. This will bring us to the point where we can think about the wide range of different offender types among juveniles and the nature and extent of their career continuity into adulthood.

Offender Typologies

A Constellation of Events vs. the Sum
Developing offender typologies (as opposed to simple measures of frequency and seriousness of offenses) and testing their validity was to be the first step in our ambitious effort to predict adult careers

from juvenile careers using scores which represented a constellation of events rather than the sums of events. At the start we examined the Gibbons (1975) typology. Would these types or, for that matter, any other constructed types found in the literature (for example, Chaiken and Chaiken, 1982) based on samples or populations of institutionalized offenders, approximate the distribution of the different types of offenders in birth cohorts? However valuable they were for other purposes, these typologies would not be very useful for predicting career continuity for cohort members because they consisted of categories of people at the serious end of the continuum of offenders.

The critics of longitudinal studies have made much of the fact that only a small percent of a birth cohort will be at the very serious end of any continuum of career seriousness or offender type seriousness.[1] We have been equally critical of research based on institutionalized populations because they have, at least in the past, dealt only with people at the most serious offense or offender seriousness end of the continuum. Most recently Gottfredson and Gottfredson (1994) have again shown us how difficult it is to predict career outcomes. They, as do we, find little justification for selective incapacitation based on the predictive efficiency of our most current devices (prior offense seriousness scales).

As our work on the development of measures or scales that encapsulate a number of variables representing delinquent and criminal careers progressed, we utilized police contact data, referral data, court dispositions, and severity of sanctions received. Members of a cohort who are at the extremes of almost any continuum based on number of offenses or seriousness of offenses (Shannon, 1980a, 1987) as juveniles were likely to be there as adults.

Some Other Facets of the Problem
The criminal career approach has been popular in recent years but controversial. There is an array of problems involved in determining who is a career criminal (high rate, dangerous vs. long-term, persistent, etc.) and how to best use these categories in the prediction problem (Chaiken and Chaiken, 1991).

Perhaps even more controversial has been the idea of types of careers which seemingly would (but need not) imply a degree of offense specialization. We and others have used computer-constructed and conceptually defined typologies, including those based on specialization vs. most serious offense. Nothing that we have done has improved prediction from the juvenile to the adult period for a cohort more than 25 percent beyond that attainable by predicting from the marginals.

If a juvenile has a serious record (numerous police contacts and/or contacts for felony-level or Part I offenses) at an early age, the likelihood of continuity is much greater. If a juvenile has reached the late teens without police contacts, the chance of future contacts (except for parking or moving vehicle violations) is small. Generally speaking, what a juvenile is like at 16 is a better basis for prediction than what he/she is like at age 6 or even age 12.

Part of the prediction problem, as previously mentioned, is the matter of skewed distributions (few people in the category to be predicted). This becomes far more important if, for example, the behavior to be predicted consists of very narrowly defined violent offenses, that is, continuity from juvenile to adult behavior among violent offender types.

Throughout their entire youth and young adult careers only 21.7 percent of the males in the 1955 Cohort had a felony-level offense in their records and most felonies do not involve violence. Although this defined only slightly more than 20 percent of the males as what could be considered serious offenders, it indicated that there were sufficient serious offenders in a large cohort for further attempts at typology construction. Our approach was to computer-construct a typology which would place cohort members in a range of types, realizing that there would be relatively few chronically serious offenders in each cohort in comparison to the proportion who would be chronic offenders in a prison population.

Examples from the Media

The prediction problem is compounded by the fact that some of the most violent crimes are committed by persons who have not had a record of previous offenses, or at least a record that would suggest violence. The Ed Gein case (1954) in Wisconsin was brought back to public attention by the media (*The Journal Times*, July 29, 1991) when it described how ' . . . police found a dozen skulls and array of ghastly items . . . chair bottoms woven from human flesh, couch legs made from the bones of human legs, bowls fashioned from skulls and a vest made from a woman's tanned torso.' Nothing in the past of this quiet Plainfield farmer would have predicted his behavior, certainly not the fact that he jested about missing persons from a local barstool. Unlike Jeffrey L. Dahmer, Wisconsin's most recent case of cannibalism and sex-oriented slayings who was convicted and sent to prison, Gein was ruled insane and died in Wisconsin's hospital for the criminally insane at the age of 81.

Even more recently an Iowa farm wife admitted shooting her spouse dead. His body had also been dismembered with a saw, his internal and sex organs removed. 'Limbs were cut from the body, most likely with a "power hand saw used in construction or home wood-working,"' the report in *The Des Moines Register*, October 8, 1991, says. There was nothing in her prior behavior that would suggested such violent behavior. 'Meanwhile residents of the usually pastoral Iowa farm town where the Friebergs lived were haunted with questions about what would drive an apparently meek woman, an insurance agent, and the mother of a young teen-ager to commit such an unspeakable crime.' She was described as 'soft-spoken, nice, and pleasant, one of the sweetest people I have ever worked with.' The media is replete with similar cases, described in the most intimate detail but seldom, if ever, have these events been predicted.

COMPUTER-CONSTRUCTED TYPOLOGIES

Extending Our Ability with the Computer

As we commenced to generate a more complex typology with the computer, it was hypothesized that inherent in each type of delinquent career would be combinations of events with varied likelihood of producing continuity into adult crime. In pre-computer days the interrelations of variables making for continuity *might* be discerned by lengthy perusal of the records of delinquents and criminals supplemented by interviews. Today computer programs can cluster cohort members into relatively homogeneous groups (the larger the number of groups, the more homogeneous is each group), rank them in a way consistent with their content, and determine which group produced the largest proportion of continuity into adult crime. Based on definitions of events, the most serious of the adult criminal types may also be determined by computer. This approach is useful, of course, in the development of typologies for application in the justice system, including program planning and evaluation (Harris and Jones, 1996).

This took us a long way from Shaw's (1931) Chicago-based model of delinquency which saw delinquency as gradually expanding from minor depredations to more serious index offenses, the slum-learned delinquent career, perhaps leading to adult crime. It was also quite different from models of delinquency which concerned themselves with specialization, offender types as it were, such as vandals, shoplifters, and, as adults, burglars and embezzlers. We would not dispute the judgment that books on hold-up men, burglars, and con men are far more fascinating than accounts based on cohort statistics.

The possibility that computer-constructed types would be more efficient as predictors than additive scale scores, weighted or unweighted, seemed reasonable because these types would represent groups of offenders with police contacts consisting of meaningful clusters of offenses rather than types with scores which could be obtained in a variety of ways but which did not tell us about the content of careers. These would seldom be completely specialized types of offenders (quite different types of offenses are often related in meaningful ways) but are types in terms of what happens in the world of misbehavior. Furthermore, the juvenile types might be more closely linked to adult types than were simple additive juvenile scores linked to simple additive adult scores, even if offense types carried different weights determined by their seriousness or by their contribution to predictability.

A Typology Based on Most Serious Offense Types

Continuity is a consequence of the process of social interaction between a number of actors (offender, police, court, social workers, court officers, judges, probation officers, and institutional personnel). Insofar as continuity develops, it is generated through social interaction as opposed to simple, willful, decision-making by certain types of people.

We commenced with a rather simple offense typology. Data on offense seriousness were subjected to the SAS FASTCLUS routine so that each person was placed in one of 23 different offender types, as shown in Table 1 for the 1949 Cohort. This gave us an idea of how well people clustered. For example, the eight most serious offender types in the 1942 Cohort contained only 5.1 percent of the cohort, but each person in these clusters had had police contacts for felonies and Part I offenses. They accounted for 80.7 percent of all felonies by members of that cohort. The 1949 Cohort produced seven types of felony/Part I offenders who constituted

Table 1.
1949 Cohort Cluster Discrimination

#	% in Cluster with		% Cohort Offenses Accounted for		Ratio % Fels to Prop. Pop. In Cluster	% Pop. in Cohort
	Fel	Part I	Felony	Part I		
11	100	100	13.1	10.6	24.9	.5
20	100	100	10.1	6.0	21.8	.4
13	100	100	10.6	7.1	10.0	.5
2	100	100	19.7	13.0	16.8	1.1
17	100	100	6.6	7.0	11.2	.5
7	100	100	12.6	7.5	8.5	1.2
21	100	100	2.0	3.3	7.7	.3
			74.7	54.5		4.5
9	100	67	3.5	1.1	5.9	.7
14	71	86	1.5	2.7	4.4	.5
6	40	100	5.6	5.9	3.8	1.2
12	38	100	2.0	2.9	2.5	.6
3	23	100	4.6	13.9	2.3	3.3
18	17	100	3.5	11.5	.8	3.7
4	100	–	–	–	3.0	.1
10	–	100	–	3.7	–	1.2
22	25	19	.5	1.1	1.6	2.1
1	8	23	.5	.5	1.0	.7
19	7	2	1.0	.2	4.8	.4
5	–	2	.5	.9	–.1	14.7
8	–	2	–	.2	–	3.6
15	1	1	1.0	.2	.1	10.6
16	–	–	–	–	–	3.0
23	1	1	1.0	.5	–.1	44.3

9.2% of 1949 Cohort has felony contacts
16.9% of 1949 Cohort has Part I contacts
56.7% of 1949 Cohort felons in pure types
    (everyone in cluster has at least one felony contact)
86.3% of 1949 Cohort Part I offenders in pure types

4.5 percent of the cohort and accounted for 74.7 percent of the cohort's felonies. It took only four types making up 5.0 percent of the 1955 Cohort to account for 75.7 percent of its felonies. If three more types were added, all felony and Part I offenders, 7.4 percent of the 1955 Cohort accounted for 87.2 percent of its felonies.

This approach enabled us to focus on a highly disproportional share of the cohort who had developed into serious offenders. For example, for the 1949 Cohort the most serious types accounted for 65.7 percent of the felonies against property but only 13.1 percent of those against persons. All cohort members in these types were

male (they constituted 8.1 percent of the males), disproportionately black, and/or socialized in the inner city. Looking at disproportionately differently, these serious offenders constituted 3.4 percent
of the whites, 10.4 percent of the Chicanos, and 18.0 percent of
the blacks. Although only a small proportion of each cohort's members were included in the serious offender clusters, they accounted
for 81.3 percent of the burglaries and 75.0 percent of the robberies.

We are far from implying that there are criminal types (persons
with a criminal propensity) or that there is something in people's
physical or psychological makeup that provides the push toward
delinquent and criminal behavior. Persons in these computer-created
offender types ranging from frequent felony/Part I offenders to non-
offenders are the products of social interaction and embody a chain
of consequent life experiences.

**Typologies Based on the Frequency and Seriousness of Offenses,
Referrals, and Severity of Sanctions**

The next step was to develop more complex juvenile and adult
typologies which would enable us to increase our predictive efficiency
over that obtained with simple scoring systems. Among these attempts
were typologies based on number systems which not only took into
account offense seriousness, referrals, and sanctions, but also the
relative frequency of events. None, however, produced juvenile/adult
relationships exceeding those obtained with various offense seriousness scores.

Although a variety of other typologies (offense typologies and
sanctions typologies) enabled us to place cohort members in sociologically meaningful career types, none permitted an improvement
in predicting the likelihood and nature of adult careers from juvenile
careers beyond that obtained with simpler measures. Some of the
typologies which arranged cohort members according to their most
frequent offenses or most serious offenses continued to produce
considerable within-types heterogeneity. But even in this period that
took youth only into the late 1960s and early 1970s, a large proportion of those who fell into the more serious types had police
contacts for drug offenses. This is a finding to which we returned
from time to time, examining the possibility that the role of drugs
within serious offender types might be the cement that linked elements of continuing careers, or might be the element that increased
severity of sanctions, indirectly leading to continuity in careers.

Our most sophisticated strategy was to conduct a canonical analysis of the major measures and typologies to see which combinations of measures and typologies for the juvenile period best accounted for which adult combinations. In other words, how is juvenile delinquency best linked to adult crime, and which variables from each group best represent the linkage? The canonical analysis revealed that the maximum amount of the relationship between the juvenile and adult periods was accounted for with each period represented by the number and seriousness of police contacts and the total severity of court sanctions. That severity of court sanctions were so important in determining future behavior can be interpreted in several ways. Has the court reacted to seriousness of behavior with severe sanctions during both the juvenile and adult periods, or has the court's reaction with severe sanctions maximized the probability of continuity? This question comes up again and again.

Little improvement in predictability was obtained when selected interview variables were added in the canonical analysis. Looking back, our earlier research clearly showed that the interview variables had different patterns of relationship to different measures of delinquency and crime depending on sex, race/ethnicity, and neighborhood of socialization so that in all probability variations in interview responses were canceled out in these uncontrolled analyses. Cernkovich and Giordano (1992) have shown, for example, how black/white differences in perception of the educational system may play a part in juvenile misbehavior, many blacks viewing the system as the embodiment of the larger society's false promises of equality even though others see education as an avenue to success.

THE COMPLEXITY OF AN OFFENSE TYPE TYPOLOGY

Examining Individual Careers

Even though the various typologies which we developed did not permit an increase in predictive efficiency from the juvenile to the adult period, they are descriptive devices that represent careers and the changing nature of careers. Tables 2 and 3 were based on official records of police contacts during both age periods. They are heuristic in the sense that complex and heterogeneous career patterns are shown in detailed form. As the various career types are presented in these tables they have been condensed somewhat from the expanded form which appears in Diagrams 1A and 1B later in this chapter with marginal subtitles in a more readable form.

There were 44 members of the 1955 Cohort in the murderer, all-around street offender (robbery with other offenses), assault with other offenses, or sexual assault types as juveniles but only nine of the 44 remained in these violent offender types as adults. Only 13 were in the drug offender and felony burglary types as adults. The prediction problem is dramatized by the fact that there were 28 in the violent offender types as adults who had been in other types as juveniles.

These types are arranged in Tables 2 and 3 without regard to the felony-level/misdemeanor-level dichotomy so that the most violent offender types (murderers, all-around street offenders, assaulters, burglars, and sexual assaulters) are at the extreme violent end of the continuum, a strategy that removes the felony/misdemeanor variable as an element in rank-ordering offender types. The modest correlation between juvenile and adult offender types of only 0.447 was reduced to 0.307 with no police contact types as both juveniles and adults removed.

What do the individual official careers of the various offender types look like. Tables 2 and 3 (only eight types of the complete typology of 24 are presented) detail the heterogeneity within juvenile and adult offender types of the 1955 Cohort. The total scores in the right-hand column of each panel shown in these tables are simple additive scores based on the number of contacts for various offenses, each having a score ranging from 1 for contact to 24 for homicide. These tables show the varied patterns of offenses that may be found in each type from murderers, all-around street offenders, assaulters down to burglars, although not shown to the extreme end of the continuum for those who have had contacts only for suspicion, investigation, or information.

Only one of the all-around street offenders in Table 2 had a felony-level police contact for drugs as a juvenile, but seven of that type in Table 3 had felony-level drug contacts as adults. Since we have been concerned about the careers of those who had felony-level drug offenses, it is important to note that many of the 27 who, as juveniles, were classified as felony-level drug offender types plus (Table 2) had offense patterns, with the exception of robbery (armed) offenses, similar to the all-around street offenders. This is also the case for the 34 who were classified as felony-level drug offenders plus as adults.

Table 2.
Cohort Members Ranked by Most Serious Juvenile Offense in
Career Score: 1995 Cohort

	Misdemeanor level												Felony level										
#	1 CONTACT	2 JUV STAT	3 DISCON	4 TRAFFIC	5 GAMBLING	8 SEX	9 FORGERY EARYD	10 THEFT	11 VPD	12 DRUGS	13 ASSAULT	14 BURGLARY	15 T AHUS TFOT	16 VPD	17 FORGERY EARYD	18 THEFT	19 BURGLARY	20 DRUGS	21 SEX	22 ASSAULT	23 ROBBERY	24 HOMICIDE	TS OC TO AR LE
								MURDERERS (1)															
1	3	16	9					30							37	40						24	173
1	3	12	18	4				40	11		26				19						69		202
1	10	14	6	12				90			26		15	17	133						46		369
1	2	14	21	12				90	11			28	60		19						46		303
1	6	20	18					10													46		100
1	4	6		4				10			13		15			18			21	23			114
1	1			3									15			19		20		23			81
1	2	14	6					110				28		17	19	247				23			465
1	3	26	18					70					60	17	18	95				23			330
1	5	18	6	16				40	11		52		30		18	76				23			295
1	2	12	6	8				10			13	14	15			76				23			179
1	1	6	6		8			30							57					23			131
1	5	10	3					210						17	36	38				23			342
1	9	26	9	8				70			13				36	38				23			232
1	2	8	21						11		13				18	38				23			134
1	3	6	3	4				50			26	70	75			38				23			298
1	2	32	3	12				70								38				23			190
1															18	19				23			61
1	7	48	45	10				60			52					19				23			282
1	1							20								19				23			63
1	1							10							18					23			56
1	7	14	33	4				20			104				18					23			223
1	1	6	6	4				20												23			78
1	3	15						10			13		15							23			79
1	6	4	6	8				40			26									23			113
1	2	6		4							13									23			48
1	4		6					20												23			47
1	3	4	6					10												23			46
1			6					10												23			39
1			3					10												23			36
1				4																23			27
1		4	9																	23			36
								ALL AROUND STREET OFFENDERS (31)															
1	6	3		4							52							20		22			108
1	4	14	33	12																22			266
1	28	6	4		8			20			13	105			75					22			136
1	3	8	6								13				19					22			71
1	2	6						10			15				19					22			40
1	12	6						ASSAULTERS (6)												22			41
1	2	10				8		60	11		13						84						138
1	4	6	12	4	16			130			13				19	63							327
1	5	20	18	4				150							76	42							359
1	2	3	4									14	60	30		21							30
1			6					SEX OFFENDERS (6)				14				21							27
1			6													21							21

All around street offenders seriousness scores (rank x frequency summed)
range from 27–465 in this type whose offenses consist mainly of robbery,
theft, burglary, and assault 31 = 3.3% of 946 cohort members with police
contacts as juveniles.

DRUG DEFENDERS + I (27)

#	1	2	3	4	5	8	9	10	11	12	13	14	15	16	17	18	19	20	21	22	23	24	Tot
1	1	6	15	12														80					114
1	2	10	12														19	40					93
1		4	6	4			9	30										40					93
1		2	3					20										40					65
1	1	4	6					10										40					61
1	2	2	3					10										40					57
1	9	8	24	4				20					15		17		114	20					231
1	2	16	6	20				40			13		15				57	20					189
1		6	6					10					15			18	38	20					113
1	8	28	15	8				110								18	38	20					245
1	2	10	6	4				40	33		13		60		34		38	20					260
1	10	20	19					20	11		26				204	18	19	20					366
1		6	6					10								18	19	20					79
1	1	2											15				19	20					57
1	1	22	3	4				30			13	28					19	20					140
1		8	3	4													19	20					54
1		2	9									14			17			20					62
1	3	8	9	4				20				14		16				20					94
1		8	3											16				20					47
1		2	3					30					15					20					70
1	3	2	3	4				10					15					20					57
1	4	24	3			8		20										20					79
1	2	6	15	8		8		10										20					69
1	1	10	3	4				10										20					48
1	4	8		4				10										20					46
1				4				10										20					34
1		2						10										20					32
1								10										20					30

DRUG OFFENDERS + II (21)

#	1	2	3	4	5	8	9	10	11	12	13	14	15	16	17	18	19	20	21	22	23	24	Tot
1	1	2				8												20					31
1	1		2	4														20					29
1		2		4														20					26
1				4														20					24
1		2	6															20					28
1	1	12	3															20					36
1		2	3															20					25
1			3															20					23
1			4															20					24
2	1	2																20					23
1		2																20					22
1	1																	20					21
7																		20					20

BURGLARS (13)

#	1	2	3	4	5	8	9	10	11	12	13	14	15	16	17	18	19	20	21	22	23	24	Tot
1	1	2	24					60			13						209						309
1	8	6						10								18	190						233
1	2	20		4							13	14				18	152						223
1	6	34	12	4				30			26		60				152						324
1	3	6	12					60			39	14	75			18	133						350
1	3	18	18	4				30			39	56			17		133						318
1	2	2						40									95						139
1	4	12	18	8				40					120			18	76						295
1	5	6	15	4				20					15			18	76						159
1	11	24	30					20					15	16			76						192
1	5	22	15	8				60	11		13			16			76						225
1	1	4	9			8		10					45				76						153
1	6	14	21	8				20			13	14	90				57						243
1	1	16	9	4				20					60				57						167
1	3	6	9					30	11				15				57						131
1	5	8	9	4				70			13						57						166
1	7	20	6	4				20									57						114
1	2							10									57						69
1	5	14	15	4				20			13					18	38						118
1	4	4	9	4				20					15		34		38						128
1	1	12	9	8				20	11		13			16			38						118
1	5	32	9					20					15				38						107
1	2	18						60			39						38						157
1	4							13									38						55
1	5	38	12					20	11								38						124
1	2	8	24	12				20	11								38						95
1	3	8	9	16				40									38						114
1	1	4	3					10									38						56
1	2	6	12	8				20			26					36	19						129
1	2	30	6					20			13		15			18	19						123
1	4	6	12	12				20			13	14				18	19						95
1	4	3	12					30								18	19						86
1	2	3						10								18	19						52
1	2	8	9	4				20								18	19						60
1	1															18	19						38
1	1	4	3					20			39				17		19						103
1		10	27	4				30	11						17		19						118
1	2	10	3					20			26		15				19						95
1	4	6	15	8				10					15				19						77
1	4	3											15				19						41
1		3	4								26						19						52
1	3	2	9					20	11		13						19						77
1		9						30			13						19						71
1	1	24	3	8							13						19						71
1	1	10		4							13						19						47
1	3	20	33	12			9	50									19						146
1	2	14	9	4				30									19						78
1	1	14	9					30									19						73
1	1	6		4				20									19						50
1	1	2						20									19						42
1	2	2	6	4				10									19						43
1		8	9	4													19						36
1	3	3						10									19						46
1	3	2	3					10									19						37
1	4							10									19						33
1								10									19						29
1	1			4													19						24
3				4													19						23
1	1	2	6														19						28
1		4															19						23
1	1	2															19						22
1		2															19						21
5																	19						19

56 lesser all around street offenders (no robbers) = 5.9% of cohort members with police contacts as juveniles.

Table 3.

Cohort Members Ranked by Most Serious Adult Offense in Career Score: 1995 Cohort

	Misdemeanor level											Felony level									
CONTACT	DIS CON	TRAFFIC	GAMBLING	LIQUOR	SEX	FOR GR EA RU YD	THEFT	VPD	DRUGS	ASSAULT	T AH UE TF OT	VPD	FOR GR EA RU YD	THEFT	BURGLARY	DRUGS	SEX	ASSAULT	ROBBERY	HOMICIDE	TS OC TO AR LE
# 1	3	4	5	6									18	19	20	21	22	23	24		

MURDERERS (4)

CONT	DISCON	TRAF	GAMB	LIQ	SEX	FORG	THEFT	VPD	DRUGS	ASLT	T	VPD	FORG	THEFT	BURG	DRUGS	SEX	ASLT	ROB	HOM	TS
1	15	4			8	10				15									161	24	273
1 1	12	16				30	11		13		34	18			40				23	24	222
1 1		8							13						20		22			24	68
1 1	12	12							13						20					24	82
1 3						10	11		15					76	40				161		316
1 7	18		8			60			13												221
1 1	60		5	6		10	11						57	20			22				261
1 2	3	16		6	9	10								20			22				157
1			4	5	8								57	20							163
1 2					8								38	20							137
1 1	30					20	33								40			44	46		174
1 4	6														40	20	21		46		96
1		8			8									57					23		80
1														19					23		80
1	6	8																	23		56
1						10													23		35
1 1	3	8			8														23		36
1 1		4																	23		

ALL AROUND STREET OFFENDERS (17)

CONT	DISCON	TRAF	GAMB	LIQ	SEX	FORG	THEFT	VPD	DRUGS	ASLT	T	VPD	FORG	THEFT	BURG	DRUGS	SEX	ASLT	ROB	HOM	TS
1	6																		23		24
1 2	9	12							39						40			44			106
1	3									15					20			22			80
1 1	12					30									57			22			85
1 2	6	12		6		10									38			22			115
1 2	21								13						19			22			95
1	33					10			26						19			22			110
1		16		6		10			13				18					22			86
1 2	24	4																22			70
1		4																22			26
1 2	9																	22			33
1	9																	22			31

ASSAULTERS I (11)

CONT	DISCON	TRAF	GAMB	LIQ	SEX	FORG	THEFT	VPD	DRUGS	ASLT	T	VPD	FORG	THEFT	BURG	DRUGS	SEX	ASLT	ROB	HOM	TS
1 3	18	8												19			21				89
1	12								13						20	21					66
1 1	12												18		20	21					52
1 3	3	4				9		11	26							21					77
1 2	6	4							26							21					59

SEX OFFENDERS (5)

All around street offenders seriousness scores (rank x frequency summed) range from 24–316. Several cohort members with lowest score in this group have no other adult offenses and are officially only armed robbers 17 = 2.0% of 863 cohort members with police contacts as adults.

#	1	3	4	5	6	8	9	10	11	12	13	15	16	17	18	19	20	21	22	23	24	
1	1		4	12			9			12							80					118
1		12															80					92
1	5	39	24		18				50	11		15				57	60					279
1		6	8							11						57	60					142
1	2	21	8		6		9				26					19	60					151
1		3									26						60					89
1											13						60					73
1																	60					70
1		3	20														60					83
1		3	4														60					67
1		3															60					64
1	1	3	20					10							36	76	40					186
1		6	4			8									18	19	40					95
1	1	6			6									17		19	40					89
1	6	9	8							22	13	13				19	40					117
1			8								13					19	40					80
1		2	8					10							18		40					78
1		3						10			13						40					66
1	1						9										40					50
1	1	3	8														40					52
1	1	3															40					44
1	1																40					41
1																	40					40
1		6										15				38	20					79
1	3	27	4								78					38	20					170
1	2	9	8				9				13					38	20					99
1	2	27									13					38	20					100
1	2	12	12								13	15			18	19	20					111
1	1	6						40							18	19	20					104
1		3	4													19	20					46
1																19	20					40
1	1																20					97
1	2	3	8					20			26				18		20					110
1	2	54	16												18		20					115
1	3	21	4	12		8				22	13	15					20					74
1		9	8							11	26						20					68
1			8														20					51
1	1	3	8					40									20					49
1	1	6	12					20									20					34
1			4					10									20					30
1								10									20					

DRUGS + I (34)

#	1	3	4	5	6	8	9	10	11	12	13	15	16	17	18	19	20	21	22	23	24	
1	1		12	6													20					39
1		6	24														20					50
3			12														20					32
1	2		8														20					30
2			8														20					28
1	2	3	4														20					29
1	1	3	4														20					28
1		3	4														20					27
1			4														20					25
7			4														20					24
1	1	27															20					48
1		9															20					29
1	1	6															20					27
1		3															20					23
3	1																20					21
10																	20					20

DRUGS II (42)

#	1	3	4	5	6	8	9	10	11	12	13	15	16	17	18	19	20	21	22	23	24	
1	3	6	4						11		13	15				57						81
1	6	3	4			8					13					38						87
1	1	18	4					20								38						74
1	3	9			6			10								38						70
1	3	6			6			10								38						61
1			12													38						50
1	1	15	8													38						62
1		3	4																			45
1	1	30	12			8						30	16	119		19						235
1	3	9	8					10							34	19						83
1		3	4					20		11				17		19						104
1	2	21	4					20			26			17		19						109
1	2	6				8		30			13	15				19						93
1												15				19						34
1	1	6			6	8				11	26					19						77
1	1	9			6	8					13					19						50
1			8					20								19						47
1		3	4					10								19						36
1	2	3	12		6		9									19						51
1			12													19						31
1		3	4													19						26
1		6														19						25

BURGLARS I (3)

76 drug offenders = 8.8% of cohort members with police contacts as adults.

All around street offenders (19) [burglary most serious offense].

Heterogeneity and Offense Switching

Tables 2 and 3 highlight the heterogeneity of offenses within offender types and the likelihood of frequent offense switching. This heterogeneity may be based on continuous heterogeneity, that is, changes in the kinds of offenses that a cohort member has had from age 6 to 18, perhaps progressing in seriousness. The kinds of offenses from age 18 to 22 (adult years in this table) may become progressively less serious in the later years as moving vehicle offenses are added during the adult period. We should not be surprised when the most serious offense category determining offender type changes between the juvenile and adult period, from drugs to burglary or from burglary to drugs. Cohort members may engage in both but be apprehended for only one or the other in a given period. Almost any typology involves some within-category heterogeneity. Casual references to offenders as burglars, robbers, assaulters, and so on, have appeared frequently in the literature, but this characterization of offenders is an oversimplification.

The all-around street offenders and assaulters (who had other offenses as well) had greater continuity than did any other type and also appeared disproportionate in the drug offender type as adults. This suggests, as we have stated before, that the drug connection should be explored further because drug use or involvement may have a catalytic effect on career continuity.

DRUG OFFENDERS VS. NON-DRUG OFFENDERS IN THE 1955 COHORT

Partitioning the 1955 Cohort

Diagram 1A (developed from diagrams in Shannon, 1991) shows the typological distribution of the 136 persons who had police contacts for drug offenses as juveniles and/or adults and Diagram 1B does so for those 2013 who did not have police contacts for drug offenses during either period.[2] Most of those who are shown in Diagram 1A are included in Sections A to I to which we shall refer as the table is discussed. About 60 percent of the cohort's most serious juvenile offender types and 45 percent of its most serious adult offender types are included in Diagram 1A which, along with Diagram 6.1B, reveals even more clearly that there is no really

Diagram 1.
Juvenile Offense Seriousness Type vs. Adult Offense Seriousness
Type: Persons in 1955 Cohort

A. With Police Contacts for Drug Offenses: 5.46% of Cohort

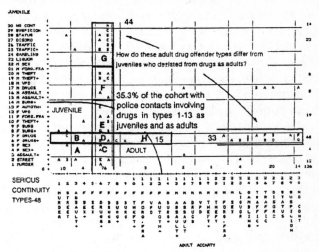

B. No Police Contacts for Drug Offenses: 94.54% of Cohort

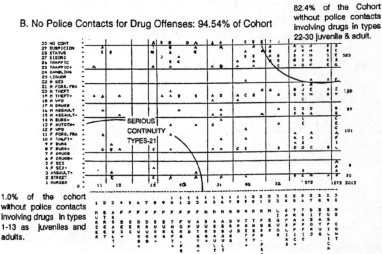

straightforward relationship between police contact patterns or types as a juvenile and police contact patterns or types as an adult. In a way, this should not be surprising because, whether delinquent/criminal or not, statuses and roles change with age in a multitude of respects.

The fact that 35.3 percent of the 1955 Cohort members with drug offenses were in the most serious offender types as both juveniles and adults while only 1 percent of those without drug offenses on their record were in the most serious offender types as juveniles and adults again suggests some relationship between drugs and continuity in delinquency and crime. Only 6 of 136 drug offender cohort members in Diagram 1A were in felony drug offender categories as both juveniles and adults, however. When both diagrams were placed together, the correlation between juvenile and adult offense seriousness types became modest, only 0.449. If those who were drug offender types had been ranked differently in Diagram 1A, their pattern of career seriousness and career continuity would have been quite different. By ranking drug offenses and offenders along with other serious offense and offender types the cards are, in a sense, stacked against drug offenders. Most drug offenses were felonies, therefore these offenders were classified as serious offenders. Placing so many drug offenders in the serious offender category produced the pattern of serious continuity in Diagram 1A.

Let us examine the data a bit further.

Drug Offenders and Career Continuity

The Most Serious Types
The very 'bad' as juveniles tended to remain 'bad' as adults (Section A of Diagram 1A) disproportionately to how many were in serious offender types as adults (although some changed for the better). All were from inner-city neighborhoods. This was one of the types of offenders whom Chaiken and Chaiken (1991) also found to more likely be high-rate offenders in their study of the selection process of cases for priority prosecution in Los Angeles County and Middlesex County in Massachusetts.

Drug Offender Types as Juveniles or Adults
Forty-eight of the 118 persons who were at one time or the other in felony drug offender types were in those types as juveniles (Sections B, D, H, and I). Most of them (42 of the 48) did not appear

in felony drug types as adults. Most of the 76 in felony drug types as adults (Sections C, D, E, F, and G) had not been in the felony drug types as juveniles. All, of course, have had drug involvement, but some had more serious offenses that placed them in other types as either juveniles or adults. Thirty-one of the 76 adult drug offender types had been in various other felony types as juveniles, but 14 had not had a police contact as a juvenile.

How do the 44 adult felony drug offender types in Sections F and G differ from the 33 in Section I who were drug offender types as juveniles but appear to have desisted from serious crime as adults? This is challenging to those who are sure that early recorded drug use is a precursor to serious criminal careers, or that adult drug involvement may be readily predicted by juvenile involvement. Cohort members in Section G were drug offender types as adults vs. those in Section I who were drug offender types as juveniles. Twelve of the 36 in this section were females and 13 were from the inner-city or transitional neighborhoods – 33.3 and 36 percent. They either had no police contacts as juveniles or their most serious contacts were for traffic offenses. Between the ages of 18 and 20, however, all had at least one police contact for possession or drug use. With one exception their adult careers were not extensive, the exception being a female with 17 contacts, eight of which were for theft (shop-lifting) and burglary and five for drugs. She exemplifies the drugs/crime relationship at ages 18–20 and then again in the updating at 28–30. This is the type of case to which people refer, as an example, rather than examining a cohort which will enable them to see the larger picture of relationships. Most of those in Section G had not been referred to the county probation department and had not been sanctioned as juveniles, but most had been referred as adults, although few were severely sanctioned as adults.

The ten cohort members in Section F were in juvenile offender types involving one or more misdemeanors from theft to burglary but in the drug offender types as adults. Only one was female. Two-thirds of the males were from inner-city or transitional neighborhoods. Two had been severely sanctioned as juveniles but, again, they were in little trouble until they were young adults, at which time half developed a sizable career. Most had drug offenses at ages 18–20, had lengthier and more serious offender careers as adults, were referred to the county probation officer, and were more severely sanctioned as adults.

The 33 cohort members in Section I should be markedly different from those in Sections F and G because they had offense careers which involved drugs as juveniles, but had either no trouble involving drugs and no or very little other trouble as adults. Sixteen (48 percent) of them were females but only 33.3 percent of those in Section I were from inner-city or transitional areas. Thus, demographically and socially they differed from cohort members in Sections F and G. Most had drug offenses at 16 or 17, had more offenses as juveniles than did cohort members in Sections F and G, and were not severely sanctioned as juveniles. They were either no worse and often better behaved as adults and, as a consequence, were not severely sanctioned after age 18. For whatever reason, it also appeared that county probation worked along with their families and these juveniles to a greater extent than it had with other types of offenders.

The 15 cohort members who, as juveniles, were drug offender types or drug offenders with other felony offenses, Sections B, D, and H, but who remained in the more serious felony types as adults differed demographically and socially from those in Section I. All were males and 57 percent were from inner-city or transitional neighborhoods. Over half were involved in serious felony-level offenses such as robbery and burglary, rather than drugs as adults, had been referred as juveniles, and had been severely sanctioned for some of their behavior. Many had been institutionalized, but had continued their serious offender careers as adults with numerous police contacts for the entire range of felonies except murder.

While drug and other felony-level offenses were intertwined in the careers of several persons in these offender types, one cannot go beyond saying that drug offenses (possession and delivery) as well as other illegal behavior had become part of their way of life. Most of this group of offender types were similar as juveniles and adults to those found in the A and C Sections (all-around street offenders) but did not have felony offenses against the person as part of their records. The range of juvenile and adult career seriousness varied but most were in serious trouble as either juveniles or adults or both.

The cohort members in Section C, more than half of whom were all-around street offenders and involved in drugs as juveniles, were in the drug offender types as adults. In most cases they had received relatively severe sanctions as either juveniles or adults or both. All were males and 55.5 percent were from the inner-city or transitional neighborhoods.

One additional group should be mentioned, those in Section E, who were in diverse felony types as juveniles but who were in the drug offender types as adults. Only three of the 16 were female and 62.5 percent were from the inner-city and transitional areas. Most had serious records as juveniles and adults and half of them had been sanctioned relatively severely in both periods, with little effect on their continuity. Although they were in the drug types as adults, their drug offenses were only part of their varied offenses, most of which were property in nature with a disproportional number of burglaries. While there are examples of a tendency toward specialization in specific Part I offenses such as burglary or theft (a male burglar and a female shoplifter, for example), in no case was this unaccompanied by numerous lesser offenses.

In sum, observation of the juvenile/adult distribution of typology types indicates that while the delinquency/crime/drugs relationship exists, it alone is probably no more the key to predicting criminal career continuity than is the fact that a cohort member has been socialized in inner-city or transitional neighborhoods. If we assume that the official records of young adults for the 1955 Cohort do not represent total careers and that self-report data will produce a more representative record – a position that can be argued – the trail is worth following.

THE RELATIONSHIP OF JUVENILE TYPES TO ADULT TYPES: SELF-REPORT DATA

The absence of interviews for 1955 Cohort members necessitated turning back to the 1942 and 1949 Cohorts: the self-report data that included the use of marijuana, the use of other drugs, and two categories on alcohol use. The typology based on the self-report data differed from that based on official data. The offense categories utilized were not the same; the official offense seriousness typology was based on the offenses in official records while the self-report typology was based on what people were willing to report about themselves in categories: 1) once or twice (very rarely), 2) occasionally, 3) frequently, and 4) all the time. The problems with categorization are known to us but this is not the point at issue here.

The Juveniles

When interviewed persons were arrayed on a self-report scale, juvenile drug use was again a part of the behavior of many serious types of offenders. For example, seven out of 17 all-around street offenders reported either hard drug and/or marijuana usage; nine out of 37 who reported carrying concealed weapons and involvement in a variety of other offenses also reported marijuana and/or drug usage; eight out of 57 who reported having stolen an automobile or used one without the owner's permission also reported drug and/or marijuana use. There were only a few such reports for the remainder of the 870 persons who submitted self-reports.

The Adults

Adult behavior differed considerably; 67 cohort members were in the hard drug offender type as adults (10.6 percent). In addition, 9 out of 15 all-around street offenders used hard drugs and/or marijuana; 49 out of 71 weapons types used hard drugs and/or marijuana; 12 out of 15 burglar types did so, as did 53 out of 89 assaulter types. A sizable proportion (86.8 percent) of those who could be defined as adult self-reported violent offender types admitted driving under the influence of drugs or alcohol. Although self-reported drug use among serious offenders is almost all-pervasive, this is overlap, not necessarily causal.

Half or more of the cohort members in each of the more serious offender types had felony drug offenses as adults (alcohol and tobacco use is even more prevalent), but unless these drug offenses were committed prior to the other offenses, knowledge of them would not be of much help in predicting serious criminal careers, even in combination with other variables.

Drug Users vs. Non-Drug Users

When the interviewed persons with continuous residence (715) were divided into those 286 who had self-reported drug use and those 429 who had none, among that 40 percent reporting drug use, the least serious official offender types as juveniles were in the least serious types as adults (86 percent of the 286). But only 46 percent of the most serious types of juvenile offenders were found in the most serious types as adults. Among non-drug users (60 percent) 96 percent were in the least serious police contact offender types as juveniles and adults but only 20 percent of the serious juvenile offenders were serious adult offenders.

In terms of the statistical relationship of alcohol and drugs to delinquency and crime, that is, a measure of the extent to which people who had substance involvement also admitted various types of offenses or had records of various types of offenses, the four self-report measures of substance involvement – hard drug use, marijuana use, liquor use, and driving under the influence of alcohol or drugs – were more highly correlated with their self-reported offense seriousness during the juvenile and adult periods than with their official records of delinquency and crime. The range of correlations between self-reported offense seriousness and self-reported measures of juvenile substance use was from 0.363 for hard drug use to 0.550 for liquor use, but for the same substance use self-report measures it was from 0.128 to 0.248 for official delinquency seriousness measures. For the 18–20 age period the self-reported offense measures produced correlations ranging from 0.569 to 0.623, but the official offense measures ranged from 0.079 to 0.351. In other words, what people reported about themselves in terms of substance use and offenses was more closely related than were what they reported about themselves in regard to substances and their official police records of offenses.

This still does not tell us as much as we wish to know about the relationship of substance involvement to delinquency and crime or to continuities in either during the 1950s through the early 1970s because most of those interviewed, drug users or not, had rather modest careers in delinquency and crime.

ADDING A PERSISTENCE DIMENSION TO TYPOLOGIES

Tables showing rates of continuation or discontinuation of offenses by contact order from the first to the tenth contact have also revealed that most juveniles desisted from most types of offense after relatively few police contacts, that is, roughly 75 percent of the males who had non-traffic contacts had desisted by the sixth or seventh police contact, including those contacts which were only juvenile status contacts or contacts for suspicion, investigation, or information. Most careers peaked at the age of 16 or 17 and desistance was rapid thereafter.

What causes people to desist and at what age is controversial. Some contend that contacts with the police result in discontinuity (Votey, 1991) and others that police contacts increase the probability of continuity. We know that there are race/ethnic, sex, and offense category differences in rates of continuation and discontinuation. The entire matter, including the possibility of increasing seriousness with age (which turned out not to be a probability for most cohort members), was dealt with in Shannon (1982).

More pertinent, however, was our finding that there were varieties of patterns of continuity and discontinuity if three age periods were considered, 6–17, 18–20, and 21 and older. Eight patterns were possible, those who had at least one contact in each age period, those who had at least one contact 6–17 and 18–20, and so on. The picture was made even more complex when separate distributions were made for all police contacts, traffic contacts only, non-traffic contacts, then felonies vs. non-felonies and for males and females. When year-by-year records were used as the time unit there were more than a dozen distinct patterns (and many more sub-patterns) of continuity or persistence. (See Chapters 10 and 11 of *Criminal Career Continuity,* Shannon, 1988.)

CONCLUSION

That enterprise which in the past attempted to explain the development of delinquent and/or criminal behavior as though the delinquent or criminal was a clinical entity was an enterprise doomed to failure, albeit a profitable one for many professionals. The idea that there are different delinquent and criminal types in terms of their patterns of behavior (offenses) has become more and more accepted over the years (Gibbons, 1975). Whether such a delinquent/criminal typology should be based on the social orientation of offenders or their pattern of offenses or some combination thereof may still be argued.

All things considered, none of the offense typologies described in this chapter, whether based on most serious to least serious types of offenses or a typology based on frequency, types of offenses, and seriousness of offenses (felony vs. non-felony), represent types and patterns of careers in such a way that they may be used for the prediction of adult behavior from juvenile behavior with accuracy. The effort has not been wasted because it does provide a strong argument against the position that the seriousness and type of adult career that an individual will have may be predicted from the seriousness and type of career that the individual has had as a juvenile, and with sufficient accuracy to be used in the decision making by persons in the justice system. This does not mean that the data are entirely without value to those who must prescribe remedial action.

NOTES

1. There has been a vast literature on measurement, prediction, classification, and typology development (Robison, 1936; Reiss, 1951; Meehl, 1954; Stott, 1960; Voss, 1963; Sellin and Wolfgang, 1964; Toby, 1965; Martin and Klein, 1965; Hirschi and Selvin, 1967; Monahan, 1978; Blumstein and Cohen, 1979 and 1987; Williams, 1980; Wilkins, 1980; Brennan, 1980; Monahan, 1981, 1982; Rhodes, Tyson, Weekeley, Conly, and Powell, 1982; Lab and Allen, 1984; Cohen, 1986; Copas and Tarling, 1986; Huizinqa and Elliott, 1986; Brownfield and Sorenson, 1987; and Farrington, 1988 and 1989, to mention a few). There have, of course, been a number of excellent assessments of the difficulties inherent in the prediction problem (Welford, 1967; Gottfredson, 1970; Chaiken and Chaiken, 1984; Gottfredson and Tonry, 1987; Schmidt and Witte, 1987, 1988). In essence, anyone who attempts to increase predictability above chance or the modal categories of the marginals must realize at the outset that it will be a difficult endeavor. Thus it is that prediction of what individuals will do in the future does not come as easily as the prediction of what proportion of a group will engage in delinquent or criminal behavior in the future.

2. A small 'A' in either diagram represents one cohort member, a small 'B' represents two members, a small 'C' represents three members, and so on.

7 Narrowing the Focus to Increase Predictive Efficiency

THE ECOLOGY OF DRUGS AND SERIOUS CRIME IN RACINE

The Spatial Distribution of Official Drug Involvement and Street Crime

We have previously concluded that, although a sizable proportion of Racine's most serious offenders, particularly as adults, had also had police contacts for drug offenses or had admitted drug involvement on their self-reports, this does not equate serious offender careers and involvement in drugs. The ecology of Racine and the changing spatial distribution of more serious types of street offenders vs. drug offenders and self-reported drug offenders will now be examined in order to better understand the relationship of drug involvement to delinquent and criminal careers.

Table 1 shows how Racine's 65 neighborhoods were arrayed within each of four major categories (inner city, transitional, stable, and peripheral) and the proportion of the all-around street offenders and drug offenders who resided in each neighborhood as juveniles and adults. Although some cohort members did not reside in the same neighborhood as both juveniles and adults, most resided in the same type of neighborhood as adults so that the effect of socialization remains, as shown in other analyses.

We commence with references to the 1955 Cohort's 1976 data. Much of the serious delinquency and crime in Racine was produced by those who resided in only ten of the 14 inner-city neighborhoods. Neighborhoods 11 through 8, seven inner-city neighborhoods, housed highly disproportionate shares of the all-around street offenders. Neighborhood 11, for example, contained only 1.4 percent of Racine's population but contained 8.4 percent of those 1955 Cohort members who were in the all-around street offender type as juveniles and 12.5 percent of that type as adults.

Table 1.
Neighborhoods of Juvenile Residence of Recorded Drug Offenders and All-Around Street Offenders: 1955 Cohort With Continuous Residence as Defined in 1976 and 1988

| NGH | % 1955 Cohort in NGH | | % All-Around Street Offenders in Neighborhood | | | | % Drug Offenders in Neighborhood | | | |
| | | | Juv | | Adult | | Juv | | Adult | |
	1976	1988	1976	1988	1976	1988	1976	1988	1976	1988
					Inner City					
11	1.4	1.5	8.4	16.0	12.5	7.7	[3.8]	[3.5]	4.5	3.9
7	2.4	3.0	3.6	4.0	15.6	23.1	—	—	7.5	9.1
13	2.8	3.1	9.6	8.0	3.1	7.7	1.9	[3.5]	6.0	7.8
12	2.3	1.9	8.4	12.0	3.1	7.7	1.9	[3.5]	7.5	5.2
9	2.5	2.9	4.8	16.0	6.3	15.4	1.9	—	6.0	5.2
17	1.8	2.3	4.8	—	6.3	—	—	—	1.5	1.3
8	2.4	2.5	6.0	12.0	3.1	—	—	—	—	5.2
10	1.5	1.7	2.4	4.0	3.1	7.7	—	—	1.5	2.6
3	.4	.4	1.2	—	3.1	—	1.9	—	1.5	1.3
2	3.2	3.5	3.6	8.0	—	—	—	—	6.0	6.5
5	2.0	2.0	1.2	—	—	—	[3.8]	[6.9]	4.5	2.6
1	.1	.2	—	—	—	—	1.9	[3.5]	—	2.6
6	1.0	1.0	—	—	—	—	—	—	1.5	—
61	.2	.2	—	—	—	—	—	—	—	1.3
SUB	24.0	26.3	54.0	80.0	56.4	69.3	17.1	20.9	45.0	54.6
					Transitional					
18	1.3	1.2	[3.6]	—	6.3	[7.7]	1.9	—	3.0	1.3
54	2.1	2.5	[3.6]	—	6.3	[7.7]	3.8	3.5	—	2.6
37	1.6	1.4	2.4	[4.0]	6.3	—	3.8	3.5	3.0	2.6
16	1.9	2.2	2.4	[4.0]	3.1	—	—	—	[4.5]	1.3
49	2.0	2.2	[4.8]	[4.0]	—	—	3.8	3.5	1.5	1.3
46	2.6	3.0	[3.6]	—	—	—	5.8	6.9	1.5	1.3
19	1.7	1.6	2.4	—	—	—	1.9	3.5	1.5	—
50	2.2	1.9	2.4	—	—	—	1.9	3.5	—	—
4	1.5	1.0	1.2	—	—	—	—	—	1.5	1.3
33	2.3	2.6	—	—	—	—	1.9	3.5	1.5	2.6
65	.2	.3	—	—	—	—	1.9	—	—	—
62	.3	.4	—	—	—	—	—	—	—	—
60	.2	.2	—	—	—	—	—	—	—	—
SUB	19.9	20.5	26.4	12.0	20.0	15.4	26.7	27.9	18.0	14.3
					Stable					
31	3.0	2.8	2.4	—	3.1	[7.7]	1.9	—	1.5	1.3
35	1.7	1.9	1.2	—	3.1	—	1.9	—	1.5	1.3
56	2.1	2.2	—	—	3.1	—	7.7	[6.9]	—	—
36	2.6	2.9	—	—	3.1	—	—	—	—	—
29	2.1	2.2	—	—	3.1	—	—	—	—	—
59	.3	.4	—	—	3.1	—	—	—	—	—
23	2.2	2.1	2.4	—	—	—	1.9	—	1.5	2.6
15	1.6	1.9	2.4	[4.0]	—	—	—	—	3.0	1.3
53	2.2	2.1	1.2	—	—	—	[3.8]	[6.9]	—	1.3
30	1.3	1.1	1.2	—	—	—	1.9	[3.5]	1.5	—
14	2.1	2.2	1.2	—	—	—	1.9	—	—	—
34	2.1	2.0	1.2	—	—	—	—	—	1.5	1.3
48	.2	.3	1.2	—	—	—	—	—	—	—

(*Continued* on page 110)

Table 1.
Continued

NGH	% 1955 Cohort in NGH		% All-Around Street Offenders in Neighborhood				% Drug Offenders in Neighborhood			
			Juv		Adult		Juv		Adult	
	1976	1988	1976	1988	1976	1988	1976	1988	1976	1988
32	3.1	3.0	—	—	—	—	1.9	—	3.0	2.6
67	.5	.6	—	—	—	—	1.9	3.5	—	—
63	.2	.3	—	—	—	—	1.9	—	—	—
64	.1	.1	—	—	—	—	1.9	3.5	—	—
21	1.5	1.5	—	—	—	—	—	—	1.5	1.3
22	1.3	1.2	—	—	—	—	—	—	—	—
20	1.0	.7	—	—	—	—	—	—	—	—
58	.6	.4	—	—	—	—	—	—	—	—
68	.4	.2	—	—	—	—	—	—	—	—
66	—	—	—	—	—	—	—	—	—	—
SUB	32.2	31.1	14.4	4.0	18.6	7.7	28.6	24.3	15.0	13.0
					Peripheral					
25	2.5	2.2	—	—	3.1	—	3.8	3.5	—	—
47	2.1	2.2	1.2	—	—	7.7	1.9	3.5	7.5	7.8
41	1.3	1.1	1.2	—	—	—	5.8	6.9	—	2.6
28	2.6	2.7	1.2	—	—	—	1.9	3.5	—	1.3
51	1.2	1.3	1.2	4.0	—	—.	—	—	1.5	1.3
38	2.7	2.5	—	—	—	—	5.8	3.5	1.5	2.6
42	1.7	1.5	—	—	—	—	3.8	6.9	3.0	—
55	1.6	1.2	—	—	—	—	1.9	—	1.5	—
27	1.3	1.0	—	—	—	—	—	—	3.0	—
57	1.3	1.1	—	—	—	—	1.9	—	—	—
39	2.0	1.8	—	—	—	—	—	—	1.5	1.3
24	.3	.4	—	—	—	—	—	—	1.5	1.3
26	1.0	.4	—	—	—	—	—	—	—	—
52	1.6	1.7	—	—	—	—	—	—	—	—
70	.5	.6	—	—	—	—	—	—	—	—
SUB	23.7	21.7	4.8	4.0	3.1	7.7	26.8	27.8	21.0	18.2
T	99.8	99.5	99.6	100.0	100.1	100.1	99.2	100.9	99.0	100.1

While five neighborhoods within the inner city had highly disproportional shares of the drug offender types as adults, there also were seven or eight transitional, stable, and peripheral neighborhoods throughout Racine with disproportional numbers of drug offenders as juveniles or adults.

Only 20.6 percent of the 1955 Cohort grew up in ten inner-city and transitional neighborhoods (Neighborhoods 11, 7, 13, 12, 9, 17, 8, 18, 54, and 37) with the highest proportions of delinquents and criminals but 55.2 percent of the juvenile all-around street offenders resided in these neighborhoods and 68.9 percent of those who were street offenders as adults also resided there as juveniles.

By contrast, as of 1976 only 19.0 percent of the juvenile and 39.0 percent of the adult cohort members with drug offenses were from these neighborhoods. What does this do to oversimplified drugs cause crime, crime causes drug involvement, or the common cause explanations of the drug/crime link? What does this mean in terms of clinically oriented explanations which define drug and other offenders as having a biophysical or genetic basis of some sort for their behavior?

The Spatial Distribution of Self-reported Drug Offenders

Not having self-report data on the 1955 Cohort, we turned back to the 1942 and 1949 Cohorts and found that 20.3 percent of those who admitted drug use as juveniles and 19.6 percent as adults were from the inner city and transitional neighborhoods just discussed. These percentages are similar to the proportion of self-reports (20.8 percent) obtained from the neighborhoods. A portion of the difference between the distribution of self-reported drug users/offenders and officially recorded drug offenders may be attributed to a difference in patterns of use and trafficking, the latter being more visible and subject to public and police notice than is drug use alone.

The widespread prevalence of drug use is further demonstrated by turning to the nine stable and peripheral neighborhoods which produced about the same proportion of self-reported drug offenders (17.9 percent as juveniles and 23.6 percent as adults) and contained the same proportion of the population (19.0 percent) as did the ten inner-city and interstitial neighborhoods to which we referred. These stable and peripheral neighborhoods, however, produced a relatively small proportion of the all-around street offenders (6.0 percent as juveniles and 9.3 percent as adults) but 26.8 percent of the officially recorded drug offenders who had their first contact for a drug offense as juveniles and 18.5 percent of those who had their first contact for a drug offense after the age of 18.

Thus, we see, there are drug offenders whose offenses are part of a larger offense career, those whose drug offenses probably have little to do with other types of recorded delinquency or crime, and those whose delinquency and crime have little to do with drugs.

PATTERNS OF SUBSTANCE INVOLVEMENT

Self-reported Specific Substances and Offenses

Other data further heightened our concern about drawing hasty conclusions from what seems to some persons evidence of a strong link between substance involvement and delinquency/crime, whether based on official or self-report data. When responses of 1942/1949 Cohort members to the four self-reported variables, liquor use, hard drug use, driving under the influence of substances, and marijuana use, were compared, the highest correlation was between hard drug and marijuana use (0.710). This was followed by driving under the influence and marijuana use (0.429), hard drug use (0.376), and liquor use (0.357). This may be surprising to those who think of driving under the influence as strictly an alcohol-involved offense when it in fact has the lowest relationship among the three to irresponsible automobile driving.

Driving under the influence of alcohol or drugs in itself produces a correlation between substance use and moving vehicle offenses which may include fleeing and eluding, resisting arrest, and so forth. When substance variables were combined in four different additive scales measuring substance involvement, the scores produced correlations with self-report offense seriousness for the juvenile period ranging from 0.590 to 0.695 and the adult period from 0.784 to 0.850. This suggests that a sizable proportion of the arrests which culminated in drug charges were a product of coterminous drug use and automobile use. The substance involvement scores, however, produced relatively low correlations with official offense measures, such as number of police contacts or seriousness of offenses including offender typologies ranging from 0.191 to 0.266 for the juvenile period and from 0.187 to 0.236 for the adult period.

The interrelationships of various self-reported substance involvements increased from age period to age period, indicating that behavioral patterns solidify, progressing from 0.189 between the ages of 6–13 and 13–17 to 0.393 between 13–17 and 18–20, and 0.545 between 18–20 and 21 and older. Simply put, multiple substance involvement increased with age.

Involvement Patterns and the Inner City

Members of the 1942 and 1949 Cohorts were also arrayed in eight different substance involvement categories by computer clustering based on self-reported liquor use, marijuana use, hard drug use, and driving under the influence of liquor or drugs. The four types representing most serious involvement were disproportionately found in six inner-city neighborhoods but they were also found in three transitional, three stable, and four peripheral neighborhoods, that is, ten of the other 51 neighborhoods.

These analyses made it clear that there were different patterns of substance use among the sample of members of the 1942 and 1949 Cohorts who were interviewed in the 1970s. Those cohort members in the most serious substance use types were disproportionately found in the inner-city and transitional neighborhoods but not all serious substance users were there. While 44 percent of the 1942 and 1949 Cohort members who were placed in a substance use type and had a definitive juvenile neighborhood were from the inner-city or transitional neighborhoods (41.5 percent of the neighborhoods were inner-city or transitional), 60 percent of the most serious substance use types were from these same neighborhoods. This pattern was accompanied by some dispersion to other neighborhoods throughout the city.

CONTINUITY IN CAREERS: NEIGHBORHOODS AND DRUG USERS/OFFENDERS VS. NON-USERS/NON-OFFENDERS

The 1942 and 1949 Cohorts

Returning to the subject of continuity in careers between the juvenile and adult periods, with the *self-report offender career typology* as the indicator of career types, the relationship of juvenile career types to adult career types was greater among inner city non-drug users (0.476) than among drug users (0.345), even less among non-inner city drug users (0.200) and non-drug users (0.323). Self-report seriousness scores for the juvenile and adult periods of each cohort member were correlated even higher for the same dichotomies, inner city (drug users 0.751 and non-users 0.752) and non-inner-city (drug users 0.454 and non-users 0.407). This indicates that self-reported seriousness scores reflected more career continuity than did the *self-report offender career typology* and that juvenile/adult career continuity was higher in the inner city than in other neighborhoods whether cohort members were drug users or not.

Most of the career continuity during the time period covered for the 1942 and 1949 Cohorts, with the exception of that based on the self-report typology, was generated by offenders with offenses other than drug offenses or in addition to drug offenses, and whose continuity existed before the spread of drugs in Racine. When the *official offender career typology* was used in place of the self-report typology the correlation indicating career continuity was highest (0.676) for inner city drug users and next for non-drug users (0.529). *Official offense seriousness scores*, the variable which represents the seriousness of offenses weighted by the frequency of these offenses, produced even greater evidence of higher inner city continuity for drug users (0.783) but also considerable continuity for non-users (0.626). In either case the non-inner city relationships were lower, ranging from 0.116 to 0.441.

The 1955 Cohort

Official ofense seriousness scores for the 1955 Cohort also produced some juvenile/adult career continuity. The highest correlations between the juvenile and adult periods were found for inner city drug offenders (0.481) and inner city non-drug offenders (0.421), followed by non-inner city drug offenders (0.371) and non-drug offenders (0.352). Since persons in the 1955 Cohort had only a few years beyond age 18, and given the stochastic nature of careers, the relatively low offense seriousness continuity for this cohort is not surprising; not enough time elapsed for many to become involved or apprehended as a consequence of their involvement.

What must be kept in mind is that findings vary when one shifts from self-report data to official data, from inner city vs. other neighborhood places of residence, and from whether members of the cohort had ever had a drug offense contact to whether the cohort member was a drug offender type. This accounts for much of the confusion and discrepancies in research reports and why it is difficult to reach simple conclusions from years of research.

ARE DRUGS AT THE CENTER OF THE CRIME PROBLEM?

Drugs vs. Other Crime

The differences between inner-city drug users/offenders and non-users/offenders were relatively small. It is questionable whether the Racine or other urban events currently headlined in the media provide a basis for directing our attention and that of the justice system to drug users/offenders as the heart of the crime problem (other than for the purpose of political posturing) rather than to serious inner-city offenders and the nature of the society that generates crime and criminals in the inner city. The latter would be too threatening to those who have accepted false explanations of the problem or benefit from blaming the victim.

One could construct a rationale for research focusing attention on drug users/offenders who work in the inner city but who reside in the suburbs (or in glitzy inner-city dwelling units) but hold such responsible positions in society that their drug use presents a greater threat to the social structure than that of the inner city poorest of the poor whose only organizing principle in life is the search for funds with which to become 'high.' Does 'cracking' down on drugs provide the poor with opportunities for integration into the larger society or with another life theme?

The delinquency/crime problem, insofar as it is one of dealing with all-around street offenders, appears to be one of how to deal with those who, as a consequence of their antecedents and ascribed/achieved characteristics, have not been integrated into the larger society. Solving the crime problem involves looking at delinquents and criminals as products of society rather than as kinds of people. Perpetuating the myth of the criminal type will do little to solve the delinquency or crime problem, however much it is satisfying to those who believe that 'bad guys' are the problem.

The Nature of the Drug-Crime Linkage

The further we examined the data from 'Prediction and Typology Development' (Shannon, 1987), the more we realized that the question of how offender type distribution and continuity varies with drug involvement and neighborhood of residence is a question of major importance. Given that drug users are far more widely dispersed throughout the community than are persons with police contacts for serious offenses and specifically for drug offenses, a combination of social structure and social process theory will be needed as the basis for generating testable hypotheses about the complex relationship of drugs to delinquency and crime.

What seems most apparent, considering the analyses that we have conducted, is that there is a linkage between drugs and a proportion of the ordinary street crime in the inner-city, but that this linkage is present to a more limited extent or is almost absent for non-inner-city areas. When a link is present outside the inner city, it probably involves different types of crimes.

The error that many have made is to look for the link rather than how different kinds of links develop. That this is what we must do should not be surprising considering the social and structural organization of society, its relationship to the social and physical ecology of the city, and variation in social processes that are related to the demographic and socioeconomic composition of neighborhoods. Without some sort of sociological framework, there is the danger of continuing to seek answers, as in the past, to simple questions like 'which kinds of people commit crimes and which kinds of people become involved in drugs?'

THE CHANGING DISTRIBUTION OF ALL-AROUND STREET OFFENDERS AND DRUG OFFENDERS

Changes in the Spatial Distribution of Offenders between 1976 and 1988

All-Around Street Offenders vs. Drug Offenders
Although we have described the distribution of delinquency and crime (events) in Racine and the changing social structure of the community, represented by the characteristics of various types of geographical areas, we have yet to fully address the changing distribution of delinquents, criminals, and drug offenders (people) represented by their numbers and proportions in various types of neighborhoods as up-dated to 1988. The data in Table 1 of this chapter provide a basis for this.

Remember that 55.2 percent of the juvenile and 68.9 percent of the adult all-around street offenders were concentrated in seven inner-city and three transitional neighborhoods during their period of socialization and that officially recorded drug offenders in the

1955 Cohort had some concentration therein but were also socialized in more of the stable and peripheral neighborhoods than were all-around street offenders. Self-reported drug offenders/users (even those who reported drug use in the category of frequently or all of the time) were socialized in neighborhoods scattered throughout the city and were distributed pretty much as were the members of the 1942 and 1949 Cohorts. This raises the question of how 1988-defined continuous residents are distributed by neighborhood of socialization or origin in comparison with the 1976-defined continuous residents from the 1955 Cohort.

Table 1 reveals that, among those who remained in 1988, there were a few more persons socialized in the inner city, 26.2 percent vs. 24 percent from the cohort as of 1976. The proportion in transitional and stable neighborhoods was essentially the same, but there were fewer left who had been socialized in the peripheral areas. Those who remained in each neighborhood within each type of cluster showed considerable variation but these small percentage fluctuations tended to cancel each other out when analyses were based on type of neighborhood. Again, the data indicate that those who remained in Racine to 1988 were fairly representative of those who were still there in 1976. But by 1988 changes had taken place in the community.

The Juvenile vs. the Adult Period
Those all-around street offenders who were continuous residents in both 1976 and 1988 were, by 1988, from the various neighborhoods of socialization in different proportions for the juvenile vs. adult periods than they had been in 1976. A larger proportion of the street offenders were from the inner city (80 percent of the juveniles vs. 69.3 percent of the adults) than in 1976 (54 percent vs. 56.2 percent). As juveniles they had been socialized in eight inner-city neighborhoods and three transitional neighborhoods had socialized another 12 percent. For those who were street offenders during the adult period, six inner-city neighborhoods had socialized 69.3 percent and two transitional neighborhoods 15.4 percent, for a total of 84.7 percent in eight of the 65 neighborhoods.

Explaining an Increasing Concentration of Offenders

The question for consideration at this juncture is why those cohort members who remained in Racine and who had all-around street offender careers were from even fewer neighborhoods than were those from the 1955 Cohort as of 1976. Aside from the fact that there were fewer street offenders among those remaining in 1988, it would be consistent with prior comparisons to say that those who were street offenders from outside the inner-city neighborhoods were more likely to have been the less serious street offender types. They were more likely to have changed their behavior for the better or to have left Racine than were more serious types socialized in the inner city. Be all that as it may, the distribution of the 1955 Cohort members by 1976 and 1988 is sufficiently similar that the skewdness of the all-around street offenders toward the inner-city neighborhoods of socialization assures us that the inner city's serious offenders have been far less mobile than their counterparts from other neighborhoods, contributing to what we have referred to as the 'hardening of the inner city.'

The picture for drug offenders was particularly interesting in that the concentration of those who had inner-city origins and who had police contacts for drug offenses as juveniles was less than half of that of those who had drug contacts as adults (17.1 percent of the juveniles vs. 48.0 percent of the adults by 1976 and 20.9 percent vs. 54.6 percent by 1988). Although juvenile and adult drug offenders who had continuous residence in 1988 were also more likely to be from the inner city than were those with continuous residence in 1976, the concentration of drug offenders in the inner city was disproportional to the distribution of cohort members only for the adult period.

Those who remained in Racine who had not had police contacts for drug offenses prior to 1976 could have acquired them in the 12 years between 1976 and 1988. The increase in inner-city origins for those who had police contacts for drugs as adults suggests that there could also have been a disproportional increase in drug offense detection between 1976 and 1988 for those who were socialized in the inner city and in all probability continued to reside there. This is another aspect of the 'hardening of the inner city.'

In summary, the concentration of drug offenders by cohort member's place of origin was most disproportional (more than expected) to the distribution of the 1955 Cohort in the transitional and peripheral neighborhoods during the juvenile period, while the adult concentration was most disproportional (more than expected) in the inner city. What is significant is that drug offenders were spatially distributed throughout the 65 neighborhoods during the juvenile period more proportionately to the 1955 Cohort's distribution than were all-around street offenders. By the adult period the drug offenders had moved closer in their spatial distribution to that of the street offenders (that is, a greater concentration in the inner city).

Comparison of the spatial distribution of all-around street offenders and drug offenders by neighborhood of socialization with the distribution of the cohort as of 1976 and 1988 suggests even more strongly that social and structural variables influence the development of different types of offender careers.

THE DEVELOPMENT OF DANGEROUS NEIGHBORHOODS

Mapping Drug and Street Offenders

Map 1 offers a visual presentation of which neighborhoods of socialization produced most of the juvenile and/or adult drug offenders and juvenile and/or adult all-around street offenders in the 1955 Cohort, that is, neighborhoods with 3.5 percent or more of the juvenile and/or 3.5 percent or more of the adult drug and/or all-around street offenders. Map 1 is for neighborhoods superimposed on Police Grids and represents the drug/street offender concentration for the cohort as of 1976.

A capital 'D' (19 'drug' neighborhoods) and/or 'S' (13 'street offender' neighborhoods) in the neighborhood on Map 1 means that of the 1955 Racine Cohort continuous residents (defined as of 1976), 3.5 percent or more of the juveniles and/or adults, drug and/or street offenders, resided in that neighborhood most of the time as juveniles. Eleven of these neighborhoods fell within six inner-city and transitional Police Grids (8, 9, 12, 13, 16, and 17); ten other 'D' and 'S' neighborhoods were in peripheral Police Grids.

THE CONTINUING DIFFERENTIAL IMPACT OF DRUG OFFENSES AND NEIGHBORHOOD OF SOCIALIZATION ON CONTINUITY

Members of the 1955 Cohort who had police contacts for drug offenses were by 1988 not only distributed disproportionately to all cohort members by neighborhood of socialization, but the proportion who were in serious offender types and the proportion who

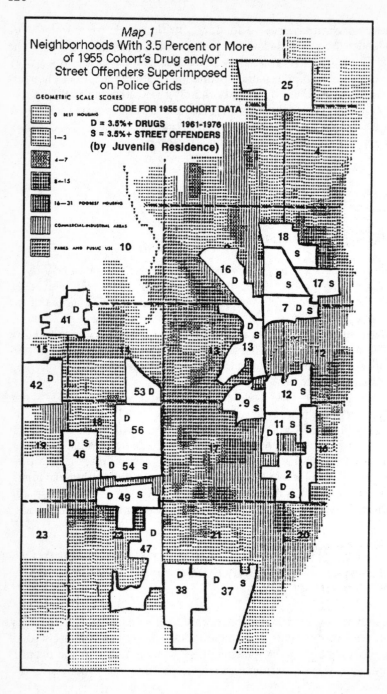

Map 1
Neighborhoods With 3.5 Percent or More
of 1955 Cohort's Drug and/or
Street Offenders Superimposed
on Police Grids

GEOMETRIC SCALE SCORES

CODE FOR 1955 COHORT DATA
D = 3.5%+ DRUGS   1961-1976
S = 3.5%+ STREET OFFENDERS
(by Juvenile Residence)

0 BEST HOUSING
1—3
4—7
8—15
16—31 POOREST HOUSING
COMMERCIAL-INDUSTRIAL AREAS
PARKS AND PUBLIC USE

Table 2.
Distribution of Juvenile Official Record Offender Types vs. Adult Types for 1976-Defined Continuous Residents vs. 1988-Defined Continuous Residents, 1955 Cohort

Inner City

Juvenile Traffic or –	Police Contacts for Drugs			No Drug Contacts		
1976	24.4	.0	.0	3.0	2.3	64.2
1988	17.8	.0	15.6	3.1	1.6	61.5
Minor Misdemeanor						
1976	9.7	.0	.0	1.3	1.3	10.9
1988	6.7	.0	17.4	.8	1.9	11.3
Major Misd & Felony						
1976	53.7	4.9	7.3	5.6	1.3	10.2
1988	37.8	2.2	8.9	6.6	1.9	11.3
Adult	Maj Misd & Fel	Min Misd	Traf or Less	Maj Misd & Fel	Min Misd	Traf or Less
1976	N – 41	C – .278		N – 394	C – .352	
1988	N – 45	C – .363		N – 259	C – .442	

Non-Inner City

Juvenile Traffic or –	Police Contacts for Drugs			No Drug Contacts		
1976	26.3	.0	.0	1.5	2.0	83.9
1988	23.6	1.8	10.9	1.7	2.2	82.8
Minor Misdemeanor						
1976	5.3	.0	6.6	.9	.5	4.7
1988	3.6	.0	3.6	.9	.5	5.0
Major Misd & Felony						
1976	30.3	3.9	27.6	1.1	.7	4.7
1988	27.3	3.6	25.5	1.3	1.3	4.9
Adult	Maj Misd & Fel	Min Misd	Traf or Less	Maj Misd & Fel	Min Misd	Traf or Less
1976	N – 76	C – .425		N – 1266	C – .287	
1988	N – 55	C – .192		N – 778	C – .281	

had continuity in their careers also varied by whether or not they had officially recorded drug offenses. Whatever concern we have about the extent to which drugs are the cause of crime or crime is the cause of drug use or concomitant involvement as a product of life experiences, drugs seem to have a catalytic effect on some criminal career continuity that takes us into processual explanations. Could it be that drug involvement was also the signal for greater monitoring and official intervention in the careers of inner city cohort members as time went on?

Table 2 takes the distribution (collapsed) of the 1955 Cohort members with continuous residence in 1976 and compares their distribution with that of those who were continuous residents in 1988. Note that the 1976- and 1988- defined continuous residents who had no police contacts for drugs had similar proportional (percent of the total number of persons) distributions. Those serious offenders who resided in the inner-city neighborhoods as juveniles and who had police contacts for drug offenses as juveniles desisted proportionately less as adults than did those who did not have drug contacts with the police or those who had contacts for drug offenses but resided in non-inner-city neighborhoods as juveniles. Note the high proportion of serious offenders who appeared to desist as adults among those who resided in non-inner-city neighborhoods as juveniles, particularly those without drug contacts. Also note that the second highest desistance rate from juvenile to adult was among the relatively small proportion who resided in the inner city and who had serious careers as juveniles but who did not have police contacts for drugs.

This leads us to even greater concern about what happens over time to those who reside in the inner city and have become involved in delinquency and crime and drugs and alcohol. How does society operate so as to make their integration ever more difficult? How little or how much do inner city residents know about what it takes to become better integrated into the larger society? The following illustrative extract from a September 1994 story in *The New York Times* illustrates, perhaps better than statistics, how achieved educational levels are related to an understanding of the organization of society.

> To make ends meet on $700 a month in welfare and disability payments, she [Vikki] rented a space to drug dealers in their first-floor apartment in the six-story tenement.
>
> A stereo system is all that remains of the drug money. Vikki and her friends spent the rest on nightclubs, clothes, taxicabs hired for two- and three-hour stretches and restaurants like Red Lobster and the International House of Pancakes.

The 'crew' of drug dealers broke all Vikki's furniture during long nights of rough-housing. She no longer has a telephone because the dealers made so many expensive calls.

And yet, *The New York Times* pointed out, 'other young people on the block regularly gather at the apartment looking for a meal, affection or advice from Vikki.' Does this sound as though Vikki is in need of psychiatric help, as though she is a medical problem? Or does it sound as though she has been socialized in an environment which has ill-prepared her for the complexities of life, even in the inner city in which she was socialized? Yet she is the legal guardian of three young cousins, ages 13, 17, and 20. *The New York Times* story describes how she has made every effort to provide a home for the youngsters, and fed them beyond all one might expect in her situation. Moreover, her door buzzer constantly rang as a parade of youngsters sought her advice and help, many with dreams so unrealistic as to make one cry.

And even Vikki has such dreams,

'I want the all-time American dream: husband, kids, a house with a picket fence, two incomes, my kids in colleges, vacations with my kids whenever I want. . . . My goal is to go into nursing and somewhere down the line be a doctor.'

She has a plan, but her voice drops with mingled embarrassment and resignation as she talks about it.

'I be thinking if I can make enough money once dealing drugs, $5,000 or $10,000, I can invest.'

Doesn't a picture such as this make involvement in drugs seem to be one of the alternatives available to people in what we have often called different walks of life than our own? Does their choice-making behavior differentiate them from persons who make choices which are more readily available to them than to persons in the inner city?

Perhaps more than anything else, data such as we have presented on the social ecology of the city highlights the argument that understanding is not a matter of clinical examination but one of sociological analyses. How does the structure of society and the nature of social processes produce the behavior that brings people into inept attempts to reach unrealistic goals and perhaps difficulty with the law? And unrealistic goals which are placed before inner-city dwellers every day are part of the problem.

CONCLUSION

We conclude that the 1988-defined continuous residents from the 1955 Cohort represent the consequences of living in various types of neighborhood in essentially the same way as did the 1976-defined continuous residents. The neighborhood differences shown in Table 1 are probably an artifact of the disproportional loss (attrition) of less serious offenders among those who had police contacts for drug offenses. Basically, however, all of the cohorts show a high neighborhood concentration of inner-city and interstitial offenders with careers in ordinary street crime, while drug offender types are more widely distributed, particularly during the juvenile period.

Those 1988-defined continuous residents (extended cohort as obtained from the original 1955 Cohort) who remained from the 1976-defined continuous residents produced essentially the same relationship between juvenile and adult careers (with the exception of those who resided in the inner city and had police contacts indicating involvement in drugs). We are now ready to give further consideration to the drug/crime relationship as a social phenomenon with ecological dimensions.

8 Thinking about the Drug/ Crime Relationship

THE DIVERSITY OF PATTERNS OF DRUG/CRIME INVOLVEMENT

Metropolitan Patterns

Contemporary research and media attention to the problems of drugs and delinquency/crime indicate that many major metropolitan areas have drug and delinquency/crime ties similar to the gangster-organized alcohol and delinquency/crime ties that were front-page news in the US and filmed in the 1920s and early 1930s (Lyman, 1989). The drug/crime connection is illustrated by the following excerpts from *The New York Times*, September 24, 1991 – about the same time that we were commencing analyses of the updated 1955 Cohort.

> With the eruption of the same kind of turf wars that marked the arrival of crack in Washington and elsewhere, 1991 is shaping into the deadliest year in Chicago history, surpassing the rate during the bloody years of the Al Capone era and even the record year of 1974, when 970 residents were killed.
>
> By the end of August, Chicago had recorded 623 murders, as against 593 by that date in 1974. The city declared last month the deadliest ever with 120 killings, more than the previous record of 117 in November 1974.
>
> ... Unlike drug distribution networks in New York, Washington and other cities with fairly diffuse trafficking systems, the network in Chicago has traditionally been tightly run by a group of major street gangs who enjoyed a long-standing monopoly on drug sales and were not inclined to introduce or – allow anyone else to introduce – a volatile new product they could not easily control, criminologists say.
>
> 'Everybody had their share of the market and there was just not room for entrepreneurs to get in like in New York,' said Dr. Jeffrey Fagan, an associate professor of criminal justice [now Professor of Criminology] at Rutgers University, who has studied

the evolution of crack in this country. 'Distributors acted like every other business and kept out the product. The fear in Chicago was that once the taste got out, it would be extremely difficult to control.'

... For most of the 1980's, as other cities writhed over mounting homicide rates, Chicago experienced its lowest murder rates since the 1960's and appeared as if it were going to escape the devastation of crack.

But now that it is here, in just two years, Chicago has gone from its lowest homicide levels in a generation to its highest ever, from a total of 661 murders in 1988 to 851 in 1989 and more expected this year.

The pattern differs from one area to another, of course. In the 1983–5 period when Klein, Maxson, and Cunningham (1991) were conducting research in Los Angeles, crack distribution was not primarily a gang phenomenon. The world of crack in Los Angeles belonged to regular drug dealers. More recently (McKinney, 1988), the juvenile gang and drug trafficking has become an established pattern with members of Los Angeles gangs found in cities across the country. The chance for fancy footwear and gold chains in the immediate future is more promising for some inner-city youth than educational programs or low-paying jobs which seem, and may be, less certain roads to a more exciting way of life.

Assistant Attorney General, Jimmy Gurule (*NIJ Reports*, June 1991), supported by a literature on increasing gang violence (Spergel and Chance, 1991), early on recommended an agency-wide Office of Justice Program 'Initiative on Gangs: Drugs and Violence in America' to be coordinated with the Criminal Division of the Department of Justice.

Small Town Patterns

The existence of a serious drug problem has been recognized for some time in Eastern, Western, and other major metropolitan areas, but not in the upper Midwest. One can understand this considering that as late as 1985 only 9.1 percent of the male first admissions (7.8 percent female) to Wisconsin Adult Correctional Institutions were regarded solely as drug offenders. Drug offenders made up only 5.0 percent of the male (13.2 percent female) readmissions, but these were primarily users and possessors, not key figures in the enterprise and these numbers failed to tell us how many offenders of other types were also drug users/offenders.

Be that as it may, the drug war in its most violent form may now be found in miniature in some middle-sized cities (*circa* 100 000) such as Racine, Wisconsin. At the time that we were bringing the official records of the 1955 Cohort up to 1989, *The Journal Times* (February 1–4, 1989) ran a series of stories illustrating Racine's drug-related violence of recent years, only a relatively few years after we and others had announced that Racine had little in the way of organized, violent crime and relatively few violent criminals.

The term 'drug war' as used at this point refers to drug-related violence. The media frequently refer to the war on drugs as the drug war. Most recently (April 5, 1997), retired General Barry McCaffery, the nation's drug czar, told the annual Governor's Conference on Substance Abuse in Des Moines, Iowa, that methamphetamine use has been soaring in Iowa and several other Midwestern states as well as in more urban states. He further stated that the battle against drugs 'may have to shed the "war image" because there is not going to be a victory over drugs in a year or three' (*The Des Moines Register*, April 16, 1997).

There has also been much concern about the relationship be- · tween drugs and delinquency/crime in smaller urban and rural areas where persons involved in drug trafficking have not yet been engaged in the deadly conflicts which have been headlined in the metropolitan media. As a consequence, persons in positions of authority, even outside of major metropolitan areas, are now eager to seize upon evidence of drug use among delinquents and criminals as the key to a successful attack on crime. Those familiar with the now voluminous literature on drug policy (*The Drug Policy Letter*, July/August 1994, for example) may take a different public position. Sociologist Elliott Currie (1985 and 1993) concludes that our only hope lies with a more profound reckoning with the underlying causes of the delinquency/crime and drug problem.

A Chain of Events

Unlike those who describe the way in which delinquency/crime and alcohol/drugs are interwoven in day-to-day life to support a simple drugs cause crime position, we have presented several reports, not only as illustrations of how the media provide a framework for public concern but to place the substance/crime involvement within a sociological framework.

The Deases case, which was headlined for months in the Iowa press, is an example of how a chain of events is sometimes presented in support of the argument that drugs lead to other types of crime, that is, drugs cause crime. We would use the same chain of events to support a more complex social and structural argument for the involvement of youth and older persons in drugs and other crime. *The Des Moines Register,* April 26, 1990 story, headlined 'DEASES: I CUT OFF GARDNER'S HEAD TO HELP HIDE BODY,' is not really representative of the day-by-day intertwining of drug use and drug-related offenses that may be found in even our largest metropolitan areas, but does show how life consists of a chain of events which may be interpreted by those involved in quite different ways, depending upon the positions that they have had in subgroups of the larger society and the larger society itself. Drug use, however, does not cause most people to become involved in other types of crime (Hunt, 1990).

Day-by-day accounts of this type are a part of the milieu that creates a public receptive to the idea that the relationship between drugs and delinquency/crime constitutes one of the most pressing problems in the nation.

> With tears streaming down his cheeks, Edward Deases haltingly recounted in court Wednesday how he severed the head of Jennifer Gardner with a fish-skinning knife as her nude body lay in the bathtub of an Ames apartment last May.
>
> ... Johnny Deases, 16, said Tuesday that after another brother, Ruben Deases, 18, had strangled Gardner with the crook of his right arm, Edward placed a looped belt around Gardner's neck and choked her when she seemed to revive.
>
> ... Believing she was dead, Edward suggested moving the body to the bathroom because he didn't want visitors who came to the house to buy drugs to see what had happened. Johnny and Edward stuffed her personal items in garbage bags and dropped them in dumpsters around Ames, he said.
>
> ... Edward said he 'freebased' or smoked crack cocaine at least seven times the day of and the day after the murder 'to keep me from thinking about what happened.' Johnny was the only one of the three Deases brothers who did not use drugs that weekend, he said.

In an earlier interview in a Texas prison near Dallas where he was serving a ten-year sentence for drug offenses (*The Des Moines*

Register, April 9, 1990) an older brother, Eustaquio, described his
drug-driven life-style.

Demand for drugs in Des Moines, Ames and the surrounding
area was astounding, Deases said, and the money cocaine brought
was as seductive as the white powder itself. Even now, he cannot say he regrets selling drugs.

'When I was growing up, we didn't have much money,' he said.
'All of a sudden, I'm carrying around $8000 in hundreds. It was
like I could do anything I wanted.

'To me, I was helping people with that money. I was able to
buy my brothers clothes, I was able to buy Jennifer clothes and
jewelry. I was able to take them out to eat when they wanted.
They had things they never, ever had. Then they went berserk
on me, and I still don't know why.'

... On Sunday, May 28, the night Gardner was killed, Deases
was in Texas, unloading drug money and picking up a new supply of cocaine and marijuana. Iowa authorities already had issued a warrant for his arrest on a cocaine delivery charge.

He had left his girlfriend and three brothers, Ruben, Edward
and Johnny, in his Ames apartment that night with $1,000 in
cash, a car, 'some drugs to party on' and alcohol.

'I left them in an ideal setting,' he said. 'And they blew it.'

Deases said he was freebasing, or smoking, cocaine early Monday
morning when he found out Gardner had been killed.

'At the time, I had $10,000 in cash, a brand new car. I was
getting high. I thought, man, I'm on top of the world right now.
Then my mom called and said, 'I don't know how to tell you
this....'

After talking to his mother, Deases said he flushed the cocaine down the toilet and got rid of the marijuana. He then tele-
phoned his brothers, who had not yet been arrested, and asked
them what happened.

Two weeks later, further drug charges were filed against him
in Kansas. A state trooper who stopped him for speeding found
more than a kilogram of cocaine and a shotgun in his trunk.
The charges brought a sentence of 10 years in prison. Deases is
appealing the case.

... Later, jurors heard from Johnny Deases that Ruben had
sex with Gardner's corpse.

.... 'She was no threat to them,' Eustaquio said of Gardner

and his brothers. 'She was mouthy, and she would pull a gun or a knife. But she would never act on it.'

.... Eustaquio said his immediate goal is to beat the federal cocaine charges.

His lawyer, Andrew Dunn of Des Moines, said the Kansas trooper violated Deases' rights when he looked into the trunk of Deases' car and found cocaine.

'Yes, I was guilty of having drugs,' Deases said. 'But I have rights. This is still America, you know?'[1]

Edward, Johnny, Ruben, and Eustaquio turned to drugs as a means and an end, and their drug-related delinquent and criminal behavior provided them with a means for living at a level which they otherwise could not have imagined. Edward is now serving a second life-without-parole term in Iowa's penitentiary at Fort Madison after a recent (November 1992) conviction for the stabbing death of another prison inmate.

It is not for us to dwell on such revolting scenes as this, real as they are, but to produce the broader picture of how alcohol/drugs and delinquency/crime may sometimes be related and, in addition, to determine if drug involvement is a useful antecedent predictor variable.

WHAT THE LITERATURE SUGGESTS

Correlates vs. Causation

Much of the literature on drugs and crime is not transferable to the more general problem of the role of drugs in continuities in delinquency and crime in the larger society. Studies of incarcerated offenders (Chaiken and Chaiken, 1982) are valuable but insufficient for an accurate estimate of the nature and extent of the wider problem of drugs outside the prison. Similarly, studies of changes in behavior during addicted vs. non-addicted periods (Ball, Shaffer, and Nurco, 1983; Anglin and Speckart, 1986 and Speckart and Anglin, 1986) are only the beginning in a barrage of studies which must be considered in developing an approach to the problem of addiction and the extent to which it plays a part in continuities in delinquent and criminal behavior.

Watters, Reinarman, and Fagan (1985) have reviewed the literature that points toward the 'drugs-cause-crime' position, criticizing the ambiguity of the relationship and concluding that the idea of causality must be rejected. It is easy to see how the 'drugs-cause-crime' conclusion could be reached by examination of institutionalized offenders who, by reason of their position in society, are likely to have early on been introduced to drugs. It is almost equally certain that people arrested in certain places at certain times are also likely to be drug users. And, as McGlothlin, Anglin, and Wilson (1978) have concluded, during periods of addiction some commit more crimes and are more likely to be arrested for them. This, too, is not surprising because offenses by persons under the influence may be more visible than similar offenses by persons who are not under the influence of alcohol and/or drugs.

White, Pandina, and LaGrange (1987), among others, have also appropriately recognized the error in jumping from the existence of a statistically significant relationship between variables (drugs and crime) to the assumption that one is antecedent to and perhaps explanatory of the other. Early and continued involvement with alcohol and/or drugs may be a significant correlate of other delinquent involvement but is neither explanatory nor an efficient predictor of future delinquent and criminal behavior. Most recently, Welte and Wieczorek's (1996) Buffalo longitudinal Study found no support for the position that drugs and alcohol use cause crime and in fact found a suggestion that causation flows in the opposite direction. Zhang, Wieczorek, and Welte (1997) describe their findings which indicate that the effect of substance use on delinquency involvement is mostly dependent on intervening and mediating social and individual contexts. They also describe how their cross-sectional research finds that daily drinking plays a moderating rather than causal role in accounting for violence – but should be followed by longitudinal research.

While some research has indicated that early illicit drug use has predictive value for illicit drug use as adults (Kandel, Simcha-Fagan and Davies, 1986) that is not always the case, was not in Racine, and is not the main issue. White *et al.* indicate an awareness of the complexity of alcohol, drugs, and delinquency relationships, pointing out in reference to their own research that 'The results indicate that serious alcohol use, drug use, and delinquency are not necessarily concentrated in a homogeneous grouping of adolescents, but rather that each group represents a somewhat unique set of individuals whose dynamic processes are qualitatively distinct' (1987, p. 736).

In the end, Watters, Reinarman, and Fagan (1985) and others have turned to the 'common-cause' position in accounting for the link between drugs and crime. Wish and Johnson (1986) concluded that determining the exact sequence of the onset of drug use and criminal behavior is a futile and perhaps trivial pursuit. Whether drugs came before or after criminal behavior is probably a function of opportunity and other social factors.

The position that the correlation of drugs and delinquency/crime is spurious, the result of similar etiological links to a common antecedent has also been supported by Elliott and Huizinga (1984) and White, Pandina, and LaGrange (1987). The latter make the crucial point that, although a majority of the serious delinquents are also serious substance abusers, only one-third of the serious users are also serious delinquents. A complete understanding of the process must also recognize its complexity and the role of alcohol in heroin abuse as described by Strug, Wish, Johnson, Anderson, Miller and Sears (1984).

Altschuler and Brounstein (1991) found that the heaviest drug users among inner-city adolescent males (387 in the 9th and 10th grades in Washington, D.C., 1988) were more likely than non-users to commit property crimes, and drug traffickers were more likely to commit crimes against persons than those who did not sell drugs. However, for every type of crime reported, only a minority of offenders stated that they had used drugs while committing the crime or said that they committed any type of crime to obtain drugs or money to buy drugs. And, for only 8 percent, could drug use have contributed to the onset of delinquency.

RECENT SURVEYS OF CORRECTIONAL FACILITIES

Going back to causation, Innes (1988) reports a variety of findings from the *1986 Survey of Inmates of Correctional Facilities* that question the idea of a widespread causal relationship between drugs and crime. About 65 percent of the inmates in this study reported that they had never been users of a major drug. Sixty percent of those who had ever used a major drug did not do so regularly until after their first arrest. Perhaps most disconcerting to those who espouse the 'drugs-cause-crime' position was the finding that 81 percent of the inmates in the study were not daily users of a major drug in the month before the offense for which they were sentenced to prison.

The *1989 Survey of Jail Inmates* (Harlow, 1989) also reported findings that added little evidence of the causal relationship so eagerly sought. Only 13 percent of the convicted jail inmates reported money for illegal drugs as a reason they had committed their offense, although nearly one-third of the robbers and burglars stated that they had committed their offenses to obtain money for drugs. Perhaps even more disappointing to those on the drug firing line was the finding that 40 percent of the convicted jail inmates who were daily users of a major drug in the month before their current offense had participated in a drug treatment program.

The fact that jail inmates were twice as likely to have ever used drugs and seven times more likely than those in the general population to be current users of drugs focuses our attention on the possibility of a relationship between crime and drugs but is not causal evidence as such.

Although a majority of those who used a *major drug regularly* began its use after their first arrest, most did report starting to use some drugs before they were arrested for the first time. Seventy percent of these jail inmates who had *ever used a drug* had used it a year or more before their first arrest. This is still not the same as being able to say that drug use leads a sizable proportion of the population to crime or to commit offenses that they would not otherwise commit so that together they constitute a major part of society's delinquents and/or criminals.

NIJ'S DRUG USE FORECASTING

The National Institute of Justice's Drug Use Forecasting (DUF) program has been a centerpiece for focusing law enforcement agencies on the so-called war on drugs as a promising approach to the war on crime. DUF reports are interesting, but do they do more than provide information of limited use for a war on drugs? Visher, writing in a special issue of *NIJ Reports* (Summer 1990), has suggested, for example, that 'Crime monitoring during pretrial release may, if coupled with appropriately strong sanctions, reduce pretrial crime and failure-to-appear for some types of offenders.' But Visher, herself a highly competent researcher, concludes that the literature indicates that experimental drug treatment programs have had conflicting results.

The DUF reports are, however, useful from a strictly informational viewpoint, particularly as they reveal regional and temporal differences

(*National Institute of Justice, DUF,* April 1991, November 1991, and Hebert and O'Neil, June 1991). That alone is something to think about – can anything but sociological, social organization explanations account for these differences? It is useful to know about self-reported sources of income, legal and illegal, proportion of arrestees weekly spending money for drug use, and range and median amounts spent. That larceny or theft was the most frequent charge for the majority of men or women followed by drug sale or possession and burglary is scarcely a surprising finding. One can only say that information about drug use among certain categories of arrestees is one thing but that knowledge about the overall alcohol/drug and delinquency/crime connection is another. In the end, biased samples of arrestees provide no evidence of a link between drugs and the offense which results in arrest (Wish and Gropper, 1990).

DUF AND THE DEVELOPMENT OF A CROSS-SECTIONAL MODEL

Let us take an even more careful look at the type of data generated by drug testing of arrestees as the source of DUF reports. Assume, for example, that our model in Diagram 1 is one with which to commence. In the upper panel we find that 90 percent of those from the inner city who have been arrested test positive for drugs. Even if 90 percent of those who have been arrested during the hours from 4 pm to midnight, or any other time for that matter, test positive for drugs, does this tell us much about the crime/ drugs relationship? These 45 persons, actual number (middle panel), constitute only a small percent of a representative sample, at best, representing only those who were arrested during this period. That we should stop with information for two of the cells in the model (50 persons consisting of 5 percent of the population sample of 1000), as there has been a tendency to do, prevents us from obtaining the data that are necessary if we are to even begin to test the hypothesis that drugs cause crime, or that crime is the forerunner of drugs, or any other hypotheses about some causal crime/ drug relationship. But this is an example of the kinds of figures that are produced by DUF. Sometimes people are pleased with figures that help support their activities whether the figures tell us what we wish to know or not!

Such a model as a starting point (all of the columns and all of

Diagram 1.
Hypothesized Distribution of Drug Test Outcome by Residence, Arrest, Self-Reported or Official Status as Offender (Other Than Drug User)

	Inner City Neighborhoods			Other Neighborhoods		
	Arrested	Offenders On Streets Not Arrested	Non-Offenders On Streets	Arrested	Offenders On Streets Not Arrested	Non-Offenders On Streets
Drug Test						
% Negative	10%	30%	50%	50%	75%	90%
% Positive	90%	70%	50%	50%	25%	10%
Total	100%	100%	100%	100%	100%	100%
Drug Test						
# Negative	5	60	125	15	75	333 (613)
# Positive	45	140	125	15	25	37 (387)
Total	50	200	250	30	100	370 (1000)
Distribution of Persons Testing Negative vs. Persons Testing Positive for Drugs						
Negative	.8%	9.8%	20.4%	2.4%	12.2%	53.4% (99.9%)
Positive	11.6%	36.2%	32.3%	3.9%	6.4%	9.6% (100.0%)
Total	5.0%	20.0%	25.0%	3.0%	10.0%	37.0% (100.0%)

the rows) may well represent the relationship of drugs to crime. Numbers are just as important as percentages which indicate a varying relationship of drugs to crime. If we hypothesize that as many as 38.7 percent of the population (387 persons) would test positive for drugs, as shown in the middle panel of the diagram, we will have identified only 45 persons of the 387 testing positive because they are in the 50 who were arrested and tested. The lower panel, which shows the numbers as percentaged by rows, indicates that the 45 persons who tested positive upon arrest were only 11.6 percent of the 387 who are drug users. They would be a small bite out of crime even if every one of them was a serious criminal. And how many were serious criminals? Altogether, there are 342 drug users who would not be identified by such a program as DUF and of these 165 (140 + 25) are drug users, an unknown number of whom are offenders. There are also 333 who would or did test negative and, of these, there are also an unknown number of other types of offenders. DUF figures, as we have said before, are interesting but do they really tell us much about what we need to know if we wish to examine the drug/crime nexus with data that can be defended as representative of the population?

BEYOND DUF AND OUTSIDE PRISON

While DUF findings are interesting, they describe only a segment of the larger society and are not even representative of the inner city. They do not enable us to learn much about the overall relationship of drugs to crime. Where would the distinguished eye surgeon, as described in *The Iowa City Press Citizen*, December 24, 1991, be placed in the model shown in Diagram 1?

Dr. James Folk, professor of ophthamology, was ordered to serve five years' probation – the maximum period allowed, perform 100 hours of community service, pay the University of Iowa $1,311 in damages, pay court fees, and continue with his rehabilitation.

The sentence means that Folk, 37, of 1241 Oakes Drive will be able to continue his ophthamology research because the charge will be stricken from his record after he completes the probation period. His research grant could have been rescinded if he was given a suspended sentence, testimony indicated.

... Folk admitted he wrote prescriptions for patients who were not at University Hospitals in order to obtain cocaine.

... He had used cocaine before for three to four weeks in 1980 at the end of his residency in Pittsburgh, Pa., he said.

Folk completed substance abuse rehabilitation earlier this year at Mayo Clinic in Rochester, Minn., and continues to follow a drug rehabilitation program through MECCA. The program includes being tested for drugs three times a week and attending group therapy sessions.

... Weingeist said the type of surgical procedures Folk performs at UI is done by fewer than 200 people in the country. Folk's expertise is valuable to the university, he said.

Thus far we have presented a variety of examples of different kinds of involvement with substances. The question is, in which ways do drug-induced behavior and delinquent or criminal behavior develop in a given milieu and in one type of milieu as compared with another? What is the role of friends and associates? How do surveillance practices net persons who are more likely to be on drugs than are others, thus resulting in delinquent and criminal defining behavior by police and others in the justice system?

THE RACINE FINDINGS AND THE BROADER PROBLEM

Our findings have been consistent with those of Elliott, Huizinga, and Ageton (1985) and Orcutt (1987), who have found strong support for the influence of associates. In the same vein, Johnson, Marcos, and Bahr (1986) have not only shown that drug using peers are the best *predictor* of drug use, but that variables from the social learning tradition have the strongest effects in a model which accounts for 49 percent of adolescent drug use. Unfortunately they apply only to the process of involvement in an on-going system with a subculture of drug use. What it is about the organization of society that explains the development and growth of the drug subculture is another matter.

Studies based on samples from subsocieties in Harlem or East Los Angeles may not be entirely applicable to an understanding of the broader problem of alcohol, drugs, and crime throughout the United States, though they are important in sensitizing us to the problem's extremes and its indirect as well as direct costs. In selected sections of New York where more people organize their lives around drugs than they do in most other metropolitan areas, the immediate or direct cost to the public of drug-related crime may not be as great as the media indicate – nor may the rewards to offenders be as great as assumed (Johnson and Wish, 1987).

Long-term drug care and policing costs are the real costs that must not be underestimated. The costs of dealing with an increasing proportion of youth who are involved is probably greater than the immediate direct costs of their property offenses. Unfortunately, the public cost is enhanced by the presumed necessity of fielding enforcement programs that increase the arrest count and number of pounds seized without even putting a dent in the number of drug traffickers and the consumption of drugs.

Part of the prediction literature suggests that concentration on a specific type of offender will pay high dividends in crime reduction. We have long been concerned about the tendency to produce very high estimates of offense frequencies among serious offenders which are inflated by high self-reports (Greenwood and Abrahamse, 1982). In some cases these are drug offenses which may occur again and again each day. On the other hand, Diagrams 1A–1E in Chapter 5 suggested that it is possible by the age of 18 to identify many of those members of a cohort who will make a disproportionate contribution to the total of adult police contacts during and after that age.

The claim that selective incapacitation of drug offenders will take a big bite out of serious crime may be misleading. On the other hand, high-rate robbers (Johnson and Wish, 1987) who commit many other offenses may be an exception to the conclusion that specific offenses should not be a basis for targeting offenders.

CONCLUSION

Although our own efforts at delinquent/criminal typology development with the Racine birth cohort data have not produced much improvement in predictive efficiency over simple measures based on offense frequency and seriousness, these efforts led to an investigation of how the *behavioral content* of some offender types in conjunction with its social context, societal setting, or neighborhood milieu may provide the cement for important linkages or be the catalyst for continuity in delinquent or criminal careers. The more that we thought about what some term the drug connection and in spite of problems with the findings based on limited and/or biased samples of the population, the more we could see the value of recoding and reanalyzing our data on substance use and involvement among the Racine cohort members. Reanalyzing the existing data would serve as a guide to recoding and bringing the 1955 Cohort up to 1988.

NOTE

1. Should the reader toss off Eustaquio Deases' call for his Constitutional rights, we refer to a story in the December 4 issue of *The Iowa City Press Citizen* about an Assistant Professor of Psychiatry who, upon arrest in a fight situation in front of Dancer's Bar, was found to have marijuana, cocaine, acetaminophen, and diazepam in his possession. Professor Barrickman was arrested on disorderly conduct charges, but his lawyer contended that there was no probable cause for search (his client was not involved in disorderly conduct) and the evidence of the drugs was the result of an illegal search and seizure. Barrickman resumed his clinical and academic responsibilities at the University of Iowa, but has since left the state for Hawaii.

9 The Relationship of Alcohol and Drugs to Delinquency and Crime in Racine

COMPARING DRUG USERS/OFFENDERS AND NON-DRUG USERS/OFFENDERS

The 1942 and 1949 Cohorts

This chapter continues our critical examination of the relationship of alcohol and drugs to delinquency and crime in the Racine cohorts. Forty percent of 715 people in the 1942 and 1949 Cohorts who filled out self-reports and had continuous residence in Racine revealed at least some marijuana and/or other drug use, but only 10 percent said that they used marijuana or other drugs 'frequently' or 'all of the time.' Only 1.8 percent had police contacts for drug offenses and half of those had only misdemeanor-level offenses. These cohorts reached the age of 16 in 1958 and 1965, before the public's attention had been focused on drugs and crime.

Police contact data for the self-reported, at least one-time, drug users produced mean *official offense seriousness scores* of 11.8 for the juvenile and 12.5 for the adult period (slightly less with drug contacts removed) in comparison to non-drug user scores of 3.2 and 6.0 for these periods. The mean *self-report seriousness scores* for these drug users of 45.0 for the juvenile periods and 60.1 for the adult period also contrasted with self-report, non-drug user scores of 21.5 and 17.4. If drug use by the self-reported drug users was removed from their seriousness scores, their scores dropped to 43.5 and 42.0, still twice as large as the mean for non-drug users. This is probably consistent with Chaiken and Chaiken's (1990) finding that persistent drug offenders commit crimes at higher rates over longer periods of time than do those who are less involved with drugs.

There were 353 people from the 1942 and 1949 Cohorts who had police contacts for offenses other than traffic or suspicion, investigation, or information. The 54 percent of this group who were at least self-reported, one-time drug users had mean *official seriousness scores* of 17.1 for the juvenile period and 17.8 for the adult period (14.6 and 16.8 with drugs removed). The non-drug users (46 percent) had scores of 7.8 and 12.8. The mean *self-report seriousness scores* of this drug user group were 52.0 for the juvenile period and 66.4 for the adult period but dropped to 50.1 and 47.0 when drug use admissions were removed from the seriousness scores. By comparison, the non-drug users had mean self-report scores of 32.3 and 20.8. This still does not tell us if drug use is followed by delinquent and criminal behavior or that delinquent and criminal behavior lead to drug use or that drug use and serious delinquency and crime are only complementary.

The 1955 Cohort

The police contact records of drug offenders in the 1955 Cohort produced *official seriousness scores* of 64.6 and 50.1 (55.1 and 30.7 with drug offenses removed) for the juvenile and adult periods, compared to 8.2 and 4.6 for all of the non-drug offenders or 18.6 and 9.6 when the means were based on 1001, 1955 Cohort members with offenses other than traffic or suspicion, investigation, or information.

No matter how we looked at it, self-reported drug users had more serious juvenile and adult careers, official and self-reported, than did those who did not report drug use. But, as we have stated, no causal implication could be drawn because we had not yet dealt with the juxtaposition of drug and other offenses or sanctions for either. It was simply a matter of recognizing that differences in careers which have been found in metropolitan areas and highly publicized in the media were also found in Racine commencing in the 1960s.

Some early nineteenth-century critics of tobacco (and really brilliant people in their fields of competence) were convinced that tobacco as well as alcohol led to immoral and eventual criminal behavior just as present-day critics of illicit drug use have been concerned about the drug/crime relationship. The media have in one way or another at one time or another extolled the positive side of tobacco and alcohol, taste, feeling, and how their use may facilitate becoming a member of a sought-after group. Drugs are effective (legal and illegal) in producing feelings of importance and are used (self-medication) in response to socioculturally induced stress. As Kaplan, Robbins, and Martin (1983) and Kaplan, Martin, and Robbins (1984 and 1985) state, there are social benefits for some because drug involvement provides people with status, and a social identity that is not too demanding. In some ways we can draw a parallel between this and cigarette or other tobacco use because smoking and, for that matter, drinking enables one to play a role successfully and it may be that some smokers and drinkers may not often be able to do so. Legal use of all manner of mood-altering prescription pills is another matter – and may be read about or seen in the media almost daily.

SERIOUSNESS SCORES FOR THE 1942 AND 1949 DRUG OFFENDER TYPES

Dichotomizing the members of each cohort on a basis of drug use or non-drug use is the same as dichotomizing them on a basis of career type. No one will argue that drug offenders/users, whether identified from official records or self-report, did not have higher total offense seriousness scores (police contact or self-report data with all reasons for police contact included) than did cohort members who were not drug offenders. However, if the 1942 and 1949 Cohorts are dichotomized as drug user or non-drug user *types* on a basis of the self-report data, the official seriousness scores and the self-report seriousness scores differ less than they do when the dichotomy is based on official police contact data, that is, had police contact for drug offenses or did not have police contact for drug offenses. Going even further, those cohort members whose admitted drug use had placed them in one of the *drug offender types* had, on the average, little or no more *serious offense scores, official or self-reported*, than did *non-drug offender types*, particularly if persons without contacts other than for traffic or suspicion, investigation, or information were removed from the analysis.

If offenses based on the drug use admissions are removed from the scores of the *adult drug offender types*, their mean offense score is lower than that for the *non-drug offender types*. This may seem inconsistent with the data presented earlier which revealed that many, if not most, of some serious types of offenders also use drugs and/or have had police contacts for drug offenses. The point here is that persons who are *drug offender types* are not always the most serious offenders overall if the drug offenses are removed in determining the seriousness of their careers.

Some of the official record differences occur because the *officially* recognized or defined drug user/offender is probably not representative of all drug users/offenders. Many are lower SES and, no matter whether engaged in crime at the moment or not, are much more likely to have had and continue to have contact with the police than are middle and upper SES drug users who may be less active or not active in crime (Part I offenses) but are placed in the drug offender type on a basis of their self-reports.

One might ask where lower SES drug users hang out in comparison with executives who purchase their drugs on the way home after a ghoulish day in Manhattan or Los Angeles? An article in *The New York Times,* March 21, 1997, described elegant Manhattan hotels and clubs as the sites for lavish drug parties for those who can afford to party and give parties. Those who frequent bars and taverns have seen and heard how things happen in real life to persons at the other end of the continuum and where to go to find a *shooting parlor.* How much of what we read and hear, particularly descriptions of lower SES depravity as a consequence of drug use, is presented as justification for the so-called war on drugs?

COMPARING THE DISTRIBUTION OF OFFICIAL AND SELF-REPORT TYPES FOR THE 1942 AND 1949 COHORTS

Of the 715, 1942 and 1949 Cohort members who filled out self-reports, 31 admitted that they had used marijuana or other drugs as *juveniles*. Forty-two percent of these (31) were classified in the *official record typology* as all-around street offenders, burglars plus, auto thieves plus, assaulters plus, thieves and thieves plus, and sex offenders. Only 12.7 percent of the 684 cohort members who did not admit drug use were in these serious offender types and they were far more frequently in the official No Contact category (58.2 percent) than were those who admitted drug use (25.8 percent).

The 279 cohort members who admitted drug use as *adults* did not differ from the 436 non-users quite so much but lower percentages were in the serious offender types, 13.4 percent vs. 5.1 percent among those who did not use drugs as adults. Only 33.7

percent of the adult drug users vs. 49.5 percent of the non-users had *not* had their names in the police records.

When the *self-report offense typology* was used in place of the official, the 31 marijuana and other juvenile drug users differed proportionately less from the 684 non-drug users than they did when classified according to the typology based on official data. Almost two-thirds of the *juvenile* drug users were included in the more serious offender types as were almost 40 percent of the *adult* drug users.

COMPARING JUVENILE AND ADULT OFFENDER TYPES IN THE 1955 COHORT

Among those in the 1955 Cohort who had contacts with the police for drug offenses as juveniles, there was little continuity to the adult period; 84.2 percent of the juveniles with police contacts for drug offenses fell in drug offender types as juveniles but of these only 12.5 percent did so as adults. The difference in the case of the 1955 Cohort may be accounted for in part by the stochastic nature of behavior and the incompleteness of official records, particularly for drug involvement in the relatively short time that their adult careers were covered by the Racine research.

The 48 who were classified as juvenile drug-offender types based on their pattern of juvenile police contacts (Diagram 1A of Chapter 6) must, as adults, have either had relatively less drug activity, have been more circumspect so as to not have had police contacts for their drug activity (24.6 percent had no police contacts as adults), or had, as in a few cases, moved into a more serious offender type. There were, however, relatively few in the serious offender types as either juveniles or adults among the 1955 Cohort members who had not had police contacts for drugs as juveniles.

Most (85.4 percent) of the 89 cohort members who had police contacts for drugs as adults were in the drug offender types as adults but had not been involved in drugs as juveniles (only 10.1 percent). Their involvement with drugs as juveniles had not been detected by the police or they had been placed in more serious offense categories (they had some offenses that were more serious than drugs). Those who had not had police contacts for drug offenses as adults appear to have had relatively little serious misbehavior as either juveniles (57.8 percent) or adults (62.4 percent). Again, these data still do not provide a basis for the claim of a causal relationship between drugs, delinquency, and crime or the development of criminal types as a consequence of drug use.

THE TEMPORAL SEQUENCE OF DRUG CONTACTS AND OTHER OFFENSES IN THE 1955 COHORT

Felony-level contacts with the police for drugs may have occurred first as a juvenile or an adult, among the 1955 Cohort members, may or may not have been preceded by a lengthy period of delinquency and crime, and may or may not have been followed by a lengthy period of delinquency and crime. Thus, patterns of delinquency and crime and drug involvement in Racine parallel those which have been described by others. For example, Chaiken and Chaiken (1990) also concluded that there is no single sequential pattern in drug use vs. delinquency and crime as more recently did Zhang, Wieczorek, and Welte (1997).

Long Career Juvenile Drug Offenders

The delinquent and criminal careers of 12 Long Career Juvenile Drug Offenders (20 or more police contacts), are shown in Diagram 1 as a chronological ordering of events. Each had a quite different patterns of police contacts involving drugs and other types of offenses. Since this computer-drawn diagram is so complex that it is difficult to follow an individual career, the career of 1955 Cohort member 0010 is shown in bold as an example.

The age of first police contact for these 12 persons ranged from 6 to 14 while the age of first drug contact ranged from 15 to 17. The lowest number of police contacts for anyone was 29 and the highest was 58. Sanctions ranged from none at all prior to first drug contact (no contacts prior to drug contact) to one year or more of institutionalization. The reasons for police contact prior to first drug offense for which institutionalization had been received ranged from truancy to burglary. Eleven of the 12 were placed in the drug offender typology as juveniles but only two remained there as adults, one had become an all-around street offender, one a felony-level sex offender, four had become burglars, and four were in lesser offense types, raising a serious question about either the idea of criminal career progression or the idea of specialization. It

Diagram 1
Long Career, Juvenile Drug Offenders
Twelve 1955 Cohort Members Whose First Felony Drug Contact Was Before Age 18

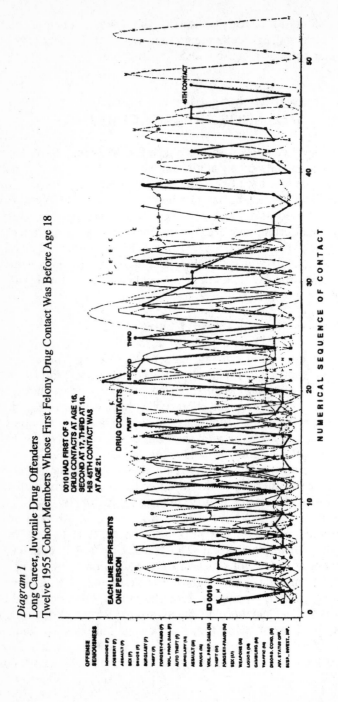

again reveals the stochastic nature of delinquent careers and gives little indication of progression in offense seriousness.

Most drug contacts charges were dismissed by the courts but three of the 12 cohort members had been institutionalized at one time or another after their first drug contact but in only one case was the institutionalization for a drug offense. Eight of the 12 received at least one sanction that was more severe after their first drug contact than had been their most severe sanction prior to a drug contact. Ninety-two percent of these long career, juvenile drug offenders were white males; only one was a female. A careful reading of the 'life story' of each failed to suggest a common thread in their lives or to indicate how they might differ from persons with similar difficulties with the police who did not have official police contacts for drug offenses.

Long Career Adult Drug Offenders

A 'Long Career Adult Drug Offenders' diagram was also constructed for persons who had their first drug contact at the age of 18 or older. Their longer careers so lengthened the diagram that computer compression to put it on a page made it almost unreadable. The first drug contact for cohort members in this group came at the average age of 19.7 years compared to 16.3 for the 12 whose first drug contact was before 18. Their average number of police contacts was 43.6 compared to 34.4 for those who started earlier and their total number of police contacts ranged from 24 to 76. Unlike the first group, 61.9 percent were black. Only two were white females and one was a black female. Even though their first drug contacts came later, their first police contacts of any kind came a bit earlier, at an average of 9.6 years of age vs. an average of 10.3 years of age for the first group. Their first drug contact ranged from being their 23rd contact to their 74th contact. Except that their first drug contact came at age 18 or older, drug contacts came at a variety of times throughout the adult offense career. Seventeen of the 21 received their most severe sanction before their first drug contact and five received their most severe sanction for a drug contact. More than half of this group received their most severe sanction for a theft or burglary contact *prior to their first drug contact.*

The range of offense seriousness and range of severity of sanctions after first drug contacts was almost the same for the juvenile and adult long career drug offenders. However, while the juvenile long career types were drug offender types as juveniles, the adult long career types were, as juveniles, in nine cases all-around street offenders and in nine other cases, burglars. As adults, 15 of the latter were drug offender types and five were murderers or all-around street offenders. Again, they provided little evidence of specialization or increasing seriousness of offenses. These 33 persons are, however, only a small proportion (3.5 percent) of either the 943 juvenile or adult offenders and only 1.5 percent of the 2149 persons in the 1955 Cohort as it was constituted in 1976.

The Chronology of Drug Offenses

The majority of the 1955 Cohort members with drug contacts did not have a contact for drugs as the first police contact of their delinquent or criminal career regardless of whether their drug offending commenced during the juvenile or the adult period. The contacts preceding any drug contact were most likely for traffic offenses, status offenses, disorderly conduct, or a previous drug offense (except for the first drug contact). With the exception of status offenses, these same contact types were also most likely to follow a drug offense. This means that if any one drug contact out of all drug contacts by the members of the cohort were chosen, the best prediction (with no knowledge of the sequential ordering of that drug contact relative to other drug contacts) of the contact types immediately preceding a drug contact would be a traffic offense. The next best prediction would be disorderly conduct, and the next best a prior drug offense. The best prediction of the contact type immediately following a drug contact would be disorderly conduct. The next best prediction would be traffic, followed by another drug offense.

Traffic offenses, status offenses, and disorderly conduct are types of activity that may be classified as low-level disruptive behavior, although status offenses are often disruptive only in the sense that responsible adults may regard them as undesirable forms of behavior for juveniles. Perhaps the switching pattern from these types of behavior to drugs and from drugs to these other behaviors present in the data indicate a need to further consider whether or not much juvenile drug involvement is just another manifestation of a tendency to become involved in low-level disruptive or non-conforming behavior (Wish and Johnson, 1986). Whatever the harmful results to the individual consumer, it is only the law that defines it as so much more serious than smoking tobacco and drinking alcohol.

Whether or not a contact type occurs before or after a drug offense is also a function of the likelihood of the occurrence of a specific contact type in the general population of cohort members. Traffic, disorderly conduct, and status contacts occur relatively frequently among all contacts generated by this cohort. Twenty-two percent of all contacts were for traffic offenses, 20 percent of all contacts were for disorderly conduct, 19 percent were for status offenses (26 percent ages 6–17), but only 3 percent of all contacts were for drugs.

We concluded that drug offenses, at least those which resulted in recorded police contacts, were not linked temporally (immediately before or after) to either property crimes, other crimes of vice, or violent predatory behavior in this cohort. Although drug offending is generally preceded by prior delinquent/criminal behavior and not the other way around, we have not yet determined that there is a special relationship between substance offenses and the larger problem of delinquency/crime. It is one thing to find that a large proportion of those who have been involved in serious offenses against the person and who have committed a property-type offense have also used various drugs or been a part of the drug enterprise, but it is quite another to say that there is a causal relationship, that one is the usual antecedent and cause of the other.

Forty-eight persons who remained in the 1988 continuous residence group had five or more police contacts as juveniles and as adults, excluding traffic, status, or contacts for suspicion, investigation, or information. While 12 of the 48 had neither drugs nor alcohol in their records, 14 had drugs, 13 had alcohol, and nine had both alcohol and drugs. Everyone in this group of 48 had police contacts for property offenses, theft and burglary for almost everyone, and robbery and auto theft for many others. Most of the 48 had numerous police contacts for low-level offenses against public order such as disorderly conduct but the order of offenses was such that neither liquor nor drugs could be seen as the cause or catalyst.

UPDATING THE 1955 COHORT AND RECODING FOR ILLEGAL SUBSTANCE INVOLVEMENT

Remember that the various analyses of the 1955 Cohort are based on four different groups: 1) residence based on ages 6–22 (2149 persons), or 2) ages 13–22 (2658 persons), both for the cohort as followed to 1976, and 3) residence based on ages 6–32 (1357 persons), or 4) ages 13–32 (1441 persons) both for the cohort as followed to 1988.

The decision to enlarge the group available for analysis would enable us to include more cohort members with the potential of having police contacts for alcohol and drug offenses but would not present a group that was significantly different in other respects from those whose continuous residence had commenced at an earlier age. Heroin use has been stable 1960–90 and cocaine has grown since the mid-1970s with freebasing and 'crack' entering the picture in the late 1980s (Johnson, Williams, Dei, and Sanabria, 1990). As a consequence, very little of the 1980s trend to cocaine derivatives and so-called 'designer drugs' will have had an impact on the 1955 Cohort's records. The 1441 persons included in this continuous residence segment of the cohort contained 29 juvenile drug offenders and 77 adult drug offenders, almost all of whom had their drug offense contacts as either juveniles or adults but not both. The distribution of offenses for this augmented group of 1441 persons is shown by age periods in Table 1.   ·

Comparison of the distribution of offense types and summary statistics with those found for the smaller continuous residence group of 1357 indicated that the 7002 police contacts for the augmented group are distributed much the same as the 6803 contacts of the smaller group. When traffic offenses, disorderly conduct, juvenile status, and contacts for suspicion, investigation, and information are eliminated, only theft, burglary, and assault exceed the proportion of contacts for narcotics and drugs combined in either cohort group. After the age of 21, the narcotics and drugs proportion slightly exceeds even theft and assault and is five times greater than burglary, again in either cohort group. As we had hypothesized, the 1955 Cohort demonstrated that narcotics and drugs have markedly increased in their proportion of the police contacts in all age periods.

VARIATION IN DRUGS AND REASONS FOR POLICE CONTACTS

Most drug contacts were classified as felonies at the time of the original contact and more were for marijuana than for other drugs. As expected, the entire range of drugs was not encountered in police

Table 1.
Distribution of Police Contacts by Age Group: Augmented Cohort*

	6–17		18–20		21+		Total	
	N	%	N	%	N	%	N	%
Traffic	319	9.0	471	30.0	776	41.1	1566	22.3
Disorderly conduct	522	14.7	438	27.9	415	22.0	1375	19.6
Suspicion, investigation, information	536	15.1	197	12.5	138	7.3	871	12.4
Liquor	88	2.5	32	2.0	32	1.7	152	2.2
Theft	459	12.9	100	6.4	100	5.3	659	9.4
Juvenile status	988	27.0	7	.7	–	–	995	14.2
Vagrancy	53	1.5	9	.6	11	.6	73	1.0
Auto theft	81	2.3	19	1.2	3	.2	103	1.5
Sex offenses	30	.8	23	1.5	20	1.1	73	1.0
Assault	90	2.5	40	2.5	100	5.3	230	3.3
Burglary	227	6.4	69	4.4	21	1.1	317	4.5
Weapons	25	.7	27	1.7	43	2.3	95	1.4
Violent property destruction	26	.7	22	1.4	49	2.6	97	1.4
Forgery and Fraud	15	.4	19	1.2	54	2.9	88	1.3
Robbery	41	1.2	31	2.0	12	.6	84	1.2
Gambling	2	.1	3	.2	5	.3	10	.1
Narcotics/Drugs	43	1.2	63	4.0	103	5.5	209	3.0
Homicide	–	–	1	.1	4	.2	5	.1
Total	3545	99.9	1571	100.0	1886	100.1	7002	99.9
CONTACTS PER PERSON		2.46		1.09		1.31		4.86
PART I	898	25.3	260	16.5	240	12.7	1398	20.0
PART I PER PERSON		.62		.18		.17		.97

* 1441 persons with continuous residence in Racine, ages 13–33.

contacts among members of the 1955 Cohort. There are, of course, a multitude of other and newer drugs on the streets in larger metropolitan areas today (and in Racine as well) but crack was not available when the 1955 Cohort was at the experimental age. Of the 204 police contacts involving drugs, 60 percent involved marijuana alone. Only 4.9 percent of the contacts involved heroin and 12.7 involved cocaine. The narcotics, depressants, stimulants, and hallucinogens combined accounted for 27 percent of the police contacts, only half of the marijuana proportion. While these numbers seem small, it must be remembered that this is one cohort born in 1955. It is the first 'drug' cohort in the Racine longitudinal research. If we think of 1970 as being the year when the most recent drug cohort would have been born, there were 17 other potential drug cohorts on the streets by 1987. These were the cohorts responsible for the sharp increase in arrests for drug offenses in Racine during recent years.

Ten of the 16 contacts by cohort members for narcotics (half for heroin) were after the age of 21, as were 24 of the 29 contacts for stimulants (cocaine). These were too few contacts for heroin or cocaine to determine if they had a special role in continuity and/or career seriousness in contrast to cannabis and other drugs. Strug, Wish, Johnson, Anderson, Miller, and Sears (1984), have reported that in a sample of Manhattan's heavy users of heroin who were also heavy drinkers, 63 percent reported themselves to be more likely, if high, to be under the influence of alcohol than drugs or a combination of them when committing crimes.

Out of the 206 drug contacts, 55.8 percent were simply for possession, 15.5 percent for possession with intent to deliver, 9.2 percent for buying, and 6.3 percent for selling. Half of all police contacts for any type of substance were for possession of marijuana and another 15 percent were for trading in marijuana. In short, the proportion of contacts for hard drug possession and/or trading was very small, little more than 20 percent. Most of the contacts during the 18–20 age period were for possession of drugs. Contacts for buying, selling, and possession with intent to deliver occurred after cohort members had reached 21, while those for possession were more evenly distributed. In short, the world of drug behavior has undoubtedly gone through a period of change since the 1980s as it has in larger metropolitan areas.

INVOLVEMENT WITH LIQUOR

When the 1955 Cohort's contacts were recoded to reflect the involvement of liquor in police contacts, the total liquor involvement rose to 316 from the 152 contacts that were strictly for liquor violations. The annualized rate for average number of contacts per year declined from 29.2 during the juvenile period to 17.7 during the 18–20 period and 13.5 for the after 21 period, a function of the legal limitation on purchasing and consuming alcoholic beverages. When the same approach was used for the drug contacts, the annualized number of contacts was 8.2, 11.4, and 8.8. Since the desistance rate increases rapidly during the twenties, dividing the 21 and older number by 12 probably generates a somewhat lower rate than should be used for comparison with the earlier periods.

SUMMARY AND CONCLUSION

Both official and self-report data for the 1942 and 1949 Cohorts produced mean average offense seriousness scores that were greater for cohort members with self-reported drug involvement than for those without drug involvement, even with the drug involvement component of their careers withdrawn when computing the means. And, no matter how we measured it, the 1942 and 1949 self-reported drug users had more serious juvenile and adult official and self-reported offense careers than did those who did not report drug use. The 1955 Cohort produced similar official record differences for those with officially recorded drug offenses vs. no recorded drug offenses.

When the 1942 and 1949 Cohorts were dichotomized as drug user types (drug offenses their most serious offenses) vs. other types, the drug offender types had more serious mean scores, or essentially the same as did the other types, or even lower mean scores than did other types of offenders, depending on each particular design for comparison.

· A variety of analyses failed to show that drug involvement usually followed other delinquent or criminal behavior or that delinquent and criminal behavior usually followed drug involvement or that there was any universal pattern of continuity between the juvenile and adult periods.

What again and again created the impression that substances, with drugs replacing or becoming equally as important as alcohol, had become a catalyst for continuity was the fact that they had become a highly visible part of the urban scene in those areas where continuity in delinquency and crime was already a more traditional form of behavior than in other types of neighborhoods. It is not that drugs and alcohol were absent in other neighborhoods. They were there and played a role in the lives of some residents of these neighborhoods, but delinquency and crime were not a part of the lives of most of the residents, certainly not enough to generate criminal career continuity in more than a small proportion of residents.

The advantage of comparable longitudinal birth cohort studies became more and more apparent because this type of data, including combinations of persons who are delinquent or non-delinquent, criminal or non-criminal, who have or have not had substance involvement, permits us to examine the hypothesized chronological interrelationship of events. This examination fails to support the hypothesis that substance involvement is the antecedent to delinquency and crime, although it could be a catalyst in some cases and an important factor in career continuity.

10 Alcohol and Drugs and Criminal Career Continuity in the 1955 Cohort

INTRODUCTION

Our numerous examples and analyses of how drug involvement may be intertwined with delinquent and criminal behavior are the kinds of evidence upon which less sophisticated citizens and many powerful politicians would build a case for a war on drugs from marijuana to cocaine and heroin. Their goal is, if not to eradicate drugs and crime, to at least reduce their prevalence in patterns so visible · that the community has great concern.

THE COHORT IN 1976 AND IN 1988

To what extent were alcohol and drugs related to continuity in delinquency and crime among the 2658 continuous residents in the 1955 Cohort as expanded from 2149 to include those with continuous residence ages 13–22? Most of the persons in this expanded cohort still had continuous residence ages 6–22 and police records differing little from the larger group who were there only through ages 13–22.

The following analyses enable us to assess the extent of the complex relationship of juvenile to adult career continuity among those who had alcohol or drug involvement and various combinations thereof. These tables show what cohort members were like as juveniles and if they changed or remained in the same offender categories as adults. We shall again show how the skewed marginals (few serious offenders as adults) make it so difficult to increase predictive efficiency beyond that already available from the marginal distribution of the cohort as adults.

155

The findings based on the expanded group are presented as a prelude to analyses of the smaller but updated 1955 Cohort (1357 with continuous residence to 1988), it, in turn, augmented by those with continuous residence age 13–32 for a total of 1441 persons.

FREQUENCY TYPES AND THE ALCOHOL/DRUG AND DELINQUENCY/CRIME RELATIONSHIP

Cohort members in more serious offender types have also had police contacts for drug and/or alcohol offenses and some whose most serious offense was for drugs have had many other lesser types of offenses. The other types, it will be remembered, ranged from murderers, all-around street offenders, and so on, to persons who had not had police contacts. This is the principal reason that birth cohort studies (there are non-offenders in the analyses) produce different conclusions about criminal career continuity than do studies of persons with court appearances or persons who have been institutionalized, all of whom are more likely to have career continuity than persons who have had little contact with the justice system.

The 1955 Cohort to 1976

The Arrangement of Cohort Members in Cells
Diagram 1 is presented for heuristic purposes as an introduction to other tables which follow. The frequent offender (chronic – a widely accepted definition) with five or more police contacts (omitting traffic, suspicion, investigation, or information and status offenses) is operationally defined as having a serious career. We have placed cohort members with police contacts for only traffic, suspicion, investigation, or information, and status offenses, unless drug or alcohol related, in the No Contact (offense) category in the table as a bookkeeping device. Persons who had no contacts or only contacts of the omitted type remain in the upper left-hand corner of the table as a part of the 2658 cohort members in the table who had a total of 7906 police contacts.

Each cell in Diagram 1 contains three figures, the number of police contacts (the total for that cell, without omissions), the number of cohort members who produced these contacts, and the mean number of contacts of all types by cohort members in that cell. In this abbreviated table persons who had from one to four contacts

Diagram 1.
Distribution of 1955 Cohort by Juvenile/Adult, Alcohol/Drug, and Frequency of Offense Status According to Official Records

Offense Behavior Type / JUVENILE (6-17)	ADULT (18 AND OLDER) SERIOUS CONTINUITY AFTER AGE 18					
		No Contacts	No Drugs/ Alcohol	Alcohol+	Drugs+	Drugs/ Alcohol+	TOTAL
No Contacts (Number of Contacts / Number of Persons / Mean Contacts per Person)	765	57	18	35	9	1523
	1744	5	2	3	1	1985
	.4	11.4	9.0	11.7	11.1	
1-4 Contacts, No Alcohol/Drugs	855	175	24	66	18	2082
	271	11	2	6	1	427
	3.2	15.9	12.0	11.0	18.0	
1-4 Contacts, Alcohol, No Drugs	158	36	17	0	0	355
	49	3	1	0	0	77
	3.2	12.0	17.0	---	---	
1-4 Contacts, Drugs, No Alcohol	51	0	0	51	18	205
	17	0	0	3	1	35
	3.0	---	---	17.0	18.0	
1-4 Contacts, Drugs & Alcohol	18	0	0	0	0	45
	3	0	0	0	0	6
	6.0	---	---	---	---	
5 or More Contacts, No Drugs/Alcohol	409	466	158	397	179	2146
	24	13	4	10	4	78
	17.0	35.8	39.5	39.7	44.8	
5 or More Contacts, Alcohol +	61	201	155	216	56	890
	2	6	4	5	1	27
	30.5	33.5	38.8	43.2 (57)	56.0	
5 or More Contacts, Drugs +	68	37	28	170	0	418
	3	1	1	4	0	15
	22.7	37.0	28.0	42.5	---	
5 or More Contacts, Drugs & Alcohol +	32	40	25	83	48	242
	3	1	1	1	1	8
	10.7	40.0	25.0	83.0	48.0	

(non-serious adults) are omitted. For example, in the first row there are 1985 cohort members who had no contacts as juveniles and, of these, 1744 had no contacts as adults and 11 who had serious careers after age 18, leaving 243 who had one to four contacts after age 18.

Note that of the 1744 persons in the 1955 Cohort continuous residence group, or drug cohort, had either no police contacts or some (765) contacts such as traffic, and so forth, an average of 0.4 contacts per person. This left 914 cohort members with 7139 contacts in eight other offender types as juveniles or adults. Each had at least one non-traffic, non-suspicion, investigation, information, or non-status police contact as a juvenile or as an adult and are in one of the other combinations of juvenile and adult careers, of which only those with serious adult careers are shown in Diagram 1. This approach places each cohort member in a category based on the frequency of certain types of police contacts but the frequency of all types of contacts for each category is still revealed by the average.

The highest averages are in the 16 cells in the lower right. Since some cells contain few cohort members, these mean numbers of offenses must be used with caution, albeit the measures are rather consistent as we go from one section of the diagram to the other.

Most cohort members in the No Contact category or with one to four police contacts, with or without alcohol or drug involvement in their records as juveniles, had little or no adult involvement in crime. All but 4.7 percent of these 427 cohort members (with one to four contacts as juveniles but no juvenile alcohol and/or drug offenses) desisted from serious careers as adults. The 118 with one to four contacts as juveniles who had alcohol and/or drug contacts as juveniles also showed little continuity to serious adult careers (7.1 percent). This should not be surprising. We and many others have found that for far more than any other reason delinquency is, at least outside the inner city, motivated by the pursuit of fun, thrills, and excitement. Wood, Arneklev, and Stephensen (1991) found that 46 percent of the property offenses were in this category, as were 43 percent of the offenses involving substances. After the age of 18, patterns of thrill-seeking become less and less likely to involve law-breaking.

Continuity among Serious Offenders

The 128 cohort members who were serious offenders as juveniles, that is, five or more contacts, had 40 percent to 60 percent continuity as adults. The 78 serious offenders who had not had alcohol and/or drug contacts as juveniles showed almost 40 percent continuity to serious adult careers. Those 50 serious offenders who were involved with alcohol and/or drugs had greater continuity, *circa* 50 percent.

The box in Diagram 1 contains 57 cohort members who, as both juveniles and adults, had five or more police contacts, 44 of whom also had police contacts involving alcohol and/or drugs as either juveniles or adults or both. If all cells were included in this introductory table, there would be cells to the left of the box for people who had serious involvement with the police as juveniles but only one to four contacts as adults. The cells above the box contain people who were serious offenders as adults but not as juveniles. The remaining cells of the table would contain those who did not have serious involvement with the police as either juveniles or adults.

There are nine cells in the extreme lower right of the diagram for those who had police contacts for alcohol and/or drugs or both as juveniles and adults but there are only 18 persons in these cells. The mean number of offenses per person is very high for each segment of that small group of 18 (only 0.7 percent of the cohort but 9.9 percent of the cohort's police contacts). Beyond that, the 1.0 percent of the cohort (26 persons) who had five or more police contacts before 18, some with substance involvement and five or more police contacts after 18 (but not necessarily involving substances as adults) was responsible for 13.4 percent of all police contacts by the entire cohort. This 1 percent also had 38.1 percent of the 2783 police contacts by persons who had five or more contacts after 18, a rather large share for only 1.0 percent of the cohort. The larger group of 57 persons who had serious offense careers as both juveniles and adults but not necessarily alcohol or drug involvement comprised only 2.1 percent of the cohort but had 28.6 percent of the cohort's police contacts.

Going back to the terrible 57 again, they comprised 2.1 percent of the cohort but had 81.2 percent of the 2783 career contacts by persons who were serious offenders after the age of 18. This was 28.6 percent of all police contacts by the cohort.

The fact is, however, that only 44.6 percent of those who, before the age of 18, had five or more police contacts, some involving liquor and some not, continued into serious offender careers during their early adult years while 55.4 percent did not. Even a serious career before 18 produced a serious career thereafter for less than half of that group. The proportional reduction in error by using the predictor, juvenile record, reduced errors by 16.4 percent over that obtained by use of the marginals.

The Extent of Dispersion

In spite of this concentration of police contacts among serious offenders it must be recognized that police contacts are also widely dispersed throughout any cohort. That 1744 (65.6 percent of the cohort) who had either no contacts or traffic and other contacts which were removed from consideration was responsible for only 9.7 percent of all police contacts. Others who had fewer than five police contacts as juveniles and adults (28.1 percent) were responsible for 36.9 percent of the police contacts. Those who had five or more police contacts as juveniles or adults but not as both (4.1 percent) were responsible for 24.8 percent of the contacts and, as previously stated, the 57 persons (2.1 percent) with five or more contacts as juveniles and adults, that is, the group with continuity from serious juvenile to serious adult careers, had 28.6 percent of the total. Depending on how widely the net is to be cast, we are most concerned with 1.0 percent, 2.1 percent, or 6.2 percent of the cohort, the latter responsible for 53.4 percent of the cohort's police contacts.

Mobility and the Changing Composition of the Cohort

The records of each person who was deceased by 1988 or who had been incarcerated for one or more years were checked to determine if either of these events could have accounted for their desistance from an adult career as of 1976. There were only 11 who had died, moved, or left the community for the armed forces so early (1973) that it would have prevented them from having a serious adult record. Of those, six were in the juvenile, no career or non-serious career categories where the probability of an adult career was small. Most who had been incarcerated had gone on to serious adult careers or had already had sufficient contact with the police to be in the adult serious offender group.

Blacks have become more and more isolated from the mainstream of life in even middle-sized cities. Thus being black and/or an inner-city resident becomes a complex explanatory variable in a sociological sense rather than in a strictly demographic and ecological sense. Even though some blacks have been able to move to almost every neighborhood (a fact which delights those who wish to minimize the problem), the proportion of the inner city consisting of black residents has been increasing (a fact which terrifies those who know the inner city for only its crime and have never experienced the warmth of its human relationships).

THE DELINQUENT CAREER AND THE ADULT CAREER: THE 1955 COHORT UPDATED TO 1988

The Effect of a Longer Career

As expected, Diagram 2 for 1357 persons from the updated 1955 Cohort showed that a longer adult career provided more career continuity than had been found for the cohort when followed only until age 22. In a sense, official continuity is based to a degree on the law enforcement officer's luck as well as his/her diligence on the 'beat.' A break in the official records for a year or so does not ensure that a person has actually desisted. This is particularly true for those with serious careers and for those who have learned to cover their tracks.

Continuity to serious adult careers (five or more police contacts) for serious juvenile offenders who did not have police contacts including alcohol or drugs (during the juvenile period) increased from 39.7 percent for those with continuous residence to 1976 to 60.9 percent for those with continuous residence to 1988. Cohort members with five or more police contacts, including some for alcohol, had an increase in continuity to serious adult careers from 59.2 percent to 66.7 percent and those with five or more contacts, some for drugs, from 40.0 percent to 54.5 percent. Those with alcohol rather than drugs in their records had more continuity than did others. Again, there was little continuity in delinquent behavior to criminal behavior among those who had fewer than five police contacts.

The 51 cohort members in Diagram 2 with five or more contacts as juveniles and as adults, while comprising only 3.7 percent of the cohort, were responsible for 34.3 percent of the cohort's 6347 police contacts. An additional 95 (62 + 33 = 7.0 percent) who were either serious offenders as juveniles or as adults, but not as both, accounted for 26.2 percent of the contacts so that the combined group comprising 10.7 percent of the cohort who were serious offenders as youths or adults, or both, had generated 60.5 percent of the police contacts. Those who were in the No Contact and 'no offense' category comprised 54.0 percent of the cohort but their minor infractions amounted to only 8.1 percent of all contacts while other persons with fewer than five contacts as juveniles and adults (35.2 percent) had 31.4 percent of the contacts.

Diagram 2.
Distribution of 1955 Cohort by Juvenile/Adult, Alcohol/Drug, and Frequency of Offense Status According to Official Records to 1988

Offense Behavior Type JUVENILE (6-17)		Offense/Behavior Type ADULT (18 AND OLDER)				
	No Contacts	No Alcohol/Drugs	1-4 Contacts Alcohol and/or Drugs	No Drugs/ Alcohol	5 or More Contacts Alcohol and/or Drugs +	TOTAL
No Contacts	514 733 .7	382 131 3.4	294 76 3.9	71 8 10.0	127 8 15.9	1388 955 1.6% SERIOUS CONTINUITY
1-4 Contacts, No Alcohol/Drugs	427 116 3.7	351 58 6.1	246 29 8.8	317 18 17.6	308 21 14.7	1649 242 16.1% SERIOUS CONTINUITY
1-4 Contacts, Alcohol and/or Drugs	129 43 3.0	86 14 6.1	78 11 7.1	13 1 13.0	127 7 18.1	431 76 10.5% SERIOUS CONTINUITY
5 or More Contacts, No Drugs/Alcohol	92 5 18.4	192 10 19.2	66 3 22.0	254 7 36.3	998 21 47.5	1602 46 60.9% SERIOUS CONTINUITY
5 or More Contacts, Alcohol and/or Drugs	30 2 15.0	183 9 20.3	135 4 33.7	105 3 35.0	822 20 41.1	1275 38 60.5% SERIOUS CONTINUITY

SERIOUS CONTINUITY AFTER AGE 18

Number of Contacts
Number of Persons
Mean Contacts per Person

33 + 62 + 51 = 10.7% of Cohort with 60.5% of Offenses

The 1273 cohort members (1211 + 62 on Diagram 2) with fewer than five police contacts as juveniles still produced 62 persons (4.6 percent of the cohort and 15.2 percent of the cohort's contacts) who had serious offender careers as adults, more serious offenders (even though proportionately less) than had been produced by the serious juvenile offenders. This is the type of finding that we have attempted to bring to the attention of those who believe that the crime problem is solved by focusing on that small proportion who, as serious juvenile offenders, are more likely to have continuity into serious adult careers. Concentration on this group may, of course, give the public the impression that the problem is being dealt with and it is undoubtedly more efficient to monitor a few with well known records than to attempt to monitor most of the community.

To be more specific, 84 cohort members had five or more police contacts, of them 46 had no substance involvement and 38 had involvement with alcohol and/or drugs. Of those without substance involvement, 28 had serious adult careers and of those with substance involvement, 23 had serious adult careers. If the marginals of the table were utilized as a basis for prediction, we would predict that no one would have a serious adult career and make 113 errors (51 + 62). If we utilized juvenile status as the predictor, 95 errors would be made, 33 false positives and 62 false negatives, less than from the marginal prediction of 113. Note that more persons who did not have a serious juvenile career had a serious adult career (62) than did those (51) who had continuity from a serious juvenile career to a serious adult career. Probability is on the side of predicting that serious delinquents continue their behavior into adulthood but there are even more (62) who have not had a serious juvenile career who have a serious adult career. The coefficient of predictability is 15.9 percent, indicating that the relationship between juvenile and adult careers results in an improvement in predicting adult behavior from juvenile behavior error but only by 15.9 percent over the errors that would have been made by predicting from the marginals of the table.

What we should consider, however, is which type of error has the greatest 'social' cost. The prediction that no one would have a serious adult career ignores 113 persons who develop serious adult careers. The prediction that what one is as a juvenile will follow into adulthood predicts 33 persons as serious adult offenders who are not and 62 as not becoming serious adult offenders who do. If juvenile behavior results in formal action which has deleterious effects, that is, crystallizes their behavior, then one would hesitate to apply such action to the 84 who were serious offenders as juveniles. The assumption that they would continue their behavior into the adult period would be correct for only 51 of the 84. If the action taken is rather benign but may turn some of the juveniles away from career continuity, then there could be less danger to the 84 members, 33 of whom do not need the intervention. Of course, we do not know which are in that category. No matter how those on the firing line look at it, the decision is difficult to make.

Going just a step further, however, of the 51 persons who had five or more contacts as juveniles and five or more contacts as adults, 41 as adults had contacts involving alcohol and/or drugs, of whom 13 had been institutionalized (31.7 percent). Of those 36 who had five or more contacts as adults including some involving alcohol and/or drugs but had not had five or more as juveniles, only three had been institutionalized (8.3 percent). This is another indication of how early and serious involvement in the judicial system may lead to more severe sanctions (which may well be consistent with dispositional procedures) but does not mean that the total who have become serious adult offenders have been equally involved and called to the attention of the system as juveniles.

Sex Differences

When Diagram 2 was partitioned by sex, only 0.9 percent of the females had five or more police contacts as juveniles and adults. All but one of this group had involvement with alcohol as juveniles. By contrast, 6.3 percent of the males had five or more police contacts as juveniles and adults. While only 3.4 percent of the females had five or more contacts as either juveniles or adults or both, 17.3 percent of the males had them. Alcohol seemed to have played an important part in female continuity but was of lesser importance among the males; 55.5 percent of the females but only 29.3 percent of the males with five or more contacts and juvenile to adult continuity had police contacts involving alcohol in one way or another. The nature of female vs. male careers can account for this difference.

THE DELINQUENT CAREER AND THE ADULT CAREER:
AUGMENTED 1955 COHORT

Diagram 2 (1357 persons 6–33) and Diagram 3 for the augmented
cohort (1441 persons 13–33) show considerable similarity. Two
relationships are consistently found: 1) the substance-involved, serious
offenders had a bit greater continuity than those serious offenders
without substance involvement and 2) the major differences in continuity between groups is the considerable difference between those
with one to four police contacts and those with five or more police
contacts.

**The Characteristics of Those with Serious Juvenile and Adult
Careers**

In Diagram 3 we readily see that 38 + 69 + 58, that is, 11.4 percent of the cohort, accounts for 63.0 percent of all offenses. Of the
58 cohort members who had five or more police contacts as juveniles and five or more as adults, 76 percent were socialized in the
inner city or transitional neighborhoods. Of those socialized in these
neighborhoods and had more serious careers than did others. 61.4
percent were black or Chicano. Only 21.4 percent of those who
were socialized in other neighborhoods were black or Chicano.

About half (48 percent) of the blacks and Chicanos in the inner
city/transitional group had been in a training school, reformatory,
or adult prison (jail terms and juvenile detention were not included)
while only 21.7 percent of the whites had been institutionalized.
Only one white member of the cohort was institutionalized during
both the juvenile and adult periods, although five non-whites had
this experience. Blacks and Chicanos constituted 76.5 percent of
the inner city and transitional group who had been institutionalized as juveniles or adults but only half of those from these
neighborhoods who had not been institutionalized.

Within each of the 16 categories collapsed into four groups in
Diagram 3 (58 persons with five or more police contacts as juveniles and adults) and for which there were persons who had been
institutionalized or not institutionalized, those who had been institutionalized had a larger number of Part I offenses on their records
than did those who had not been institutionalized. Although the
range in number of police contacts was almost the same, whether
institutionalized or not, the mean for those institutionalized was
20 and was 10.2 for those who had not been institutionalized.

Diagram 3.

Distribution of 1955 Augmented Cohort by Juvenile/Adult, Alcohol/Drug, and Frequency of Offense Status According to Official Records to 1988

Key (for each cell):
Number of Contacts / Number of Persons / Mean Contacts per Person

Offense/Behavior Type JUVENILE (6-17)	Offense/Behavior Type ADULT (18 AND OLDER)						
	No Contacts	1-4 Contacts — No Alcohol/Drugs	1-4 Contacts — Alcohol and/or Drugs	5 or More Contacts — No Drugs/Alcohol	5 or More Contacts — Alcohol and/or Drugs +	SERIOUS CONTINUITY AFTER AGE 18	TOTAL
No Contacts	521 / 770 / .7	397 / 137 / 2.9	308 / 79 / 3.9	71 / 7 / 10.1	127 / 8 / 15.9	1.6% SERIOUS CONTINUITY	1424 / 1001
1-4 Contacts, No Alcohol/Drugs	462 / 126 / 3.7	364 / 61 / 6.1	251 / 30 / 8.4	317 / 18 / 17.6	397 / 27 / 14.7	17.2% SERIOUS CONTINUITY	1791 / 262
1-4 Contacts, Alcohol and/or Drugs	141 / 44 / 3.2	90 / 15 / 6.0	78 / 11 / 7.1	13 / 1 / 13.0	140 / 8 / 17.5	11.4% SERIOUS CONTINUITY	462 / 79
5 or More Contacts, No Drugs/Alcohol	99 / 6 / 16.5	267 / 12 / 22.3	66 / 3 / 22.0	279 / 8 / 34.9	1084 / 23 / 47.1	59.6% SERIOUS CONTINUITY	1795 / 52
5 or More Contacts, Alcohol and/or Drugs	39 / 3 / 13.0	206 / 10 / 20.6	135 / 4 / 33.8	105 / 3 / 35.0	1106 / 24 / 46.1	61.4% SERIOUS CONTINUITY	1591 / 44

1273

Circled values: 38, 69, 58

38 + 69 + 58 = 11.4% of Cohort with 63.0% of Offenses

But let us go further. Among the inner city and transitional neighborhood people, the blacks and Chicanos had a mean of 16.8 Part I offenses and the whites 9.9. There were too few blacks in other neighborhoods for comparison on this measure but these whites had a mean of 8.7, only a bit below their counterparts in the inner city and transitional neighborhoods. The consistency of race/ethnic differences becomes even more apparent as we see that among those socialized in the inner city, whites who were institutionalized had a mean of 17.7 Part I offenses while blacks had 22.9. Among those not institutionalized, whites had a mean of 8.1 and blacks 10.6.

The complexity of the situation is even further increased if we look at the characteristics of the 58 cohort members in 16 career offender cells collapsed in Diagram 3. In the four cells for juveniles who had neither officially recorded alcohol nor drug involvement as juveniles the proportion of those who were black or Chicano was 62.5 percent, 75.0 percent, 37.5 percent, and 71.4 percent. Eleven of the 27 who were in the cells involving alcohol as juveniles were blacks or Chicanos (40.7 percent), generally a lower proportion than for cells not involving substances.

What we have here is an indication that during the 1960s, 1970s, and 1980s, blacks and Chicanos in the inner city were more involved in the ordinary, garden variety street crime (Part I offenses) and less involved than were whites in offenses which are based on substance use, production, or trafficking. What has appeared in the media for some time to be greater black involvement may be a product of their lack of criminal sophistication and late entry into the field, thus becoming visible only at the lower levels, as described in some of the newspaper stories which we have quoted.

While most of those in the substance involved categories as juveniles continued to have contacts involving substances *if* they continued in crime, substances in themselves did not constitute the most serious offenses in their criminal careers. These comparisons reveal that the proportion of blacks with criminal career continuity follows a different pattern from that of the whites and that this was even more apparent in the 1955 Cohort as we brought it up to 1988.

Cohort Members with Five or More Police Contacts as Juveniles But No Contacts for Alcohol/Drug Offenses

Non-Serious as Adults
Sometimes the reader examines a complex table and then asks, 'where are the people?' Here we anticipate this response by examining the people in some illustrative cells. Some may say that this detail is superfluous but we differ. Let us look at the people in a few cells.

There were 12 cohort members who had five or more police contacts as juveniles but none for drugs or alcohol and one to four contacts as adults but none for drugs or alcohol. As juveniles in all cases except one they had contacts which involved taking property from others. There were three robbers, three burglars, four thieves, and two auto thieves. One had an assault as his most serious offense. Along with these offenses they had numerous status contacts and contacts for disorderly conduct. As adults none had police contacts for robbery or burglary. Two were in trouble for assault, four for theft, two for violent property destruction, and four for disorderly conduct; all in all a very limited repertoire in comparison with their youthful misbehavior. They, as juveniles, had a median of 11.5 police contacts and a median of 1.0 as adults. All but two had been on probation, eight had been fined, but only two had been institutionalized, one of whom died in 1983.

Serious as Adults
Only 41.7 percent of the 12 offenders whom we just mentioned were from inner-city or transitional neighborhoods in comparison with 87.5 percent of this group of eight who had five or more contacts as juveniles and five or more contacts as adults (no alcohol or drugs). This group had a median of 19 contacts with the police as juveniles and a median of 12.5 as adults. As juveniles they were involved in robbery and burglary and continued in burglary, theft, and robbery to a greater extent than did the first group. They also contained four people who had contacts for assault as adults. This group was skewed toward more serious offenses and they were found in the serious offender types as adults. All but one had received probation or more, all had been fined, most of them repeatedly, and one had been in and out of institutions without evidence of any positive change in his behavior.

No Alcohol/Drugs as Juveniles but Alcohol/Drugs as Adults

Serious and Alcohol as Adults
Persons in the next group of 23 had five or more police contacts as
juveniles and substance involvement as adults. There were eight
with at least one contact involving alcohol as adults and 87.5 percent were from the inner city or interstitial areas. Its members also
had a median of 19 police contacts before 18 and 20.5 after 18.

Is it the effects of alcohol pure and simple, or is it a way of life
and a pattern of alcohol involvement or some combination of them?
What else do we find? Half of the group was engaged in felony-
level offenses as juveniles and adults, a larger proportion than in
the other groups, seven of the eight had burglaries as juveniles
and were involved in robbery, burglary, assault, and theft as adults.
Most had numerous status and/or disorderly conduct contacts as
juveniles. Although all had at least one contact for a liquor offense
as an adult, the official record gives no indication that liquor played
a part in the seriousness of their careers. All had engaged in the
same or similar kinds of offenses as juveniles. Since their median
number of juvenile offenses was larger than that for the previously
described groups and all save one were from the inner city or transitional neighborhoods, it would be reasonable to propose that this
group is simply a more serious offender group whose extensive juvenile activity continued into the adult period where it flourished
into the 1980s for most offenders.

Serious and Drugs as Adults
The next group of eight is similar to the last but, as adults, they
had contacts for offenses that involved drugs. The same proportion of its members (87.5 percent) came from inner city and transitional neighborhoods and all were males. The length of their careers
were also similar except that one member received a life sentence
plus 25 years for murder at the age of 20. All were in the most
serious offender types as juveniles and adults. As juveniles, four
were armed robbers, three were burglars, and one was an assaulter.
As adults the burglars were still burglars but two of the robbers
changed, one to murder and the other to drug offenses as their
most serious offenses. The assaulter still had assault as his most
serious contact type. Besides this, almost all of them were continu-
ously involved in a variety of street offenses, theft, auto theft, and

assault, somewhat more extensively than were those in the group that had contacts as adults for offenses involving alcohol.

Compared to the alcohol group, the drug group's median number of contacts was 38.5 vs. 19 for those with alcohol involvement before age 18. Both had a median of 20.5 after that age. Everyone in this group had received referrals, probation, and some institutionalization, most continuing their serious illegal activities. Their heterogeneous careers involving continuous switching from offenses against property to offenses against persons to offenses against public order were apparently not deterred by the inconsistent efforts of those in the justice system. In the early years the members of this group were status offenders, were contacted for disorderly conduct, released, and/or referred again and again. The Racine County Probation Department worked with most of them during their juvenile years. Some were sent to the training school, some made the next step to the reformatory, and several were sent to adult prisons for burglary, theft, auto theft, armed robbery, and murder. Some were heavily fined again and again, more than ten times.

Serious and Drugs and Alcohol as Adults
The last group to which we refer includes seven who, as adults, had police contacts involving alcohol and drugs. All were from inner city or transitional neighborhoods, only one was female and she had the longest record of any female in the study. Although their array of offenses was very heterogeneous, all except one had robbery or burglary as their most serious juvenile offenses, along with theft. They were involved in burglary, robbery, assault, and theft as adults and all had contacts with the police indicating that substance involvement of one kind or another played a part in their lives, even though it could not be said that their non-substance offenses were a function of substance involvement. This is an important difference if a war on drugs is believed to reap great benefits in crime reduction.

Here, again, these people were basically all-around street offenders and had become involved with drugs and alcohol in the sub-society of which they were a part. All were well known to the police and the county probation system before they had a police contact for alcohol or drug involvement. All had been fined, most of them repeatedly. As juveniles they had also been status offenders (runaways and truants) and as adults most of them had been disorderly, in fights at home, in the street, or in the taverns. Most had been in jail, in the juvenile training school, in the reformatory, and some ended up in the Wisconsin State Prison.

It is the continuity in their careers, regardless of what had been done by the justice system, which gives the impression that alcohol and drugs were a catalyst. The fact that their careers were in full bloom before their recorded police contacts for involvement in alcohol and drug offenses is good reason to question drug involvement as an easy explanation of their criminal careers.

Serious Offenders with Substance Involvement as Juveniles

Non-Serious as Adults
There were fewer cohort members in this group but there were seven who had five or more contacts before 18 including at least one involving alcohol. They enable us to consider alcohol's role in increasing career seriousness and continuation. They had from one to four contacts with the exclusions mentioned and no further alcohol or drug contacts; 71.4 percent were from the inner-city or transitional neighborhoods. All had been in the burglary, robbery, theft, or assault type as juveniles and/or adults, all but one had offenses at the felony level as juveniles, all had been referred, and half had extensive probation with some institutionalization. This group was not systematically more serious nor dealt with more severely than were persons with similar records who did not have early involvement with alcohol.

Serious and Alcohol as Adults
The last group consisted of nine who had five or more police contacts including those involving alcohol before and after age 18. This is the first group with continuity from the juvenile to the adult period in what might be called disruptive behavior involving alcohol. Two-thirds of this group were from inner-city or transitional neighborhoods and all but one was male. Four had been involved in armed robberies as juveniles and had, as juveniles and/or adults, also been involved in various kinds of theft and burglary. All had at least one offense involving liquor as juveniles but this was not their major reason for trouble except in two cases and, of these, only one also had liquor offenses as a major part of his difficulty as an adult.

Most of this group were involved in ordinary street crimes as both juveniles and adults with an inordinate number of contacts for disorderly conduct. Most had been on probation, some quite frequently, and only one had never been sanctioned. Sanctions ranged from probation and fines (one person had been fined 18 times) to sentences in the Wisconsin State Prison. Two-thirds continued their misbehavior into the 1980s.

Again, inspection of their offender careers as arranged chronologically provided little evidence that alcohol played a causal role and in only a few cases did it appear that it had a catalytic effect. In one case the person had 19 police contacts, of which five were for burglary, five for auto theft, and one for robbery before a contact at age 15 involving liquor. Throughout this person's career (including 23 Part I offenses and 15 disorderly conducts) he had four contacts for liquor, two of which were driving while intoxicated. Among his sentences were one for 40 months in the Wisconsin State Prison.

A similar person had his first contact involving liquor at age 16, having previously been on probation and then in the reformatory for burglary and robbery. Another member of the cohort was in trouble almost every year from age 10 to 33, 18 of his police contacts for disorderly conduct but only three in which liquor was given as the reason. Yet he received 18 fines and days in jail as well.

Another person with a career of similar length, age 11 to 31, had 25 police contacts for disorderly conduct. Still another had been sentenced to four years in the Wisconsin State Prison for theft and burglary at 19, again for eight years for robbery at 24, at 31 to two years and six months for robbery, and ultimately had 28 police contacts for Part I offenses. His lengthy career commencing at age 12 was marked with status offenses interspersed with Part I offenses such as theft, robbery, auto theft, and burglary, but the record showed only one liquor offense before 18. Considering the chronology of events in their lives, without more complete information about their involvement with alcohol, it would still be difficult to say that alcohol played a causal role in the careers of persons in the group.

CONTINUITY AMONG MALES FROM INNER-CITY AND TRANSITIONAL NEIGHBORHOODS

The inner city and transitional neighborhood males with continuous residence to 1988 are shown in Diagram 4. A similar diagram for males from other neighborhoods is not included but compares with Diagram 4 as follows. To begin, while 77 males (Diagram 4), 28.0 percent of all of those with inner city and transitional residence as juveniles, were in the No Contact category as juveniles and adults, 239 (54.4 percent) of those from other neighborhoods were in that category. Thirty-eight males (13.8 percent) of those socialized in the inner-city and transitional area had serious careers as juveniles and adults but there were only seven (1.6 percent) similar males from other neighborhoods. Also note that 32 males from the inner city and transitional area who did not have serious careers as juveniles did have serious careers as adults, only a small proportion (14.6 percent) of the 219 (187 + 32) who did not have serious careers as juveniles. Among those from other areas there were 18 males (4.3 percent) and an even smaller proportion who had serious careers as adults but not as juveniles.

In sum, the probability of a serious career as a juvenile or an adult or both is related to neighborhood of residence. More than that, juvenile behavior is a better predictor of adult behavior in non-inner-city/transitional areas for those who were well behaved as juveniles than it was for those well-behaved juveniles who were socialized in the inner city and transitional areas. Even then, most juveniles who stay out of trouble as juveniles will continue to do so regardless of their neighborhood.

Serious juvenile misbehavior, however, is a better predictor of continuity to serious adult misbehavior in the inner city and transitional neighborhoods than in other neighborhoods. Thirty-eight of 56 inner city males, that is, 67.9 percent of those who were in the serious offender category as juveniles, continued as serious offenders as adults. In other neighborhoods only seven of 19 (36.8 percent) of the serious offenders continued to serious adult crime.

Seventy-three percent of these cohort members from the inner city and transitional areas who had serious juvenile careers but no recorded substance involvement continued to serious adult careers but only 11.1 percent of those from other neighborhoods did so. There were few cohort members in some cells, but it is apparent that substance involvement for serious juvenile offenders has about the same relationship to continuity, whether causal or not, for those males who were socialized in the inner city and transitional neighborhoods as it does for those socialized in other neighborhoods. In short, 'good' kids from both kinds of areas are likely to stay good, although inner city kids are less likely to do so. 'Bad' kids

Diagram 4.
Distribution of 1955 Cohort Males With Inner City or Transitional Neighborhood Residence by Juvenile/Adult, Alcohol/Drug, and Frequency of Offense Status According to Official Records to 1988

Offense/Behavior Type JUVENILE (6-17)	ADULT (18 AND OLDER)			SERIOUS CONTINUITY AFTER AGE 18		TOTAL
	No Contacts	1-4 Contacts No Alcohol/Drugs	1-4 Contacts Alcohol and/or Drugs	5 or More Contacts No Drugs/Alcohol	5 or More Contacts Alcohol and/or Drugs +	
No Contacts	87 / 77 / 1.1	80 / 22 / 3.6	91 / 16 / 5.7	91 / 7 / 13.0	20 / 2 / 10.0	369 / 124 — **7.2% SERIOUS CONTINUITY**
1-4 Contacts, No Alcohol/Drugs	94 / 25 / 3.8	133 / 21 / 6.3	107 / 12 / 8.9	165 / 9 / 18.3	185 / 13 / 14.2	684 / 80 — **27.5% SERIOUS CONTINUITY**
1-4 Contacts, Alcohol and/or Drugs	25 / 7 / 3.6	27 / 3 / 9.0	29 / 4 / 7.3	0 / 0 / ---	18 / 1 / 18.0	99 / 15 — **6.3% SERIOUS CONTINUITY**
5 or More Contacts, No Drugs/Alcohol	55 / 3 / 18.3	124 / 5 / 24.8	43 / 2 / 21.5	254 / 7 / 36.2	978 / 20 / 48.9	1454 / 37 — **73.0% SERIOUS CONTINUITY**
5 or More Contacts, Alcohol and/or Drugs	0 / 0 / ---	79 / 4 / 19.8	124 / 4 / 31.0	77 / 2 / 38.5	402 / 9 / 44.7	682 / 19 — **57.9% SERIOUS CONTINUITY**

187

Circled figures: 18   32   38

Number of Contacts
Number of Persons

Mean Contacts per Person

18 + 32 + 38 = 32.0% of Inner City Cohort Males with 79.5% of Offenses

from the inner city and interstitial areas are more likely to remain bad. 'Bad' kids from other areas are less likely to remain 'bad' unless they have been involved in alcohol and/or drugs.

SUMMARY

We have frequently referred to the possibility that drug involvement may sometimes be the catalyst for continuity in careers from the juvenile to the adult period, differing depending upon the number of police contacts that cohort members had during the juvenile period. Involvement with alcohol and drugs may increase career continuity, but being socialized in the inner city in itself produces the highest proportion of persons with officially recorded career continuity.

Alcohol and drug involvement call attention to a person and may be a catalyst because police officers believe that formal action is more appropriate in substance involved offenses or for substance involved offenders. Here again we must conclude by asking to what degree is career continuity based on justice system decisions as well as on offender behavior?

11 Summary and Conclusions

A FRAMEWORK WITHIN WHICH TO EXAMINE PATTERNS AND RATES OF DELINQUENCY AND CRIME

The first chapters in this book provided the foundation for our most recent research. Let us go back to the beginning and briefly summarize the findings and their meaning. Differences in offense rates, police contact rates, arrest rates, and incarceration rates from state to state are so large that the underlying causes of delinquency and crime are best understood within a sociological, social and structural framework.

Social and structural variables include the opportunity structure and the institutions which exist for the maintenance of order, the socialization of the young, the use of leisure time, and the problems generated in so doing. More important than most people realize is how the society is organized for the production and distribution of goods and services and the determinants of how people acquire their initial positions in society. During the process of socialization people become aware of their statuses and how to play the roles expected of them. To the extent that they have not been integrated into the larger society and absorbed into the economy they learn to behave, to play roles quite differently, and become more and more defined as a problem. Thus, delinquency and crime are problems of the larger society rather than simply character problems of the individual.

Social and structural variables differ markedly within urban areas, between urban areas, by states, within regions, and between regions. Moreover, spatial differences in delinquency and crime rates were even greater when specific offenses were considered, suggesting more surely that social and structural factors underlie these differences.

As Haapanen (1988) has summed it up,

The less deeply one is entrenched in the social network, the fewer the expectations to conform, and the less one would have to lose by 'cheating' at the social game – even by committing the unsavory,

176

and particularly unpleasant kinds of crime of primary interest to proponents of selective incapacitation. . . . The reduced social bonds serve to increase the viability of criminal behavior as one of the individual's options by giving him less reason not to take the most expedient and/or direct path to his desired ends in particular situations.

If explainable within a sociological framework, what proportion of the variation in rates and measures may be assigned to the delinquents or criminals, to the victim, to the operation of the justice system, and, of course, to the organization of society, the social system itself?

VARIATION IN DELINQUENCY AND CRIME RATES

Perhaps startling to some who have a complex theoretical rationale for variation and fluctuation in crime rates was the fact that seasonal fluctuations from January to July of each year were greater than the variation from the same month in 1969 to the same month in 1979. This type of fluctuation, just as other types of fluctuations that may be related to exogenous variables, argues for social and structural rather than individual-oriented explanations of delinquency and crime. It is not the temperature in itself but patterns of time use and behavior that have been generated in a society that has developed in an area with marked climatic changes.

The Racine cohort data, its time series data, and data for the United States make it apparent that changing rates and patterns (the incidence and prevalence) of delinquency and crime are products of human interaction within the social and physical environment, varying by sex, place of residence, age, cohort, and time period. It is the social components of sex and age, as well as residence, cohort, and time period, including those related to the opportunity structure, that determine rates and patterns of delinquency and crime.

When samples of the population of the United States were interviewed during the late 1980s, it was apparent that while delinquency and crime and alcohol and drugs were considered serious problems, there was little agreement on how to deal with them. Members of professional organizations have never agreed, nor have our highest-ranking elected officials and representatives, and much less the multitude of minor functionaries who profess to be involved in the war against delinquency, crime, alcohol, drugs, and tobacco, on how to ameliorate whatever is defined at the moment as a pressing social problem. Many have firm opinions, often untouched by scientific evidence.

Reducing the supply of drugs coming into the United States has been and remains a favorite approach by some politicians of both major political parties. Many scholars (for example, Moore, 1990) and other knowledgeable people, some in American and European governments, and as recently as 1997 the US General Accounting Office, have concluded that supply reduction efforts have been a failure.

THE ECOLOGY OF DELINQUENCY AND CRIME

Changes and fluctuations in Racine's delinquency and crime rates in spatially delineated areas provided the evidence of how delinquency and crime are tied to the social organization of the Racine community. During the period from 1950 to 1980 the inner city, interstitial, and transitional police grids declined from having *circa* 50 percent of Racine's population to 20 percent but its proportion of the Part I offenses known to the police showed very little change. Similarly, while peripheral, middle, and upper SES areas increased from *circa* 6 percent to 28 percent of Racine's population, their share of the Part I offenses rose very little.

Maps, diagrams, and tables strengthened the social and structural explanations of the genesis and continuity of delinquency and crime, suggesting once again that programs for amelioration of the problem must rest on a causal framework that has its roots in an understanding of the nature and organization of society.

THE EFFECTIVENESS OF THE JUSTICE SYSTEM

Examination of a number of official data sets on state expenditures and measures of crime, arrests, and incarcerations provided little evidence of a straightforward relationship between remedial efforts and measures of delinquency/crime. The idea that spending more produces less crime, that spending means deterrence or effective control, may be an incorrect assumption at the outset. It is interesting that many politicians and their constituents have decided that we have thrown money at social problems, for example, programs targeting the poor without success, but are sure that we must spend more on law enforcement and prisons as a solution to the delinquency/crime problem. Will Sherman and Gottfredson's (1997) *Preventing Crime: What Works, What Doesn't, What's Promising*, a lengthy report mandated by the United States Congress and commissioned by the Department of Justice's National Institute of Justice, be carefully read by people high in government and have an impact on decision-making? This is another example of how personal convictions, however unsupported by scientific evidence, may have greater weight in policy formation than a scientific review of existing research.

More specifically, our Racine research found no evidence that sanctions were effective as applied to males. In fact, the more severe the sanctions, the more serious was the misbehavior of males in the period following. For females, half responded to sanctions by increasing seriousness of their behavior and half did not. At every turn we met with evidence of the complexity of the problem and the futility of expecting an easy answer.

THE PREDICTION PROBLEM

Numerous measures of juvenile careers did not greatly reduce the number of errors in predicting what adult careers would be like beyond what could be achieved from the modal category of the adult marginals. It became apparent that prediction suffers from either lack of theory or from theory that directs researchers to variables that account for only a modest proportion of the variance in rates of delinquency and crime.

Analyses which revealed that race/ethnicity, sex, and place of socialization produced different patterns of relationships between delinquency/crime and other variables descriptive of cohort members (associations, education, attitudes toward social institutions, employment experiences, access to automobiles) explained in part why efforts to predict for the entire juvenile population rather than for separate segments have produced such large negative and positive errors.

TYPES OF DELINQUENT AND CRIMINAL CAREERS

Criminologists have developed delinquent and criminal typologies, most often with data from incarcerated offenders. Some of the types in the typologies that we constructed tended to be quite heterogeneous consisting of burglars plus lesser offenses, armed robbers plus lesser offenses, and so forth. Our goal has been to develop delinquent and criminal typologies that permit assignment of the entire range of cohort members to categories from least serious to most serious offender types, from never to occasional to continuous offenders, to offender and/or offender-justice system response categories. Hopefully, this would permit determination of the extent to which transition from one behavior/justice system involvement type to another type takes place in a sufficiently orderly fashion to be predicted.

The specialization and/or offense transition hypothesis has been a contentious matter, agreement on the degree of specialization evading researchers for a variety of reasons, including disagreement on categories selected, the extent and manner in which specific offenses have been collapsed, and the validity of prison populations as representative of those who are offenders. One could argue, particularly after examining a large number of careers, that specialization in itself is not an important concern, that it is a remainder from the period when criminologists wrote interesting books about con men, burglars, bank robbers, hold-up men, and embezzlers.

THE RACINE COMPUTER-CONSTRUCTED TYPOLOGIES

Computer-constructed typologies produced offender types whose members were at the extremely serious end of the continuum and responsible for a large proportion of the Part I offenses, the felonies, or, even more specifically, such offenses as armed robbery. One of the computer-constructed typologies based on offense seriousness placed each person in each cohort in one of 23 different offender types. Eight of the most serious offender types in the 1942 Cohort contained only 5.1 percent of the cohort but this group of offenders had police contacts that accounted for 80.7 percent of all felonies for that cohort. The 1949 Cohort produced seven types of serious offenders who constituted that 4.5 percent of the cohort responsible for 74.7 percent of the felonies. Four types making up

5.0 percent of the 1955 Cohort accounted for 75.7 percent of their felonies. Adding three more types resulted in 7.4 percent of the cohort accounting for 87.2 percent of its felonies.

Other offender types were developed for the juvenile period and the adult period but in no case could adult careers be predicted from juvenile careers more efficiently than by simply using the number or seriousness of police contacts or the total severity of court sanctions. Little overall improvement in predicting adult careers was obtained when selected interview variables were added in a series of canonical analyses because most of the variables addressed in the interview schedule had effects which differed by race, sex, and place of residence. The latter is one of the most important findings from our research and is consistent with the more recent conclusions of others.

Our typologies were, whether predictive or not, descriptive devices which laid the foundation for a sociological approach to prediction. Types may represent kinds of offender records and are an advance beyond simple additive scoring systems. The inclusion of drug offenses in a large proportion of the cohort with serious offender careers or the admission of drug use by cohort members whose self-reports placed them in serious offender types suggested, but did not establish, that drugs have a catalytic effect on career continuity. The continuity in careers for offenders who were also involved with drugs may in part be a function of the increasing direction of attention to these offenders by the justice system – so, in a sense it is an indirect catalytic effect.

DRUGS, DELINQUENCY, AND CRIME AND THE ECOLOGY OF THE CITY

The focus of our narrative narrowed when we explored the relationship of drug offenses and offenders to serious street level crime, more specifically to all-around street offenders. All-around street offenders were more highly concentrated in the inner city than were other types of offenders (20.6 percent of the 1955 Cohort lived in inner-city neighborhoods that socialized 55.2 percent of the all-around street offenders as juveniles and 68.9 percent of those as adults). Drug offenders were less concentrated in the inner city. The concentration of all-around street offenders was greater among those who were continuous residents to 1988 than among those with continuous residence to 1976. Eighty percent of the remaining all-around street offenders as juveniles and 69.3 percent as adults had been socialized in eight inner city neighborhoods (65 neighborhoods total) but among those in this group in Racine back in 1976 it was only 54 percent and 56.2 percent.

Although the drug offenders with continuous residence to 1988 continued to be spread throughout the city by neighborhood of socialization, place of socialization and continued residence of drug offenders was becoming more similar to that of all-around street offenders. Recent developments in Racine indicate that drug offenses are now playing a larger role in the inner city's delinquency and crime.

Serious offenders with continuous residence to either 1976 or 1988 who resided in the inner city as juveniles and had police contacts for drug offenses as juveniles desisted less from serious offender careers than did persons socialized outside the inner city or without police contacts for drug offenses as juveniles. Could we early on have seen this as a product of inner city socialization where for many of its residents the distribution of illegal goods and services had become even more a part of that way of life and for some, drugs the newest and most available source of pleasure and wealth, but despair for others?

THE DRUG/CRIME RELATIONSHIP AND CAREER CONTINUITY

The Racine cohort research has not dealt with the mechanics of how drug involvement leads to other delinquent and criminal endeavors or how various patterns of criminal behavior lead to involvement with drugs. Drug involvement can exist independently of other delinquent and criminal behavior and the latter can exist independently of drug involvement.

The juxtaposition of police contacts for drugs and other offenses led us to conclude that, for the most part, drug contacts were preceded and followed by contacts that could be classified as low-level disruptive behavior. Since approximately two-thirds of the police contacts involving drugs were for marijuana, this bundling of low-level offenses was consistent with other research findings from metropolitan areas. There is also evidence that both (drugs and some types of crime) are generated in the same social environment.

Official offense seriousness scores of those in the 1942 and 1949

Cohorts who admitted drug involvement were at least twice as high as were those who did not admit drug involvement. Their self-reported seriousness scores were also at least twice as high for self-reported drug offenders as for non-offenders.

It is equally important to remember that 1942 and 1949 drug user types developed from self-report data with drug use admissions or other drug offenses *omitted* had official and self-report seriousness scores that were similar to those of non-drug user types. Not comparable to self-reports, of course, but by contrast, official offense seriousness scores for drug offenders from the 1955 Cohort were from two to six times higher than for non-drug offenders, depending on controls utilized for comparison.

What has happened is that the incidence of officially recorded drug offenses rose from cohort to cohort and constituted a high proportion of the 1955 Cohort's officially defined serious offenses. That almost two-thirds of the police contacts for substances involved marijuana and less than 20 percent were for heroin and cocaine suggested that drug offense involvement at this time, although a part of a large proportion of the serious offender careers of 1955 Cohort members, did not yet play an important role in career escalation or continuity of careers. Rather, as we had indicated in citations from the literature, drug involvement would be a part, particularly involvement in marijuana, in other low-level infractions against public order, much the same as liquor. In fact, there has been considerably more involvement with liquor (316 contacts) but with much the same continuity into serious adult offender careers.

Most juvenile drug offenders and/or those who were in juvenile offender types failed to turn up as adult drug offenders or in adult drug offender types. Most adult drug offenders and drug offender types had not been juvenile drug offenders or juvenile drug offender types. This suggests that official records for the Racine cohorts (the 1950s, 1960s, and 1970s period) did not provide a complete representation of the extent to which youth and adults had become involved with drugs, particularly those from neighborhoods outside the inner city. Although sanctioning tended to become more severe for juveniles after they had drug contacts, those who were drug offenders as adults had their most severe sanction before having had a drug contact.

Although users/offenders had longer official careers than did non-users/non-offenders, removal of contacts for drug-related offenses reduced the differences. No matter how the data were examined, however, those who were involved in drugs in one way or another had more involvement with the justice system than did those who were not involved with drugs. As we have said, drug use in itself increases visibility and the probability of involvement with the law.

ALCOHOL VS. DRUGS AND CAREER CONTINUITY

The Concentration of Continuity

A series of detailed tables enabled us to observe career continuity for categories of persons in the cohort based on their number of police contacts, as juveniles and as adults, and the presence or absence of alcohol and/or drug involvement among different combinations of juvenile and adult careers. Each table had 81 cells to represent the different combinations of contact frequency as juveniles and adults with or without the presence of alcohol and drug involvement. Abridged versions of several tables were presented and discussed in the last chapter.

Desistance was high among those with little juvenile involvement in delinquency and continuity was high among those with high juvenile involvement, a bit more so if involvement also included police contacts for alcohol and drug offenses. That this pattern existed when the cohort had been followed only to age 22 once again made us consider the alcohol/drug and delinquency/crime relationship as being one in which career continuity was enhanced by substance involvement, perhaps during periods of heavy substance involvement.

Although not a surprise, that small percent (−1 percent) of the expanded 1955 Cohort with substance involvement and serious juvenile and adult careers (five or more police contacts) was responsible for 9.9 percent of all police contacts by the 1955 Cohort up to 1976. When the 1357 cohort members with continuous residence to 1988 were augmented to 1441 by including those ages 13–33, the findings were similar. Dealing with these groups, while involving a disproportional share of the misbehaviors, would seem to take only a small bite out of the most serious crime because much of their total consisted of substance offenses and offenses against public order. Casting the net more widely would involve even a greater percent of the crime, of course, but fill the prisons more rapidly and at a greater cost per serious street offense prevented by incapacitation.

What is so apparent is that a small proportion of the cohort with serious delinquency had rather high continuity and that the great majority of the cohort had very little involvement with the police and little or no continuity. Furthermore, although proportionately fewer, there are as many or more who are serious offenders as adults from the non-serious groups than there are serious offenders as adults who had always been serious offenders. Essentially the same situation that we noted before with other measures and typologies is found again, too many false positives and too many false negatives.

The Offense Share of Continuers

Juvenile offenses, although they may be classified as Part I or Felonies or as both, may not be as serious as adult offenses similarly classified. Those with continuity from serious juvenile misbehavior to serious adult misbehavior, with or without alcohol and drug involvement, were responsible for a highly disproportionate share of the adult offenses. Remember that 1 percent (26 persons) of the expanded 1955 Cohort with substance involvement and five or more police contacts before 18 and five or more contacts after 18 (but not necessarily involving substances as adults) was responsible for 38.1 percent of the career police contacts by persons who had *five or more contacts after age 18 and before 23*, a period of considerable activity for the cohort.

When we cast the net a bit wider to include those who had five or more police contacts before 18 and five or more police contacts after 18 (without regard to substance involvement), we netted 2.1 percent of the cohort (57 persons) with 28.6 percent of the cohort's police contacts. They also constituted 59.3 percent of the 96 serious adult offenders and were responsible for 81.2 percent of the career offenses of the serious adult offenders. Remember, this is only 57 out of 2658, 1955 Cohort members.

The 1955 Cohort's 1357 members, as extended to 1988, produced 113 serious adult offenders, 51 (45.1 percent) of whom were serious juvenile and adult offenders. This 3.7 percent of the cohort was responsible for 34.3 percent of the cohort's offenses and 69.3 percent of the career offenses of the serious adult offenders. Thus, a small group of juveniles who were serious offenders as juveniles and adults committed a highly disproportionate share of the cohort's offenses and the career offenses of adult offenders. But again, this is an after-the-fact finding; 55 percent of the serious adult offenders did not have a serious juvenile career. We could not have predicted their adult careers from their juvenile careers.

While it was still necessary to maintain a critical stance in terms of increasing predictive efficiency, dichotomizing juvenile and adult careers at fewer than five police contacts or five or more did reveal that serious juvenile careers (as represented by number of police contacts for behaviors other than traffic offenses, status offenses, or suspicion, investigation, or information) identified those who would be responsible for a large proportion of the police contacts by adults.

Delineating Continuity

Continuity from the juvenile period to the adult period in serious offender careers was consistently found as we moved from the 2658 members of the 1955 Cohort with continuous residence to 1976 to those who had continuity to 1988, whether it be the 1357, 1955 Cohort members with continuous residence to 1988 or the augmented group of 1441 with a later entry point giving them continuous residence from age 13 to age 33. Although continuity from the serious offender type as a juvenile to the serious offender type as an adult was increased somewhat more for those who also had at least one drug involvement, the proportion with continuity was similar to that of those who were serious offenders but who did not have substance involvement and still less than that for those with a police contact involving alcohol.

We could continue the summary of findings in more detail but the essence is that five or more contacts as juveniles delineated a group of serious offenders with almost as much continuity to adult seriousness as did the same number with substance involvement added.

CONCLUSION

The 1955 Cohort, the first drug cohort, reveals that the role of drugs had been on the rise for some time before the 1980s when drug-related homicides were becoming a visible product of inner city life. What we saw was some serious criminal career continuity after the juvenile period as a fixture of inner city life that could readily be transformed into a somewhat higher degree of visible continuity by adding drug/alcohol involvement in everyday life.

When substance involvement becomes a part of everyday life it becomes as difficult to eliminate as does the business martini, late afternoon scotch and water, or pre-dinner cocktail. Perhaps it is even more difficult because while those who reside outside the inner city have a multitude of exciting diversions, drugs may be one of the most important organizing principles in the lives of those who dwell within the inner city. It is their patterns of substance use, and other types of misbehavior, which disturb the middle class and tend to make them highly visible, particularly if they are also involved in patterns of delinquency and crime that include the production and distribution of drugs. Drug use alone, although a felony or misdemeanor depending on each state's criminal code, came to be considered a disease, chemical dependency, but only later when it spread to youth, and then adults, outside the inner city and transitional areas. Now that Iowa is one of the gambling capitals of the US it is not surprising that addiction to it is a 'disease.'

The numerous analyses presented and our discussion of the delinquency/crime and alcohol/drug problem may imply that drug and alcohol involvement are closely related to career continuity, or at least to have been a catalyst for continuity. For some cohort members this may have been the case. Observation of the records of numerous serious career offenders from the 1955 Cohort still does not enable us to specify exactly how it may have been the catalyst for continuity or greater continuity than that already generated by other patterns of misbehavior and illegal activity. Even when those whose police contacts include problems with liquor and/or drugs, and there is some indication that substances played the catalytic role that we have suggested, this is not the same as saying that substance use causes delinquency and crime or the opposite. The fact is that substance involvement is defined as delinquency and crime and that in itself may be a major part of the problem, just as was the illegality of liquor – but that was a long time ago.

While we do not subscribe to shoebox sociology (clippings from newspapers), it may be well to conclude with several excerpts, first from *The Des Moines Register* (December 13, 1994) and then from *The New York Times* (December 13, 1994) which illustrate both the suburban and inner city urban phenomena which so often call the problem to public attention. Then we shall ask you some crucial questions, the answers to which you should have now acquired from this small book.

Urbandale is a middle- to upper-class bedroom city adjacent to Des Moines, Iowa.

> After determining residents of two Urbandale houses were away, burglars cleaned them out, stealing furniture, cars, even a 32-inch TV set. . . .
>
> A caller ID box, a big-screen TV, an answering machine, jewelry, and a long list of other items were stolen.
>
> A car was taken from the C—— home, too.
>
> David C—— said the burglars emptied every drawer in the house onto the floors and put cigarettes out on the carpets. . . .
>
> At the S—— residence the burglars apparently used a four-wheel-drive vehicle to back up her driveway. Police found no slippage in the unplowed driveway, despite the fact that it is on an incline. Included in the booty from her residence was a love-seat and an oversized chair. . . .

How do burglars learn the skills of the trade? Is their school the tavern with postgraduate study in the state prison? Do not take their rudeness in putting out cigarettes on the carpet as evidence of a social deficit which explains their criminal behavior. How many of us have seen university professors and other supposedly properly socialized persons do the same thing? The author did not purchase white carpeting for the living room until he had passed the cocktail circuit period in life.

Would you recognize these burglars (women do not become involved in crimes of this nature very often so that narrows it down a bit) as criminals if you met them in the neighborhood tavern or kneeling in their local parish church?

Let us once again turn to the inner city of metropolis. *The New York Times* story is titled 'Crack's Legacy of Guns and Death Lives on.' As you read this, think about the alternatives that are available and the one that you might have selected if you had been in Jovan's shoes.

> On a spring morning four years ago in a dead-end neighborhood in Chicago, it was Jovan Roger's turn to sell a little bag of crack that, added to the bags that he figured were sure to follow, would buy him gym shoes and girlfriends and maybe keep the electric company from turning off the lights at his mother's apartment again. . . .
>
> He was too young to work at McDonald's. And anyway, in his

neighborhood, the biggest employer is the drug business, which pays him more in a day than flipping hamburgers would in a month. . . .

Jovan soon found that he had more than just the police to worry about. With crack came violence. And before he was finally arrested for drug dealing and put on probation in 1992, he had lost a half-dozen friends in gunfire, witnessed executions and fired on rival gang members in turf wars. In his business, it was understood that there would be casualties.

Violence caught up with Jovan when he was shot in an early morning rampage by rival gang members two years ago when he was barely 17. After that, he never left home without his .38. Without it, 'you feel empty, bare, naked,' he said, 'because you ain't got your friend with you.'

Teen-agers who might have otherwise stuck to hustling or shoplifting suddenly had a shot at the big time. As kingpins and upstarts competed for prime locations, disputes were settled with violence. With more guns on the street, homicides skyrocketed.

Ask Jovan Rogers why he got into the drug business and he will tell you about the three younger sisters he has to take care of, about his mother, an on-again, off-again welfare recipient who gave birth to him at 14 and had trouble making ends meet, about her boyfriend who went to prison for selling drugs, about the family refrigerator that did not have enough food in it, and an apartment with no electricity because his mother lacked money to pay the light bill.

'You feel sorry,' Jovan said of the times his mother had asked him to help. 'If there's nothing to eat at night, who's going to go buy something to make sure something is there? I was the only man in the house and they had to eat. They knew I was out there hustling for us.'

Ask him about crack, and he will also tell you about the seductive idea of being somebody when you have nothing. 'If you sell drugs, you had anything you wanted. Any girl, any friend, money, status. If you didn't, you got no girlfriend, no friends, no money. You're a nothing. . . .'

Over time, Jovan got used to the job, became good at it and started selling drugs himself, independently of the gang. He learned that all he had to do was to stand at his spot, and grown-ups in the neighborhood would flock to him for a 20-minute high. Mothers would bring their children with them, offering food stamps for crack. Men, who in another day and place would tell boys like him to go inside and behave themselves, would give him their cars as collateral for a few bags of crack. . . .

Jovan was a retailer, not a drug lord. He was never one of the wildly successful ones who had lines outside a crack house of his own, pulling in hundreds of thousands of dollars a week. But crack did to him what it had to thousands of inner city boys. It transported him into the violent orbit of gangs and guns. . . .

Does this account seem all too familiar to those who have their metropolitan newspaper on the doorstep every morning and to those who, although not in metropoles, read the daily metropolitan newspapers – or, for that matter, view these as real and/or manufactured life stories on their television?

Would you respond that a low IQ, a genetic defect, a 'tortured' mind lies behind these behaviors and thus categorize it as a medical problem? Who should you call, the doctor, the psychiatrist, the precinct captain – or your Congressman, your Senator, or the President? And what should you tell them?

I would tell those persons in positions of power and authority in the justice system, and in the political system as well, that I am aware of the violent and horrifying consequences of addictive drug use, cocaine and its derivatives, crack and crank (methamphetamine), and do not condone their use. I would also tell those who believe that a war on drugs is tantamount to a war on delinquency and crime that they should seriously consider the findings that have been generated by the last 30 years of sociological and other empirical research on the subject. They should consider the complexities of our findings and others' as they plan and expound upon how they will spend other people's money, that is, the taxpayers' dollars.

Before they decide what to do about the problems of alcohol and drugs, delinquency and crime, they should examine the research that at least gives a clue to how these behaviors are generated in segments of society where people are excluded from the larger society and segments where people are seemingly a part of the great society. Effort should then be exerted in more creative ways that will bring a greater proportion of the population into the activities of the larger society and also modify their behavior.

Dealing with those who are a part of the great society but still can become involved in all manner of disapproved behavior is a different matter. The latter may involve working with smaller groups of individuals while changing those who are not a part of the larger society may call for programs which involve major changes in the organization of society. The integration of inner-city residents will not be an easy task considering the many years that we have neglected the hardening of the inner city. This among other things may well involve a complete revision of our 'war on drugs' and its wasted billions, as argued by Tonry (1995), let alone the havoc that the war has dealt to the poorest of the poor in the inner city. Last of all, but just as important, remember that programs for amelioration of problem behavior should target those who are outside the larger community rather than be a vehicle for further upward mobility by those who have already made it.

Bibliography

Altschuler, David M. and Paul J. Brounstein, 'Patterns of Drug Use, Drug Trafficking, and Other Delinquency among Inner-City Adolescent Males in Washington, D.C.,' *Criminology*, 29(4), November 1991, pp. 589–622.

Anglin, M. Douglas and George Speckart, 'Narcotics Use, Property Crime, and Dealing: Structural Dynamics Across the Addiction Career,' *Journal of Quantitative Criminology*, 2(4), December 1986, pp. 355–75.

Ball, John C., John W. Shaffer, and David R. Nurco, 'The Day-to-Day Criminality of Heroin Addicts in Baltimore: A Study in the Continuity of Offense Rates,' *Drug and Alcohol Dependence*, 12(1), 1983, pp. 19–142.

Becker, Howard, S., 'FOI POR ACASO: Conceptualizing Coincidence,' *The Sociological Quarterly*, 35(2), May 1994, pp. 183–94.

Blumstein, Alfred and Jacqueline Cohen, 'Estimating Individual Crime Rates from Arrest Records,' *Journal of Criminal Law and Criminology*, 70(4), Winter 1979.

Blumstein, Alfred and Jacqueline Cohen, 'Characterizing Criminal Careers,' *Science*, 237(4818), 1987, pp. 985–91.

Brennan, Tim, *Multivariate Taxonomical Classification for Criminal Justice Research*, 1980. Final Report to the National Institute of Justice, Office of Research Evaluation Methods, Project No. 78-NI-AX-0065.

Brownfield, David and Ann Marie Sorenson, 'A Latent Structure Analysis of Delinquency,' *Journal of Quantitative Criminology*, 3(2), June 1987, pp. 103–24.

Bureau of Justice Statistics, *National Update*, US Department of Justice, 2(1), July 1992.

Bureau of Justice Statistics, *Drugs, Crime and the Justice System*, US Department of Justice, December 1992.

Bursik, Robert J. Jr., 'Urban Dynamics and Ecological Studies of Delinquency,' *Social Forces*, Vol. 63, 1984, pp. 393–413.

Bursik, Robert J. Jr., 'Ecological Stability and the Dynamics of Delinquency,' in Albert J. Reiss, Jr. and Michael Tonry (eds.), *Communities and Crime* (Chicago: The University of Chicago Press), 1986a, pp. 35–66.

Bursik, Robert J. Jr., 'Delinquency Rates as Sources of Ecological Change,' in James M. Byrne and Robert J. Sampson (eds.), *The Social Ecology of Crime* (New York: Springer-Verlag), 1986b, pp. 63–74.

Bursik, Robert J. Jr., 'Social Disorganization and Theories of Crime and Delinquency: Problems and Prospects,' *Criminology*, 26(4), November 1988, pp. 519–32.

Bursik, Robert J. Jr., 'Political Decision-Making and Ecological Models of Delinquency: Conflict and Consensus,' in Steven F. Messner, Marvin D. Krohn and Allen E. Liska (eds.), *Theoretical Integration in the Study of Deviance and Crime* (Albany: State University of New York Press), 1989.

Bursik, Robert J. Jr. and Harold G. Grasmick, 'Longitudinal Neighborhood Profiles in Delinquency: The Decomposition of Change,' *Journal of Quantitative Criminology*, 8(3), September 1992, pp. 247–63.

Bursik, Robert J. Jr. and Harold G. Grasmick, *Neighborhoods and Crime: The Dimensions of Effective Community Control* (New York: Lexington Books), 1993.

Bursik, Robert J. Jr. and Jim Webb, 'Community Change and Patterns of Delinquency,' *American Journal of Sociology*, Vol. 88, 1982, pp. 24–42.

Burton, Velmer S., Francis T. Cullen, T. David Evans, and R. Gregory Dunaway, 'Reconsidering Strain Theory: Operationalization, Rival Theories, and Adult Criminality,' *Journal of Quantitative Criminology*, 3(10), September 1994, pp. 213–39.

Cappell, Charles L. and Gresham Sykes, 'Prison Commitments, Crime and Unemployment: A Theoretical and Empirical Specification for the U.S., 1933–85,' *Journal of Quantitative Criminology*, 7(2), June 1991, pp. 155–99.

Cernkovich, Stephen A. and Peggy C. Giordano, 'School Bonding, Race, and Delinquency,' *Criminology*, 30(2), May 1992, pp. 261–91.

Chaiken, Jan M. and Marcia R. Chaiken, *Varieties of Criminal Behavior: Summary and Policy Implications*. Prepared for the National Institute of Justice (Santa Monica, California: Rand), August 1982.

Chaiken, Jan M. and Marcia R. Chaiken, 'Drugs and Predatory Crime,' in Michael A. Tonry and James Q. Wilson (eds.), *Drugs and Crime – Crime and Drugs: Review of Research*, Vol. 13 (Chicago: The University of Chicago Press), 1990, pp. 203–39.

Chaiken, Marcia and Jan M. Chaiken, 'Offender Types and Public Policy,' *Crime and Delinquency*, Vol. 30, 1984, pp. 195–225.

Chaiken, Marcia and Jan M. Chaiken, 'Priority Prosecution of High-Rate Dangerous Offenders,' *Research in Action*, National Institute of Justice, March 1991.

Chilton, Roland, 'Twenty Years of Homicide and Robbery in Chicago: The Impact of the City's Changing Racial and Age Composition,' *Journal of Quantitative Criminology*, 3(3), September 1987, pp. 195–214.

Cloward, Richard A. and Lloyd Ohlin, *Delinquency and Opportunity* (New York: The Free Press), 1960.

Cohen, Jacqueline, 'Research in Criminal Careers: Individual Frequency Rates and Offense Seriousness,' Appendix B in Alfred Blumstein, Jacqueline Cohen, Jeffrey Roth, and Christy Visher (eds.), *Criminal Careers and 'Career Criminals'*, Vol. 1 (Washington: National Academy Press), 1986, pp. 292–418.

Cohen, Lawrence E., 'Throwing Down the Gauntlet: A Challenge to the Relevance of Sociology for the Etiology of Criminal Behavior,' a preview essay of *Crime and Human Nature* by James Q. Wilson and Richard J. Herrnstein (eds.), *Contemporary Sociology*, 16(2), 1987, pp. 202–5.

Copas, John B. and Roger Tarling, 'Some Methodological Issues in Making Predictions,' in Alfred Blumstein, Jacqueline Cohen, Jeffrey Roth, and Christy Visher (eds.), *Criminal Careers and 'Career Criminals,'* Vol. II (Washington: National Academy Press), 1986, pp. 291– 313.

Currie, Elliott, *Confronting Crime: An American Challenge* (New York: Pantheon Books), 1985.

Currie, Elliott, *Reckoning: Drugs, the Cities and the American Future* (New York: Hill and Wang), 1993.

Daily Iowan, The, September 4, 1992, p. 1.

Denton, Nancy A. and Douglas S. Massey, 'Patterns of Neighborhood Transition in a Multiethnic World: U.S. Metropolitan Areas,' *Demography*, 28(1), February 1991, pp. 41–63.

Des Moines Register, The, April 9, 1990, pp. 1A and 10A.

Des Moines Register, The, April 26, 1990, p. 2A.

Des Moines Register, The, October 8, 1991, pp. 1A and 3A.

Des Moines Register, The, December 13, 1994.

Des Moines Register, The, April 16, 1997, p. 5M.

Drug Policy Letter, The, Drug Policy Foundation, The (Washington, D.C.), July/August 1994.

Elliott, Delbert S. *et al.*, *The Prevalence and Incidence of Delinquent Behavior: 1976–1980*, National Youth Survey Report No. 27 (Boulder, CO: Behavioral Research Institute), 1983.

Elliott, Delbert S. and David H. Huizinga, *The Relationship between Delinquent Behavior and ADM Problems* (Boulder, CO: Behavioral Research Institute), 1984.

Elliott, Delbert S., David H. Huizinga, and Suzanne S. Ageton, *Explaining Delinquency and Drug Use* (Beverly Hills, CA: Sage), 1985.

Elliott, Delbert and Harwin L. Voss, *Delinquency and Dropout* (Lexington, MA: D.C. Heath), 1974.

Fabricant, Michael, *Deinstitutionalizing Delinquent Youth* (Cambridge, MA: Schenkman Publishing Co.), 1980.

Farrington, David P., 'Advancing Knowledge About Delinquency and Crime: The Need for a Coordinated Program of Longitudinal Research,' *Behavioral Sciences and the Law*, 6(3), 1988, pp. 307–31.

Farrington, David P., 'Long-term Prediction of Offending and Other Life Outcomes,' in Herman Wegener, Friedrich Losel, and Jochen Haisch (eds.), *Criminal Behavior and the Justice System: Psychological Perspectives* (New York: Springer-Verlag), 1989.

Farrington, David P., Robert J. Sampson, and Per-Olaf Wikstrom, *Integrating Individual and Ecological Aspects of Crime* (Stockholm, Sweden: National Council for Crime Prevention), 1993.

Farrington, D. P. and D. J. West, *The Cambridge Study in Delinquent Development*, Institute of Criminology (Cambridge: University of Cambridge), 1977.

Felson, Marcus and Lawrence E. Cohen, 'Human Ecology and Crime: A Routine Activities Approach,' *Human Ecology*, Vol. 8, 1980, pp. 309–406.

Gibbons, Don C., 'Offender Typologies – Two Decades Later,' *British Journal of Criminology*, 13(2), April 1975, pp. 140–56.

Gibbs, Jack P., 'Review Essay of Crime and Human Nature by James Q. Wilson and Richard J. Hernstein,' *Criminology*, 23(2), May 1985, pp. 381–8.

Glueck, Eleanor T., 'Efforts to Identify Delinquents,' *Federal Probation*, 24(2), 1960, pp. 49–56.

Glueck, Sheldon, 'Ten Years of Unraveling Juvenile Delinquency,' *Journal of Criminal Law, Criminology and Police Science*, Vol. 51, 1960, pp. 301–7.

Glueck, Sheldon and Eleanor Glueck, *Unraveling Juvenile Delinquency* (Cambridge, MA: Harvard University Press), 1950.

Gottfredson, Don M., 'Assessment and Prediction Methods in Crime and Delinquency,' in James F. Teele (ed.), *Juvenile Delinquency* (Itasca, Illinois: F. E. Peacock), 1970, pp. 401–24.

Gottfredson, Don M. and Michael Tonry (eds.), *Prediction and Classification: Criminal Justice Decision Making* (Chicago: The University of Chicago Press), 1987.

Gottfredson, Steven D. and Don M. Gottfredson, 'Behavioral Prediction and the Problem of Incapacitation,' *Criminology*, 32(3), August 1994, pp. 441–74.

Graham, Mary, 'Controlling Drug Abuse and Crime: A Research Update,' *Drugs and Crime*, National Institute of Justice Reports, March/April 1987, pp. 2–4.

Greenwood, Peter W. and Allan Abrahamse, *Selective Incapacitation*. Prepared for the National Institute of Justice (Santa Monica, California: Rand), August 1982.

Gurule, Jimmy, 'OJP Initiative on Gangs: Drugs and Violence in America,' *National Institute of Justice Report*, June 1991, pp. 4–5.

Haapanen, Rudy A., *Selective Incapacitation and the Serious Offender: A Longitudinal Study of Criminal Career Patterns*, Department of Youth Authority, State of California, 1988.

Haapanen, Rudy A., Kathy Houstin-Hencken, and Mary Duncan, *Patterns of Violent Crime: A Longitudinal Investigation*, Department of Youth Authority, State of California, 1991.

Harlow, Carolina Wolf, *Drugs and Jail Inmates, 1989: Special Report*, Bureau of Justice Statistics, 1989.

Harris, Philip W. and Peter R. Jones, 'Differentiating Delinquent Youths for Program Planning and Evaluation.' Paper presented at the Annual Meetings of the American Society of Criminology, Chicago, Illinois, November 12, 1996.

Hebert, Eugene E., III and Joyce A. O'Neil, 'Drug Use Forecasting: An Insight Into Arrestee Drug Use,' *Research in Action*, National Institute of Justice, No. 224, June 1991.

Hirschi, Travis and Hanan C. Selvin, *Delinquency Research: An Appraisal of Analytic Methods* (New York: The Free Press), 1967.

Hoyt, Homer, *The Structure and Growth of Residential Neighborhoods in American Cities* (Washington: Federal Housing Administration), 1939.

Huizinga, David and Delbert S. Elliott, 'Reassessing the Reliability and Validity of Self-Report Delinquency Measures,' *Journal of Quantitative Criminology*, 2(4), November 1986, pp. 293–327.

Hunt, Dana E., 'Drugs and Consensual Crime: Drug Dealing and Prostitution,' in Michael A. Tonry and James Q. Wilson (eds.), *Drugs and Crime – Crime and Justice*, Vol. 13 (Chicago: The University of Chicago Press), 1990, pp. 159–202.

Innes, Christopher, 'State Prison Inmate Survey, 1986: Drug Use and Crime,' *Special Report*, Bureau of Justice Statistics, July 1988.

Iowa City Press Citizen, The, December 4, 1991, p. 1C.

Iowa City Press Citizen, The, December 24, 1991, p. 1C.

Johnson, Bruce D., Terry Williams, Kojo A. Dei, and Harry Sanabria,

'Drug Abuse in the Inner City: Impact on Hard-Drug Users in the Community,' in Michael A. Tonry and James Q. Wilson (eds.), *Drugs and Crime – Crime and Justice: Review of Research*, Vol. 13 (Chicago: The University of Chicago Press), 1990, pp. 9–67.

Johnson, Bruce D. and Eric D. Wish, 'The Robbery-Hard Drug Connection: Do Robbers and Robberies Influence Criminal Returns and Cocaine Heroin Purchase?' Paper presented in Criminology Section of the American Sociological Association, Chicago, 1987.

Johnson, Richard E., Anastasios C. Marcos, and Stephen J. Bahr, 'The Role of Peers in the Complex Etiology of Adolescent Drug Use,' *Criminology*, 25(2), May 1986, pp. 323–40.

Journal Times, The, February 1–4, 1989.

Journal Times, The, July 29, 1991, p. 2A.

Journal Times, The, February 13, 1992, pp. 1–2.

Kandel, D., O. Simcha-Fagan, and M. Davies, 'Risk Factors for Delinquency and Illicit Drug Use from Adolescence to Young Adulthood,' *Journal of Drug Issues*, 16(1), 1986.

Kaplan, Howard B., Steven S. Martin, and Cynthia Robbins, 'Pathways in Adolescent Drug Use: Self-Derogation, Peer Influence, Weakening of Social Control, and Early Substance Use,' *Journal of Health and Social Behavior*, Vol. 25, 1984, pp. 270–89.

Kaplan, Howard B., Steven S. Martin, and Cynthia Robbins, 'Toward an Explanation of Increased Involvement in Illicit Drug Use: Application of a General Theory of Deviant Behavior,' *Research in Community and Mental Health*, Vol. 5, 1985, pp. 205–52.

Kaplan, Howard B., Cynthia Robbins, and Steven S. Martin, 'Toward the Testing of a General Theory of Deviant Behavior in Longitudinal Perspectives: Patterns of Psychopathology,' *Research in Community and Mental Health*, Vol. 3, 1983, pp. 27–65.

Kasarda, John D., 'Inner City Concentrated Poverty and Neighborhood Distress: 1970 to 1990,' *Housing Policy Debate*, 4(3), 1993, pp. 253–67.

Klein, Malcolm W., Cheryl L. Maxson, and Lea C. Cunningham, '"Crack," Street Gangs, and Violence,' *Criminology*, 29(4), November 1991, pp. 623–50.

Lab, Steven P. and Roy B. Allen, 'Self-Report and Official Measures: A Further Examination of the Validity Issues,' *Journal of Criminal Justice*, Vol. 12, 1984, pp. 445–55.

Lottier, Stuart, 'Distribution of Criminal Offenses in Sectional Regions,' *Journal of Criminal Law and Criminology*, 29(3), 1938 pp. 329–44.

Lyman, Michael D., *Gangland: Drug Trafficking by Organized Criminals* (Springfield, IL: Charles C. Thomas, Publisher), 1989.

Maguire, Kathleen and Timothy J. Flanagan (eds.), *Sourcebook of Criminal Justice Statistics – 1987*, Bureau of Justice Statistics, 1988.

Maguire, Kathleen and Timothy J. Flanagan (eds.), *Sourcebook of Criminal Justice Statistics – 1988*, Bureau of Justice Statistics, 1989.

Martin, R. I. and M. W. Klein, *A Comparative Analysis of Four Measures of Delinquency Seriousness* (Los Angeles: University of Southern California, Youth Studies Center), 1965.

Maume, Michael O., 'Disorder and the Fear of Crime: Linking Objective and Subjective Factors.' Paper presented at the 1996 annual meeting of the American Society of Criminology, Chicago.

McCord, Joan, 'Crime in Moral and Social Contexts – The American Society of Criminology, 1989 Presidential Address,' *Criminology*, 28(1), February 1990, pp. 1–26.

McGlothlin, William H., M. Douglas Anglin, and Bruce D. Wilson, 'Narcotics Addiction and Crime,' *Criminology*, 16(4), November 1978, pp. 293–315.

McKinney, Kay C., 'Juvenile Gangs: Crime and Drug Trafficking,' *Juvenile Justice Bulletin*, Office of Juvenile Justice and Delinquency Prevention, September 1988.

Meehl, Paul, *Clinical vs. Statistical Predictions: A Theoretical Analysis and a Review of the Evidence* (Minneapolis: University of Minnesota Press), 1954.

Monahan, John, 'The Prediction of Violent Criminal Behavior: A Methodological Critique and Prospectus,' in Alfred Blumstein, Jacqueline Cohen, and Daniel Nagin (eds.), *Estimating the Effects of Criminal Sanctions on Crime Rates* (Washington, D.C.: National Academy of Sciences), 1978, pp. 244–69.

Monahan, John, *Predicting Violent Behavior: An Assessment of Clinical Techniques* (Beverly Hills, CA: Sage), 1981.

Moore, Mark H., 'Supply Reduction and Drug Law Enforcement,' in Michael A. Tonry and James Q. Wilson (eds.), *Drugs and Crime – Crime and Justice: Review of Research*, Vol. 13 (Chicago: The University of Chicago Press), 1990, pp. 109–57.

Morgan, Kathleen O'Leary, Scott Morgan and Neal Quitno (eds.), *Crime State Rankings 1994* (Lawrence, Kansas: Morgan Quitno Corporation, 1994).

Mott, Joy, 'Young People, Alcohol and Crime,' *Research Bulletin* (London: Home Office), No. 28, 1990, pp. 24–8.

Mulford, Harold, 'Rethinking the Alcohol Problem: A Natural Process Model,' *Journal of Drug Issues*, Winter 1984, pp. 31–43.

Nagin, Daniel S. and David P. Farrington, 'The Stability of Criminal Potential from Childhood to Adulthood,' *Criminology*, 39(2), May 1992, pp. 235–60.

National Institute of Justice, *Research in Action*, 'Drug Use Trends,' DUF: Drug Use Forecasting, April, August, and November 1991.

National Institute on Drug Abuse, *Perceived Alcohol and Drug Problems in the 1995 Household Survey*, US Department of Health and Human Services, 1989.

New York Times, The, February 11, 1992, p. C1.

New York Times, The, September 24, 1991, pp. A1 and A14.

New York Times, The, February 16, 1992, p. 1

New York Times, The, September 13, 1992, pp. A1 and A14.

New York Times, The, September 9, 1994, pp. A1 and A12.

New York Times, The, December 13, 1994, pp. A1 and A13.

New York Times, The, April 16, 1997, p. D23.

Nimick, Ellen H., 'Juvenile Court Property Cases,' *OJJDP Update on Statistics*, Office of Juvenile Justice and Delinquency Prevention, November 1980, pp. 1–5.

Orcutt, James D., 'Differential Association and Marijuana Use: A Closer Look at Sutherland (With a Little Help from Becker),' *Criminology*, 25(2), May 1987, pp. 341–58.

Peele, Stanton, *Diseasing of America: Addiction Treatment Out of Control* (Lexington, MA: Lexington Books), 1989.

Peeples, Faith and Rolf Loeber, 'Do Individual Factors and Neighborhood Context Explain Ethnic Differences in Juvenile Delinquency?' *Journal of Quantitative Criminology*, 10(2), June 1994, pp. 141–57.

Petersilia, Joan, 'Criminal Career Research: A Review of Recent Evidence,' in Norval Morris and Michael Tonry (eds.), *Crime and Justice: An Annual Review of Research* (Chicago: The University of Chicago Press), 1980, pp. 321–79.

Reiss, Albert J. Jr., 'The Accuracy, Efficiency and Validity of a Prediction Instrument,' *American Journal of Sociology*, Vol. 56, 1951, pp. 552–61.

Rhodes, William, Herbert Tyson, James Weekley, Catherine Conly, and Gustave Powell, *Developing Criteria for Identifying Criminals*, US Department of Justice, Office of Legal Policy, Federal Justice Research Program, September 1982.

Robison, Sophia M., *Can Delinquency Be Measured?* (New York: Columbia University Press), 1936.

Roncek, Dennis W. and Pamela A. Meier, 'Bars, Blocks, and Crimes Revisited: Linking the Theory of Routine Activities to the Empiricism of "Hot Spots,"' *Criminology*, 29(4), November 1991, pp. 725–53.

Sampson, Robert J. and John H. Laub, 'Crime and Deviance Over the Life Course,' *American Sociological Review*, 55(5), October 1990, pp. 609–27.

Schmidt, Peter and Ann Dryden Witte, 'Some Thoughts on How and When to Predict in Criminal Justice Settings.' Working paper developed from the Distinguished Scholar Lecture Series of the School of Justice Studies at Arizona State University, March 1987.

Schmidt, Peter and Ann Dryden Witte, *Predicting Recidivism Using Survival Models* (New York: Springer-Verlag), 1988.

Sellin, Thorsten and Marvin Wolfgang, *The Measurement of Delinquency* (New York: John Wiley and Sons), 1964.

Shannon, Lyle W., 'The Problem of Competence to Help,' *Federal Probation*, 25(1), 1961, pp. 32–9.

Shannon, Lyle W., 'The Spatial Distribution of Criminal Offenses by States,' *The Journal of Criminal Law, Criminology and Police Science*, 45(3), 1954, pp. 264–73.

Shannon, Lyle W., *Assessing the Relationship of Adult Criminal Careers to Juvenile Careers*, 1980a. Final Report to the National Institute for Juvenile Justice and Delinquency Prevention, Department of Justice, Grants Number 76JN-99-0008, 76JN-99-1005, and 79JN-AX-1101.

Shannon, Lyle W., 'Assessing the Relationship of Adult Criminal Careers to Juvenile Careers,' in Clark C. Abt (ed.), *Problems in American Social Policy Research* (Cambridge, MA: Abt Books), 1980b, pp. 232–46.

Shannon, Lyle W., *The Relationship of Juvenile Delinquency and Adult Crime to the Changing Ecological Structure of the City*, 1981. Final Report to the National Institute of Justice, Department of Justice, Grant Number 79NI-AX-0081.

Shannon, Lyle W., *Assessing the Relationship of Adult Criminal Careers to Juvenile Careers*, US Department of Justice, Office of Juvenile Justice and Delinquency Prevention, National Institute for Juvenile Justice Delinquency Prevention, 1982.

Shannon, Lyle W., *The Development of Serious Criminal Careers and the Delinquent Neighborhood*, 1984. Revised and expanded final report to the National Institute of Juvenile Justice, Grant Number 82JN-AX-0004.

Shannon, Lyle W., *A More Precise Evaluation of the Effects of Sanctions*, 1985a. Final Report to The National Institute of Justice, Department of Justice, Grant Number 84IJ-CX-0013.

Shannon, Lyle W., 'Risk Assessment vs. Real Prediction: The Prediction Problem and Public Trust,' *Journal of Quantitative Criminology*, 1(2), June 1985b, pp. 159–89.

Shannon, Lyle W., 'Ecological Evidence of the Hardening of the Inner City,' in Robert M. Figlio, Simon Hakim, and George F. Rengert (eds.), *Metropolitan Crime Patterns* (Monsey, NY: Criminal Justice Press), 1986, pp. 27–54.

Shannon, Lyle W., *Prediction and Typology Development*, 1987. Final Report to the National Institute of Justice, Grant Number 85IJ-CX- 0019.

Shannon, Lyle W., *Criminal Career Continuity: Its Social Context* (New York: Human Sciences Press, Inc.), 1988.

Shannon, Lyle W., *Changing Patterns of Delinquency and Crime: A Longitudinal Study in Racine* (Boulder, CO: Westview Press), 1991.

Shaw, Clifford R., *The Natural History of Delinquent Careers* (Chicago: The University of Chicago Press), 1931.

Shaw, Clifford R., Frederick M. Zorbaugh, Henry D. McKay, and Leonard S. Cottrell, *Delinquency Areas* (Chicago: The University of Chicago Press), 1929.

Sherman, Lawrence W. and Denise Gottfredson, *Preventing Crime: What Works, What Doesn't, What's Promising*, Office of Justice Programs, National Institute of Justice, February 1997.

Sickmund, Melissa, 'Juvenile Court Drug and Alcohol Cases: 1985–1988,' *OJJDP Update on Statistics, Juvenile Justice Bulletin*, Office of Juvenile Justice and Delinquency Prevention, December 1991, pp. 1–11.

Sickmund, Melissa, 'Offenders in Juvenile Court,' *OJJDP Update on Statistics, Juvenile Justice Bulletin*, Office of Juvenile Justice and Delinquency Prevention, February 1992, pp. 1–11.

Smith, Douglas A. and Patrick R. Gartin, 'Specifying Specific Deterrence: The Influence of Arrests on Future Criminal Activity,' *American Sociological Review*, 54(1), 1989, pp. 94–105.

Snyder, Howard N., 'Arrests of Youth in 1990,' *OJJDP Update on Statistics, Juvenile Justice Bulletin*, Office of Juvenile Justice and Delinquency Prevention, January 1992, pp. 1–12.

Speckart, George and M. Douglas Anglin, 'Narcotics Use and Crime: A Causal Modeling Approach,' *Journal of Quantitative Criminology*, 2(1), March 1986, pp. 3–28.

Spergel, Irving A. and Ronald L. Chance, 'National Youth Gang Suppression and Intervention Program,' *National Institute of Justice Reports*, June 1991, pp. 21–4.

Steffensmeier, Darrell J., *The Fence: In the Shadow of Two Worlds* (Totowa, NJ: Rowman and Littlefield), 1986.

Stott, D. W., 'The Prediction of Delinquency from Non-Delinquent Behavior,' *British Journal of Delinquency*, Vol. 10, 1960, pp. 202–10.

Strug, David L., Eric D. Wish, Bruce D. Johnson, Kevin Anderson, and Tom Miller, 'The Role of Alcohol Use in the Crimes of Heroin Abusers,' *Crime and Delinquency*, 30(4), 1984, pp. 551–67.

Sunday Telegraph, The, October 13, 1996, p. 30.

Taylor, Ralph and Jeanette Covington, 'Neighborhood Changes in Ecology and Violence,' *Criminology*, 26(4), November 1988, pp. 553–89.

Tittle, Charles R. and Robert F. Meier, 'Specifying the SES/Delinquency Relationship,' *Criminology*, 28(2), June 1980, pp. 271–99.

Toby, Jackson, 'An Evaluation of Early Identification and Intensive Treatment Programs for Predelinquents,' *Social Problems*, 13(2), 1965, pp. 160–75.

Tonry, Michael (ed.), *Malign Neglect: Race Crime and Punishment* (New York: Oxford University Press), 1995.

Triplett, Ruth A. and G. Roger Jarjoura, 'Theoretical and Empirical Specification of a Model of Informal Labeling,' *Journal of Quantitative Criminology*, 10(3), September 1994, pp. 241–76.

U.S. Bureau of the Census, *Census of Housing: 1970, BLOCK STATISTICS*, U.S. Government Printing Office (Washington D.C.).

Vila, Bryan, 'A General Paradigm for Understanding Criminal Behavior: Extending Evolutionary Ecological Theory,' *Criminology*, 32(3), August 1994, pp. 311–59.

Visher, Christy A., 'Incorporating Drug Treatment in Criminal Sanctions,' *NIJ Reports*, Summer 1990, pp. 2–7.

Voss, Harwin L., 'The Predictive Efficiency of the Glueck Social Prediction Table,' *The Journal of Criminal Law, Criminology and Police Science*, 54(4), 1963, pp. 421–30.

Votey, Harold, L. Jr., 'Employment, Age, and Crime: A Labor Theoretic Investigation,' *Journal of Quantitative Criminology*, 7(2), June 1991, pp. 123–53.

Ward, David and Charles R. Tittle, 'IQ and Delinquency: A Test of Two Competing Explanations,' *Journal of Quantitative Criminology*, 10(3), September 1994, pp. 189–212.

Watters, John K., Craig Reinarman, and Jeffrey Fagan, 'Causality, Context, and Contingency: Relationships Between Drug Abuse and Delinquency,' *Contemporary Drug Problems*, Fall 1985, pp. 351–73.

Welford, Charles F., 'The Prediction of Delinquency,' Chapter 2 in William F. Amos and Charles Welford (eds.), *Delinquency Prevention: Theory and Practice* (Englewood Cliffs, NJ: Prentice-Hall, Inc.), 1967.

Welte, John W. and William F. Wieczorek, 'Two-Wave Three Variable Causal Models of Alcohol, Drugs and Crime.' Paper presented at the Annual Meetings of the American Society of Criminology, Chicago, Illinois, November 1996.

White, Helene Raskin, Robert J. Pandina, and Randy L. LaGrange, 'Longitudinal Predictors of Serious Substance Use and Delinquency,' *Criminology*, 25(3), August 1987, pp. 715–40.

Wilkins, Leslie T., 'Problems with Existing Prediction Studies and Future Research Needs,' *The Journal of Criminal Law & Criminology*, 71(2), 1980, pp. 98–101.

Williams, Kirsten M., 'Selection Criteria for Career Criminal Programs,' *The Journal of Criminal Law & Criminology*, 71(2), Summer 1980, pp. 89–93.

Wilson, James Q. and Richard J. Hernstein (eds.) *Crime and Human Nature* (New York: Simon and Schuster), 1985.

Wish, Eric D. and Bernard A. Gropper, 'Drug Testing by the Criminal Justice System: Methods, Research and Applications,' in Michael A. Tonry and James Q. Wilson (eds.), *Drugs and Crime – Crime and Justice: Review of Research*, Vol. 13 (Chicago: The University of Chicago Press), 1990, pp. 321–91.

Wish, Eric D. and Bruce D. Johnson, 'The Impact of Substance Abuse on Criminal Careers,' Chapter 2 in Alfred Blumstein, Jacqueline Cohen, Jeffrey Roth, and Christy Visher (eds.), *Criminal Careers and 'Career Criminals'* (Washington: National Academy Press), 1986.

Wolfgang, Marvin, Robert Figlio, and Thorsten Sellin, *Delinquency in a Birth Cohort* (Chicago: The University of Chicago Press), 1972.

Wolfgang, Marvin, *From Boy to Man – From Delinquency to Crime* (Chicago: The University of Chicago Press), 1987.

Wood, Peter B., Bruce J. Arneklev, and Marci Stephensen, 'Thrillseeking and Delinquency: Toward a Theory of Intrinsic Rewards,' presented to the American Society of Criminology, November 1991.

Wright, Kevin N. and Karen E. Wright, *Family Life, Delinquency, and Crime: A Policymaker's Guide* (Washington: Office of Juvenile Justice and Delinquency Prevention), 1994.

Zhang, Lening, William F. Wieczorek, and John W. Welte, 'The Impact of Age of Onset or Substance Use on Delinquency,' *Journal of Research in Crime and Delinquency*, May 1997.

Index